AN
ANTHROPOLOGY
OF ARCHITECTURE

AN
ANTHROPOLOGY
OF ARCHITECTURE

Victor Buchli

B L O O M S B U R Y
LONDON · NEW DELHI · NEW YORK · SYDNEY

Bloomsbury Academic

An imprint of Bloomsbury Publishing Plc

50 Bedford Square   1385 Broadway
London   New York
WC1B 3DP   NY 10018
UK   USA

www.bloomsbury.com

Bloomsbury is a registered trade mark of Bloomsbury Publishing Plc

First published 2013

British Library Cataloguing-in-Publication Data

A catalogue record for this book is available from the British Library.

ISBN: HB: 978-1-8452-0782-3
PB: 978-1-8452-0783-0
ePub: 978-0-8578-5301-1
ePDF: 978-0-8578-5300-4

Library of Congress Cataloging-in-Publication Data

Buchli, Victor.
An anthropology of architecture / Victor Buchli.
p. cm.
Includes bibliographical references.
ISBN 978-1-84520-783-0 — ISBN 978-1-84520-782-3 —
ISBN 978-0-85785-300-4 — ISBN 978-0-85785-301-1
1. Architecture and anthropology.   I. Title.
NA2543.A58B83   2013
306.4'7—dc23   2013012954

Cover image: copyright the artist, courtesy Sadie Coles HQ, London
Typeset by Apex CoVantage, LLC, Madison, WI, USA
Printed and bound in Great Britain

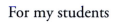

For my students

CONTENTS

List of Illustrations   ix

Introduction   1

1   **The Long Nineteenth Century**   19

2   **Architecture and Archaeology**   47

3   **Social Anthropology and the House Societies of Lévi-Strauss**   71

4   **Institutions and Community**   89

5   **Consumption Studies and the Home**   117

6   **Embodiment and Architectural Form**   137

7   **Iconoclasm, Decay, and the Destruction of Architectural Forms**   157

Postscript   179

Notes   187

Bibliography   189

Index   203

LIST OF ILLUSTRATIONS

Figure 1   A Maori meeting house interior   p. 9
Figure 2   Viollet le Duc's first hut   p. 20
Figure 3   Laugier's primitive hut   p. 22
Figure 4   Semper's Carib hut   p. 24
Figure 5   The Crystal Palace, 1851   p. 26
Figure 6   Pitt Rivers's weaponry   p. 31
Figure 7   Morgan's Iroquois longhouse   p. 33
Figure 8   Lake Zurich dwellings   p. 36
Figure 9   Field tent   p. 40
Figure 10   Upper Paleolithic dwelling at Gagarino   p. 49
Figure 11   William Paca Garden, Annapolis, Maryland   p. 60
Figure 12   Stonehenge   p. 68
Figure 13   The Acropolis   p. 69
Figure 14   A *tavu* house altar   p. 82
Figure 15   Paris barricades   p. 91
Figure 16   Paris arcade   p. 93
Figure 17   Bonaventure Hotel, Los Angeles   p. 97
Figure 18   Brasília   p. 100
Figure 19   Astana skyline   p. 101
Figure 20   A gated community   p. 103
Figure 21   Viennese *Flakturm*   p. 110
Figure 22   Postwar Soviet interiors   p. 126
Figure 23   Luzia's "throwntogetherness"   p. 128
Figure 24   Daniels's Japanese house   p. 133
Figure 25   Da Vinci's Vitruvian Man   p. 138
Figure 26   Camera obscura as architectural chamber   p. 140
Figure 27   DeSilvey's abandoned Montana farmhouse   p. 160
Figure 28   Edensor's ruined industrial building   p. 162
Figure 29   Gonzalez-Ruibal's abandoned farmhouse, Galicia, Spain   p. 165

Figure 30   World Trade Center   p. 171
Figure 31   Cathedral of Christ the Savior, Moscow   p. 174
Figure 32   Berlin Wall fragment   p. 175
Figure 33   Hage's pavilion   p. 180

INTRODUCTION

I

If buildings make people, as the numerous studies in this book suggest, then it is the writing about these buildings that in turn endeavors to make up what is generally human, its condition, and its infinite creative complexity. This book, therefore, is not a comprehensive survey, which would be impossible to encompass meaningfully within one volume. I defer to other colleagues whom I have learned from for thorough summaries of the arc of anthropologically inflected studies of architectural form. Indispensable sources are Paul Oliver's magisterial multivolume work (1997); the vast output of the journal *Traditional Dwellings and Settlements Review*, published by the International Association for the Study of Traditional Environments; Suzanne Preston Blier's state-of-the-art survey in Tilley et al. (2006); Setha Low and Denise Lawrence-Zúñiga's (2003) review of the anthropological and wider literature pertaining to the study of house forms; the reviews of both Mike Parker Pearson and Colin Richards (1994) as well as Ross Samson (1990) of architecture within archaeology; Claire Melhuish's cross-disciplinary exploration of architects and anthropologists (1996); Donna Birdwell-Pheasant and Denise Lawrence-Zúñiga's edited volume on Europe (1999); and Trevor Marchand's (2009) ethnography of mud brick construction. All of these works must be consulted for a more wide-ranging discussion of the scope of architectural studies relevant to anthropology.

Rather, this book aims to engage with the more specific question of the materiality of built form in its various material registers (Thrift 2005). The emphasis on material register is an attempt to understand architectonic and architectural forms in particular, not merely in terms of immediate empirically evident material form—as an assemblage of certain kinds of building materials such as wood, concrete, or mud or building techniques such as mass-industrialized housing or mud brick—but in terms of how architectonic forms might be understood additionally in different registers such as image, metaphor, performance, ruin, diagnostic, or symbol and how the specific material conditions of these registers—their materiality—enables human relations.

In short, how does the materiality of built form in its great variety make people and society? What does the materiality of built form in its various material registers do socially? As abstracted concept? As lived building? As metaphor? As mind, as sign, as environmental adaptation, as fossil, as performance, as ruin, as iteration, as destroyed object, as image, as flow and movement?

Toward the engagement with these issues, this book—beginning with this introduction and ending with a postscript—is organized as follows. Chapter 1, "The Long Nineteenth Century," examines the currents in eighteenth- and nineteenth-century thought and anthropological practice that have influenced the anthropological analysis of architecture. It charts the development of thought starting from the work of the Abbé Laugier and his primitivist fantasies, Pitt Rivers, Gustav Semper, and Lewis Henry Morgan, to the rise of postwar vernacular studies in the mid-twentieth century. In particular it examines the prevailing "fossil metaphor" characterizing understandings of architecture and material culture. It considers how these investigations served to demonstrate the nineteenth-century concept of the "psychic unity of man" and inspired later modernist ideals and the material terms by which social reform (notably Marxist) could be imagined. Following the waning of material culture studies and architecture in the wake of early-twentieth-century social anthropology's preoccupation with social structure, the chapter examines the theoretical disengagement with architectural form and material culture and then charts its reemergence and reconstitution with new effects in the postwar period. This period represents a radical update of earlier approaches. It is here that we see the return of nineteenth-century linguistic analogies with the "linguistic turn" and the rise of structuralism and the recurrent understanding of architecture as an aspect of mind. The question of why such a renewed focus should emerge is asked in relation to changes in postwar social life and the new meanings architectural questions pose for anthropological thought. This chapter identifies those enduring themes of universalism and modernization, which still frame (as well as obscure) debates in the present.

In Chapter 2, "Architecture and Archaeology," archaeology is discussed as that traditional subfield of anthropology that has concerned itself most emphatically with the study of material culture and architecture in particular. Especially within the area of ethno-archaeology emerging from the New Archaeology of the postwar period, the interface between people, material culture, and architecture assumed a renewed methodological and theoretical significance for the study of society. This chapter examines this tradition along with postprocessual responses to the New Archaeology. Beginning with the reevaluation of nineteenth-century evolutionary theories, this chapter examines how these trends within archaeology introduced a new dimension to the understanding of mind, cognition, and representation over the long term that is distinctive from ethnographic approaches and the "ethnographic snapshot." Such an approach emphasizes the deep-time perspective that archaeology enables and that allows us to consider the radically different ways material registers can change and function over time. In particular, the significance of archaeology's understanding of the changes associated with the rise of the Neolithic and enduring built forms are discussed when sedentism and agriculture emerge, resulting in changed social relations and new material forms of dwelling. Similarly, archaeology's engagement with deep time and culture change enabled the imagination of radically new modern forms of architecture to facilitate social reform as well as determine the condition of "basic needs" at the heart of wider developmental and modernization discourses. Later poststructuralist approaches emphasizing performance and the iterative nature of architectural forms over time suggested a shift from a fossil metaphor to a palimpsest metaphor, shifting the focus to what architectural forms *do* rather than *represent* and their attendant changing material registers over time.

With Chapter 3, "Social Anthropology and the House Societies of Lévi-Strauss," we examine the postwar period and how architectonic contexts begin to reassume a central significance in the understanding of human societies, notably in reference to Lévi-Strauss's concept of "house societies." This chapter considers in particular the understanding of dwellings and the institutions associated with house societies as inherently "illusory objectifications," as Carsten and Hugh-Jones note (1995: 8), of social relations created to resolve social conflict. The structural analogies between dwellings and human and cosmological bodies and their interrelationship are explored in terms of the increasing significance of the body and its metaphors for the understanding of architectural space within anthropology—taking on the observation of Carsten and Hugh-Jones that bodies and buildings are inherently difficult to meaningfully disentangle. The chapter examines the house as an architectonic regulator of generative substances looking at such diverse substances as foodstuffs and bodily fluids following the insights of Marilyn Strathern in her work (1999). The chapter considers how the regulation of such generative flows involves the work of architecture in diverse material registers and their attendant dynamics, such as those facilitating immobility, commensality, backgrounding and foregrounding, mobility, and dematerialization.

Chapter 4, "Institutions and Community," examines institutional forms and their role in the development of anthropological thought. The chapter returns to the Crystal Palace and the ethnographic museum and our understandings of modern consumerism. Jeremy Bentham's panopticon and Foucault's notion of governmentality are at the heart of approaches through which institutions such as prisons, schools, shopping malls, and factories have been engaged anthropologically. The chapter examines how such approaches have attended to the unexpected consequences of material forms as they are experienced. It considers how attachments and detachments are created that produce social life and how new neoliberal practices such as those concerned with regulation and management replace classic Foucauldian understandings of discipline. Here we see a shift from material architectonic forms of regulation to new principles of self-management and regulation through new immaterial practices such as the actuarial regulation of populations. The unexpected consequences of planning in Brasília; the effects of generic material forms such as those encountered in gated communities, and phenomena such as sick building syndrome are examined in addition to the more recent impact of digital technologies imbricated with the conventional "bricks and mortar" of architectural forms to create new material terms of sociality.

Chapter 5, "Consumption Studies and the Home," discusses the rise of consumption studies in the built environment as it relates to the home. The home is the primary context as well as the object of most consumer practices. This chapter explores the role of changing consumer practices and gender relations, especially the impact of feminism and changing understandings of materiality on the architecture of the home. Within such a setting the issues surrounding daily life are emphasized with reference to the work of Pierre Bourdieu, Mary Douglas, and Marcel Mauss. Hygiene and its structuring qualities are examined in relation to the experience of domestic space and how materially attachments and detachments and wider flows are produced to create social relations and understandings of moral personhood. Similarly, qualities of domestic space, centered on neutrality and color (such as whiteness) and the flows and the values they enable, are also understood in relation to the body and capitalist financial instruments such as mortgages. Additionally, the qualities of genericism and interchangeability are examined in terms of their ability to facilitate flows and habitation within neoliberal globalizing contexts and the novel forms of moral personhood that emerge under these conditions.

In Chapter 6, "Embodiment and Architectural Form," the inherent ambiguity between the body and architectural form is examined. In particular the evident anthropomorphism of architectural form is discussed in its wider aspects. The chapter first examines this relationship from within the Western perspective—considering the Cartesian mind/body split that has shaped understanding of the relation of the body to architectural form and emergent technologies of representation of the time such as the camera obscura that enabled this disembodied form of engagement. The discussion then moves to phenomenological accounts that work to overcome this division, with reference to numerous non-Western examples where the imbrication of bodily and built form are deeply intertwined. In light of this, a reexamination of Western contexts is addressed through the phenomenological tradition. The problem of dwelling identified by Heidegger is considered in addition to feminist approaches in the postwar period that have examined the intimacy of built and bodily form as it pertains to the construction and maintenance of architecture in a variety of ethnographic contexts. Here the work of Pierre Bourdieu and his notion of habitus and its insights into the nature of embodiment is examined. In contrast, forms of disembodiment are discussed. These are associated with rituals of divestment that are necessary for the production of social relations as well as the role of architectural forms as ephemeral and generic shells for the regulation of the material and generative flows that enable social life.

Chapter 7, "Iconoclasm, Decay, and the Destruction of Architectural Forms," is the final chapter. As the previous chapter examines how architectural forms are in fact animate and alive, this chapter considers the consequences of "killing" architectural forms. It understands destruction as an "animatory" practice through the work of Alfred Gell and explores the wider anthropological implications regarding the actual destruction of architectural forms. The chapter also considers the destruction of architectural forms, from prehistory to the modern practice of "urbicide." In particular, it considers the productive and socially generative capacities of decay and destruction to constitute novel forms of social life. The chapter examines the Berlin Wall, decaying farmsteads and factories, and the wider political aesthetics of ruins in their various forms as well as the productive consequences of absence formed in the wake of destructive practices. Here one of the pressing issues is the examination of legitimate and illegitimate forms of destructive violence, especially as it relates to urbicide and the unexpected consequences of destructive practices to generate novel political and social identifications.

In the postscript, the consequences of emerging technologies such as three-dimensional printing are considered in relation to the previous themes discussed, such as the role of architectonic forms for the regulation of the flows that constitute social life. Such new technologies challenge the stability of architectural forms compared to other ethnographic examples where such forms are similarly unstable. This final section considers such architectonic forms as a productive "fetish" in light of Lévi-Strauss's "illusory objectification" (Carsten and Hugh-Jones 1995). Such forms accommodate multiple conflicting "commitments" (Rouse 2002) related to the objectifications that architectural forms facilitate and the constitution of social life in novel material registers that anthropology has always been attentive to, and the myriad ways that architecture makes people.

As can be gleaned from this overview, the extent of architectural forms discussed here is mostly limited by the scope of anthropological research, which tends to privilege the domestic, which methodologically results from the intimate ethnographic scale in which this research takes place. Since the postwar period, however, anthropologists have expanded their scope of inquiry to include institutional settings such as offices, airports, and shopping malls, but the domestic is still the predominate site for research in keeping with the anthropological understanding of the domestic realm as the primary realm within which people and social relations are forged. Similarly, questions of materiality have not been problematized in anthropological inquiries until relatively recently. As such, the materiality of built forms and wider architectonic contexts have been underanalyzed in favor of focusing on immaterial abstracted social processes, overlooking the role of the material toward the formation of those processes. For this reason, traditionally, anthropological texts have been rather limited in their material description and discussion of architectural forms with very few images indeed. But this was not always the case. Nineteenth-century discussions of built forms were particularly rich with images drawn and collected by ethnologists, stemming from a reliance on visual representations that were at the heart of nineteenth-century theory building. As we shall see in subsequent chapters and in the postscript, image and built form become increasingly more difficult to segregate meaningfully with the rise of new technologies in the late twentieth and early twenty-first centuries.

2

As concerns the question of the materiality of built form, this book takes note of Tim Ingold's (2007) problem with recent work on materiality in architectural form that has underplayed at times the actual material qualities of things in favor of focusing on the discursive, semiotic, or mental aspects of form. Ingold rather, sees material qualities as having an inherently relational quality—not reducible to some empirical material quality such as a building material or mental construct, but existing within what he describes as a relational context of action, material, and environment, reminiscent in certain ways of the philosopher of science Karen Barad's (2007) notion of "intra-action."

Three thinkers are key to this discussion of built form and subsequent understandings of its materiality: Alfred Gell's (1998) work on the Maori meeting house as a distributed object and distributed mind; Claude Lévi-Strauss (1987) on house societies and the concept of the house as an "illusory objectification" (Carsten and Hugh-Jones 1995) and Pierre Bourdieu's (1977, 1990) work on the Kabyle house and the notion of habitus. These thinkers attend to the question of the multiplicity of registers and the inherently conflictual nature of house forms in terms of these multiple registers and the house's centrality in the negotiation of competing social claims and the productive value of these conflicting claims for the sustenance of social and biological life. Register must be understood here in different ways. The material register of built form can be understood as text, as sign system, as embodied experience; visually, tactilely, aurally, and so on; and in its variously configured material forms, lived building, construction tradition, text, visual image, sound-scape, model, and so on. Within these authors' works, the key themes of flows and registers and the shift from register to register pervade their discussions. It is within this anthropological tradition that the empirical dwelling, the architectural object/artifact—the analytical category—both emically and etically can be seen not as a self-evident enduring and stable material entity but as a momentary stoppage (following Gell 1998) within such flows both from the point of view of the anthropological observer and the inhabitant. Such stoppages enable social life, as Marilyn Strathern (1999) has demonstrated in aspects of her work on Melanesia. And, more importantly, as Strathern has noted in another context (1990), this stoppage, this momentary snapshot of the architectonic conditions of social life, is primarily an analytical category born out of Euro-American concerns. These concerns are specific to the conditions of Euro-American society, but whose power and ubiquity, especially when recruited as a form of governance, require an engagement with such forms regardless of what preexisting local or indigenous conditions might otherwise require.

The regulation of such flows is understood by an insight from Lévi-Strauss (1987) regarding the more specialized notion of house societies. Here the institution of the house, which encompasses relations of kinship, hierarchy, and the physical entity of the house itself, is presented as what Carsten and Hugh-Jones (1995) describe as an "illusory objectification" of contradictory interests producing a common object from antagonistic commitments to that object (i.e., the architectural object and the relations it embodies). Carsten and Hugh-Jones (1995: 8) note how Lévi-Strauss attempts to introduce a notion of fetishization in Marx's sense to describe these conflicted interests. William Pietz (1985), in his discussion of the fetish, notes that a fetish as such is a peculiar category—the anxious product of a cultural clash of incommensurable values and understandings of materiality and immateriality on the western African coast. It is a clash regarding the proper material (and social) attachments that constitute social life, resulting from "the encounter of radically heterogeneous social systems" (Pietz 1985: 7). Pietz's work on the fetish sees it as a misrecognition of a relation, but a productive misrecognition—one that enables complementary and at times conflicted and conflicting materialities and social claims to coexist. As the numerous examples of classical anthropological accounts of dwellings attest, there is an inherent and contradictory complementarity of gendered roles associated with built forms; these contradictions are productive of the wider terms of social life and its hierarchies and asymmetries. These are the "inversions" described by Bourdieu in terms of gender conflicts and complementarity; these are also the more manifold and unstable "incommensurablities" (following Povinelli 2001) that characterize the experience of modernity (or the "parallax" as suggested by Žižek [2006]).[1] The changing, shifting, opposing, and complementary nature of various material registers are precisely the lived terms by which productive categories of social life are at times variously committed to, sustained, overcome, and rearticulated.

This question of the fetishization of the house and the productive nature of this misrecognition can be seen to function in Gell's (1998) discussion of the Maori meeting house (see Figure 1) in his magisterial work *Art and Agency* (I am indebted here to the discussion of Hicks and Horning [2006] of Gell's Maori meeting house). The arc of Gell's discussion of an anthropology of art culminates in his discussion of the Maori meeting house, which closes the work. The house as an architectural entity, as would befit traditional vernacular approaches, loses its centrality and even its monumental materiality and dissipates when considered as an embodiment in Gell's terms of a "distributed object" over time and space, within another material register, as "oeuvre" and as distributed "mind" (Gell 1998). In fact, Gell (1998: 255) offers the image produced by Roger Neich (1996), which Gell posits as the more authentic representation of the meeting house from the Maori perspective, which sees it as a mere stoppage (following Duchamp) in a series of many stoppages before and many more to come as a result of open-ended competition to enact even more elaborate houses over time. What is important to note, however, is that the Maori meeting house as distributed "object" and "mind" over time is itself a product of the colonial encounter, where competing groups found themselves reduced to competition and display in terms of the construction of these houses (Gell 1998: 251). The Maori meeting house thus is an "illusory objectification" (Carsten and Hugh-Jones 1995) in Lévi-Strauss's sense of these conflicting tensions and similarly an inherently conflicted fetish—as Pietz would have it, a misrecognition of value and material signification as the result of a colonial encounter. But as Lévi-Strauss observes, such "illusory objectifications" (Carsten and Hugh-Jones 1995) produce commitments to certain modes of sociality—they become the means by which conflicted entities are brought into relation to one another and become visible and intelligible in both built and embodied form as a consequence. Architectural form as discrete empirical object is rather problematic in light of the insights of Lévi-Strauss and Gell.

The central premise of this book is an examination of understandings of the materiality of architectural forms and their various registers within the anthropological tradition. Through the wider return to the material within the social sciences (see Brown 2001), a renewed emphasis on the materiality of things emerged. More widely this has been part of an examination of materialism (see Coole and Frost 2010) within the social sciences. Within anthropology, and notably material culture studies, the question of the nature of the material that the term *materiality* refers to has achieved a central role (Miller 2005).

Figure 1 A Maori meeting house interior. *Source*: Daniel Bellhouse, Dreamstime.com.

In relation to this emergent discussion of materiality, there has been a considerable deal of controversy over the status of the "real" as regards material phenomena (see Barad 2007; Hacking 1983; Latour 1999; Rouse 2002). Recent work on materiality has called into question the role of the material—not as passive recipient of our social projections but as co-constitutive of the very worlds we live in (Barad 2007; Butler 1993; Foucault 1977; Hacking 1983; Latour 1999, Miller 2005). The privileging of the social within material culture studies (Miller 2005) has meant that the co-constitutive aspects of materiality have been rather underanalyzed. The "real"—as "thingness," as it is often referred to—has a somewhat mysterious and ambiguous quality that thinkers as far back as Locke have been at pains to observe.

It has often been noted of late that when we stop thinking of certain items of material culture as sign, text, or sensual vehicle, then what we are left with is a certain implacable thingness, an "untranscended materiality" (following Pietz 1985)—a thingness that is "figural" (following Pinney 2005), a thingness that contains a delimited but open-ended "bundling" of attributes (following Keane 2005), or the implacable material agency of things that Sansi-Roca (2005) identifies in his discussion of Candomblé stones that embody saintly spirits in Afro-Brazilian Candomblé ritual practices. The particular stone of Sansi-Roca's discussion was originally seen as "evidence" of a criminal pathology of occult practices like witchcraft, then exhibited for a time in a city museum of history and culture as an artifact associated with Candomblé culture. But as such, the stone can never be publicly viewed in Candomblé ritual; neither is it possible to reinstate it to its original context, which is now broken and lost, and thus the stone is hidden in storage—it can never be artwork or artifact or "saint" stone; it exists in limbo. This thingness is an implacability that one might understand in Whitehead's (1978) terms as a "stubborn fact" when considering the nature of materiality. The fact that Sansi-Roca's Candomblé stone ought to be easily reincorporated but cannot, because of the specificity of its historical emergence, requires that it be engaged with in an ambiguous but nonetheless nonarbitrary way. This is an example of the sort of realism Barad (2007) and Rouse (2002) attempt to delineate—that things such as indigenous art forms (Myers 2004) or Candomblé stones, despite their seeming instability and interstitiality, neither in one realm nor the other (see Strathern 1990), possess a certain implacability, or stubbornness, that, like the stubbornness of the facts of natural science, exhibits a materiality that cannot be reduced—will not quite go away despite what social constructionists might say. As Lesley McFadyen has argued about the archaeological record (personal communication), even if a thing might be inscrutable, it is nonetheless irrefutable and "must" be engaged with in circumscribed terms—not just any story will do.

The Marxian legacy, which focused on embodied praxis and materialism, has been somewhat sacrificed in various engagements with poststructuralism and its preoccupation with meaning and signification. This legacy requires a reengagement and recommitment to a sense of realism and the empirical, which recent discussions concerning the question of materiality have attempted to do. This is not a return to some form of essentialism but an account of these commitments to the empirical, in Hume's terms, an account of those regularities that we are beholden to[2] and that form the basis of what Karen Barad calls the "intra-actively" produced worlds in which we live (see Barad 2007; Rouse 2002). These insights resonate with those of Whitehead, who, in keeping with Locke,[3] argues for the metaphysical nature of any statement of "substance," which is ultimately arbitrary but which is necessary for the coherence of our ideas about the world (Whitehead 2000: 22–3). According to Whitehead, our received notions of substance and matter and materiality as they are more widely understood in the philosophy of science are a consequence of what he calls a misplaced "Ionian effort to find in space and time some stuff which composes nature" (Whitehead 2000: 19)—the search to find, citing Aristotle, "the ultimate substratum which is no longer predicated of anything else" (Whitehead 2000: 18). He states, "It is the history of the influence of Greek philosophy on science. That influence has issued in one long misconception of the metaphysical status of natural entities" (Whitehead 2000: 16). This is an effort that is always troubled: "Accordingly, it would seem that every material entity is not really one entity. It is an essential multiplicity of entities" (Whitehead 2000: 22). Hence the inherent multiplicity of registers in which materiality functions. What I would like to draw attention to throughout the chapters of this book are the often conflicted modes in which a given empirical entity—such as architectural form—might function, particularly in the regulation of "generative substances" and their "flows" as developed by Marilyn Strathern to which the discussions in this book are heavily indebted as well as the works of Gabrielle Ackroyd, Anna Hoare, and Fiona Parrott who have examined similar issues regarding flow and substance in different ways relating to the house.

In this respect, the field of material culture studies tout court might be said to need to continuously justify itself (following Rorty), emerging as it did in the nineteenth century with its attendant ways of being and attention to the terms of materiality, as it emerges under present conditions. Yet it is important to consider why the field emerged as it did in the nineteenth century—what its productive capacities were then, and how historically one might consider how these capacities were configured differently as well as ethnographically in terms of the alternative ontologies Viveiros de Castro (1998) has championed (see also Vilaça 2005); keeping in mind what is at stake in these productive capacities, what are their costs, and how they enable as well as disable (as we shall see in a number of the examples presented here).

The language of philosophers of science such as Barad and her emphasis on "agential realism" and "intra-action," as with Whitehead's emphasis on "events," provide useful remedies with which to break out of such unproductive distinctions and vacillating turns. The general language proposed by these scholars is useful partly because of the conceptual impasses within the philosophy of science itself that have necessitated rather robust means with which to think through these impasses, which in turn can aid anthropological studies of material culture. One might argue that anthropology did not need to have to struggle so much with these impasses and therefore did not need to create such robust tools. So why do anthropologists still need this? Simply put, anthropologists, not having had to develop such conceptual tools, have found themselves mired in some of the same dilemmas, while anthropological material culture studies, in a similar way, have historically and rather ironically been rather inattentive to the physical conditions of the material world and materials themselves, leaving this to the natural sciences, which in turn have been in the thrall of certain "Ionian" misconceptions regarding "material" and "substance" according to Whitehead (2000). Anthropology is in a better position by virtue of its focus on the ethnographic method to engage with these issues. To put it simply, philosophers of science and philosophers of mind (such as Rorty and Thalberg) have basically thrown these issues back onto anthropology, whose scales and scopes of analysis are precisely suited to engage with them—focusing on the ontology of the "man on the street," as Rorty would have it (Rorty 1970: 422–4). From Sassen's "imbrications" to Barad's "intra-actions" and Rorty's "matters of taste," all these recourses are calls to anthropology to engage with these issues at the scales the discipline knows best: the micro, the intimate, and the embodied. The question of material culture needs to be thought through specific material registers—reengaging with the discursive as a particular register in play. This is especially important now when things, rather than being textlike, are in fact simply both: the STM atom and IBM brand name as described by Barad (2007: 351–61) or the artifact in three-dimensional printing emerging as both thing and code, reconfigured into a novel assemblage whose affordances and enabling and disabling properties are not yet fully understood (see Buchli 2010a and Carpo 2001).

The philosopher of science Joseph Rouse suggests an understanding of scientific phenomena to which our objects of material culture study can be related: "scientific practices disclose natural phenomena rather than objects, in a sense in which scientific practices are themselves understandable as natural phenomena" (Rouse 2002: 309). He suggests that we think of objects alternatively as "practically constituted components of repeatable phenomena" (2002: 313). How we think about material culture, and in particular the distinctions we make between material registers, is part of these phenomena as well. The question of thingness in its inscrutable ambiguity and materiality "matters to us," citing Rouse, because "[w]e are responsible for our choices not because we constitute them, but because we are involved in them with stakes to which we are accountable, epistemically and politically" (2002: 347). For this reason Rouse argues that there are palpable boundaries (or a "constitutive outside," following Butler [1993]) that we are beholden to—what he refers to as norms—and that such norms are not arbitrary; we are constituted "intra-actively" within them (Rouse 2002: 355). The vexed materiality of the Candomblé stone's thingness is a symptom of the fact that it "matters" (following Rouse 2002)—how this is so is precisely at the heart of its controversial and ambiguous status. It cannot be placated. Its thingness and ambiguous material registers are in some sense perceived as mystically intransigent. It is not some metaphysical guarantor, but merely the acknowledgement that through our complex and historical "intra-actions" within the world (following Rouse 2002), thingness and the complex and often conflicted conditions of materiality, when it comes to that point of time and history when the Candomblé stone merges as it does in Sansi-Roca's (2005) discussion, matter most emphatically because we are "practically constituted" (Rouse 2002: 313) within thingness in many different ways—and, in the particular case of the Candomblé stone, in many incommensurable ways (see also Povinelli 2001; Strathern 1990). Thingness is what remains, what is remaindered, what is in excess, what cannot be assimilated, when the many registers of its complex and conflicted materiality cannot be resolved to one or the other—in short, a fetish (following Pietz) attesting to its inherently conflicted and contested materiality. However, thingness, when we consider Locke and Whitehead, in terms of substance just means that we have a normative commitment (following Rouse 2002): that things—and, with relevance to this book, architectural forms—and the diverse registers in which they function are necessary for the way we are practically constituted. Thingness and its apparent immanence are merely the effects of our practical commitments to these objectifications. But this excess is merely the historical effect of being constituted within these practical terms. Such "excesses" are a call to be responsible to ourselves and the communities and individuals constituted within them (Rouse 2002: 347)—they can offer no guarantees.

When considering the multiplicity of conflicted registers in which a given material phenomenon emerges such as architectural form, Pietz's discussion of the fetish draws particular attention to the productive capacities of such conflicts (echoing of course Marx's own demonstration of the productive capacities of such fetishes to sustain the relations emergent within industrialized capitalism). Pietz notes that a fetish as such is a peculiar category—the anxious product of a cultural and economic clash of incommensurable values. These are objects that are displaced by such clashes, much like the stone of Sansi-Roca's (2005) Candomblé—held in limbo in storage but out of view, as irrefutably meaningful but unassimilable to any existing context; as a result, it is radically abject and undimensionable (Sansi-Roca 2005). But like most artifacts of material culture, and especially architecture in its greater complexity, they are inherently overdetermined and irreducible to one register or another except as part of a given historical and contingent productive strategy.

The fetish in Pietz's sense in many ways describes what is conflicted and overdetermined of any material culture phenomenon. And as Carsten and Hugh-Jones (1995) have noted vis-à-vis the house, architectural form in Lévi-Strauss's work fetishistically serves to obscure the interests of the various agencies and groups that converge and commit to the "house," even as its conflicted nature makes it productive and enduring. As Althusser (2006a) notes in relation to ideology and the real conditions of existence, their relation is imaginary, misrecognized, but this very misrecognition is productive and what enables subjects to exist: "all ideology represents in its necessarily imaginary distortion not the existing relations of production (and the other relations that derive from them), but above all the (imaginary) relationship of individuals to the relations of production and the relations that derive from them" (Althusser 2006a: 111). Therefore, "*all ideology hails or interpellates concrete individuals as concrete subjects*, by the functioning of the category of the subject" (Althusser 2006a: 117). All matter has an ideological existence: "an ideology always exists in an apparatus, and its practice, or practices. This existence is material" (Althusser 2006a: 112) and "that 'matter is discussed in many senses,' or rather it exists in different modalities" (Althusser 2006a: 113).

Althusser (2006b) discusses the slippages or "swerves" that constitute the "brief encounters" that then emerge into the world and make up the objects of history and social life, in terms suggestive of Rouse's discussion of slippages along anaphoric chains. Rouse (2002: 202) describes these chains as comparable to how pronouns work in the way they enable us to retain commitments to previous statements without having to reiterate their content:

> Anaphoric expressions such as pronouns enable a discursive performance to inherit the inferential commitments and entitlements of another performance without having to articulate its specific content. Such expressions are crucial to keeping track of discursive commitments, because one can use them to talk about whatever someone else is talking about, without having to understand or endorse the concepts she used to talk about it. Anaphora are the linguistic expressions that enable communication to proceed in the absence of shared meanings.

Hence a "name" might refer back to a commitment to the generative potential of ancestral forest lands, as we shall see in McKinnon's (2000) account of Tanimbarese dwellings, without having to reiterate such lands but whose generative capacity the name commits to, stands in for, and sustains without in fact being forest lands. Rouse offers the material example of a stick from Brandom (1994):

> One can grasp an anaphoric chain as one grasps a stick; direct contact is achieved only with one end of it, and there may be much about what is beyond that

direct contact of which one is unaware. But direct contact with one end gives genuine if indirect contact with what is attached to the other end . . . A *tactile* Fregean semantic theory . . . incorporates, as two sides of one coin, both the possibility of ignorance of and error about our own concepts and the possibility of genuine aboutness of those concepts and genuine knowledge of the [phenomena]. (Brandom 1994: 583 cited in Rouse 2002: 296)

In more conventional material culture terms, we might see this stick as the originary stick of Pitt Rivers's famous weaponry illustration from "On the Evolution of Culture" (1875a) (Figure 6). Though we might grasp such a related artifact in the present, say, one of the actual weaponry sticks in Pitt Rivers's collection invariably used to constitute this scheme, one's phenomenological grasp of the stick, despite the immediacy of the encounter, betrays a commitment to the originary schema at the other end several times removed. In fact our grasp of material culture tout court emerges without sharing, for example, a belief in evolutionary theory but nonetheless a common commitment to the objects that constitute it at one end. Thus, multiple registers are at play—some foregrounded, some backgrounded, but they nonetheless coexist in a complex, nonarbitrary relation to one another, slipping from one register to the next (platonic form to phenomenological encounter) and emergent within a very specific historical trajectory and genealogy within contracting and expanding notions of time and space (following Munn 1977). The productive capacities (following Strathern) of these registers slip between these different anaphoric chains, but these capacities are nonetheless entailed in relation to one another.

3

The question of diverse material registers can be traced most fruitfully to Althusser's (2006a) discussion of differing material registers and his call for their theorization. Reinterpreting Pascal's formulation of ideology—"Kneel down, move your lips in prayer, and you will believe" (Althusser 2006a: 114)—Althusser uses a more explicit Marxist vocabulary. Regarding the individual subject,

> *His ideas are his material actions inserted into material practices governed by material rituals which are themselves defined by the material ideological apparatus from which derive the ideas of that subject.* Naturally the four inscriptions of the adjective "material" in my proposition must be affected by different modalities: the materialities of a displacement for going to mass, of kneeling down, of the gesture of the sign of the cross, or of the *mea culpa*, of a sentence, of a prayer, of an act of contrition, of a penitence, of a gaze, of a hand-shake, of an external verbal discourse or an "internal" verbal discourse (consciousness), are not one

and the same materiality. I shall leave on one side the *problem of a theory of the differences between the modalities of materiality.* (Althusser 2006a: 114, my italics)

"The problem of a theory" is what has motivated more recent anthropological work to investigate the differences between the "modalities of materiality" or material registers.

Nancy Munn's (1977, 1986) foundational work on Gawa explicitly engages with such shifting material registers in her discussions of the transformations from forest trees to canoes and the ensuing and shifting registers of what she describes as "spacetime" (Munn 1986: 9) that emerge. Here the productive capacities of specific registers in relation to intensities and extent ("spacetime") reprise what Althusser refers to as "modalities of materiality." Munn describes the transformations of raw materials, such as wood worked into canoes and the transformations of those canoes into modes of travel that expand social relations that produce other objects, such as highly prized *kula*-shell valuables, as part of a wider process of transforming closed island "spacetime" into wider open inter-island "spacetime." This is a process of the transformation of substances both prosaic and sublime (see Carsten [2004] on substance and kinship in anthropology), whereby the genital blood of the mythical matrilineal ancestor produces the red-colored wood that is worked on by traveling men, fed by island-bound female kin, and the wood in turn ventures forth as the canoe with these men to bring other goods and valuables back to the island and their female kin through their journeys and trade networks. Thus, canoes traverse diverse material qualities of heaviness and femaleness associated with wood and land and the lightness and speediness of men traveling across water. Canoes are embodied with both masculine and feminine qualities, but when "adorned" and carved and made to be beautiful, "lightning-like" and light, it is the preeminently masculine qualities of beauty whose "radiance" attracts and expands social space back onto Gawans themselves through masculine overseas travel and exchange (Munn 1977).

By contrast, it is worth noting Georges Bataille's *Story of the Eye* (1987 [1928]), which functions in a similar fashion as an investigation into the anaphoric chains describing shifts in material register (I am indebted here to Pinney's discussion of Barthes on Bataille's tale [2005: 267]). Bataille's story echoes the workings of Piercean quali-signs and Munn's own discussion of such quali-signs in her work on Gawa. The linear form of the anaphoric chain in both Bataille's and Munn's account, as the unfolding of the quali-sign in various registers, enables differential engagements—that is, differing attachments or commitments (in Rouse's sense) that attach to the same mutually intelligible phenomenon. Bataille writes how "elementary" and "obscene" images (Bataille 1987 [1928]: 92) in his pornographic tale facilitate the shifting associations between eggs, a saucer of milk, urine, testes, and eyes. From this emerges his wild and ecstatic tale of different encounters, pairings, sacrilegious mergings, and so on. In this confounded and ecstatic tale, which is accelerated out of control by unhinged but by no means arbitrary erotic desire, various anaphoric associations are produced along the axis of eggs, testes, and eyes and with them wildly divergent spatial, sexual, social, and sacrilegious configurations. These are utterly upsetting and refiguring of what Munn might refer to otherwise as the various "spacetimes" and intensities produced by Bataille's pornographic tale "where certain images coincide, the elementary ones, the completely obscene ones" (Bataille 1987 [1928]: 92). In both accounts, Bataille's and Munn's, genital secretions radically reconfigure and animate in reference to their animatory, spatially and temporally transformative and expansive productive capacities—one normative, the other transgressive, but both equally nonarbitrary.

Objects, as material culture, do something similar: they enable differential commitments to the same phenomenon, demonstrating the qualities of an "illusory objectification" (Carsten and Hugh-Jones 1995) in Lévi-Strauss's terms or the conflicted encounters that produce the fetish (Pietz) (becoming an assembly of otherwise differential elements that constitute the "assembly" of the *Ding* as "thing" [Latour 2005]). The notion of the assembly attests to these inherently heterogeneous and conflicting commitments. In fact, it might be argued that it is precisely the intensity of such converging differential commitments that in fact produces the phenomenon of the material thing and sustains it as something that requires constant engagement. The architectural form of the house, that "illusory objectification" (Carsten and Hugh-Jones 1995) par excellence identified by Lévi-Strauss, maintains its ability to perform its productive work precisely because of the convergence of these differential commitments and identifications. Hence Mary Douglas's (1991) observation regarding the multiplicity of engagements that the "house" enables, which unfold at differing scales, within different temporal frames and different material registers, yet all accommodated and assembled in that complex, unstable, but constantly emergent thing/*Ding* (or assembly, as Latour calls it) that is built form and the "generative substances" (following Strathern) that built form regulates.

These anthropological questions in relation to the material registers of human activities call into question many of the received analytical categories that have structured analysis in the social sciences. It is the contention of this book that architectural form is part of this modern understanding and investment in the material world. What I hope to describe is how this particular understanding of the architectural as an analytical category serves as a very specific material register producing social lives and modes of governance—one that is distinct not only from those encountered ethnographically and archaeologically but also from those understandings of built forms that have emerged in more recent ethnographic studies in and outside the Euro-American tradition and experience.

1 THE LONG NINETEENTH CENTURY

1

This chapter examines the nineteenth-century European preoccupation with the origins of architecture and the role played by prehistoric and non-European forms that can be said to date back to the writings of the ancient Roman architectural writer and theoretician Vitruvius. His *Ten Books on Architecture* speculates on origins and concludes that they are derived from "primitive" archetypal forms born out of the processual assembly of disparate elements into the conditions that produce the social and the human (consider Viollet le Duc's version of the first "hut"; Figure 2):

> The men of old were born like the wild beasts, in woods, caves and groves, and lived on savage fare. As time went on, the thickly crowded trees in a certain place . . . caught fire . . . and the inhabitants of the place were put to flight. . . . After it subsided, they drew near and . . . brought up other people to it, showing them by signs how much comfort they got from it. In that gathering of men, at a time when utterance of sound was purely individual, from daily habits they fixed upon articulate words just as these happen to come; then, from indicating by name things in common use, the result was that . . . they began to talk, and thus originate conversation with one another. (Vitruvius 1914: 38)

Thus, as Hvatuum (2004: 30) observes apropos Vitruvius, investigations into the origins of these forms were inseparable from investigations into the origin of human society and what it means to be human—signaling an enduring interpretative problem surrounding the nature of this relation between humans and nature, the status of built forms, and their relation to the production of social life and human life in general. In addition, the major themes of language, human social organization, and morality are seen early in Vitruvius as being intimately implicated and constitutive of one another within an architectural nexus (Hvatuum 2004). In these respects, architectural forms assume the status of the artifact par excellence for understanding the nature and structure of human society. As one enters the debates of the nineteenth century, architectural form itself becomes the most significant analytical category

The First Hut.—Fig. 2.

Figure 2 Viollet le Duc's first hut. *Source*: Viollet le Duc, *The Habitations of Man* (London: Sampson Low, Marston, Searle, & Rivington, 1876).

with which to consider the questions of origins and ideal forms of human society and human habitation both in the past and the future. In fact, the two idealizations are really opposite sides of the same analytical coin. The result of this, of course, is that architecture established itself in the nineteenth century as a particular analytical form that was foundational to the discipline of anthropology and one that has remained in various guises to this day. However, this nineteenth-century category emerged within specific conditions to meet specific intellectual needs—needs that have changed considerably through the development of anthropology and, though related and similar to those in the present, are distinctly different from contemporary concerns. At stake here is the idea of the universalism of human being in its various guises, from the nineteenth-century concern with the "psychic unity of man" (Stocking 1995) to notions of universalism in the twentieth century. This analytical category thus needs to be reconsidered more directly in terms of its origins so that one might make better sense of it and its use in the present. Although the uses of this analytical category have changed considerably, the commitment to it remains strong.

By way of an earlier example, Joseph Rykwert (1981) notes how European commentators such as the seventeenth-century Bishop de Lobkowitz reaffirmed Vitruvius in the wake of explorers' observations. De Lobkowitz described the indigenous architecture in Hispaniola (Haiti) and the palace of the cacique of Hispaniola in classical terms. Rykwert notes that the bishop might have been aware of the stone traditions in other parts of the Americas but probably chose to ignore them. Instead, de Lobkowitz's purpose was to describe the universalism of the analytical trope of the "primitive hut" within the Vitruvian tradition, which evolved into the classical orders (Rykwert 1981: 137). By cataloging the evidence of these recurrent (if not at times imperfect) manifestations of the "primitive hut" of timbers, de Lobkowitz argued for the universalism of the classical orders for all of humanity from a distinctly ethnocentric European perspective as being the most evolved manifestation of these eternal principles that are in evidence everywhere, as the anthropological evidence would indicate—as could at once be seen in Haiti as well as within the European past and present.

It is later in the eighteenth century with the writings of the Abbé Laugier that speculation on the origins of architecture and the significance of the Vitruvian "primitive hut" regains increased significance (Figure 3). In the wake of European exploration and colonization and its encounters with other peoples and building traditions, the position of European forms was not so self-evident (Hvatuum 2004: 37). Only by peering beyond the surfaces, into the ethnographic "other" and the archaeological "other" of antiquity could the significance of forms be discerned. The question of the origin of architectural form was inseparable from the question of the origin of human social formations. Language, social order, and architecture were seen in this

Figure 3 Laugier's "primitive hut." *Source*: British Architectural Library, Royal Institute of British Architects.

Vitruvian tradition as inextricably linked. In the eighteenth century, Enlightenment-era thought was founded on the quest for origins to establish the foundations of rational thought. As Hvatuum notes, this is the tradition of rational certitude that we associate with Cartesianism: to find the fundamental unassailable principle upon which one can secure and found our reason and actions (Hvatuum 2004: 30–4). This preoccupation with form and its origins, however, was more importantly linked to early modern European concerns in relation to the emergence of new technologies—especially the printing press, which, as Carpo (2001) argues, emphasized visual form over other concerns. As Carpo notes, visual form through line drawing as advanced by the printing press and the radical spread of books proved the most effective means for the development, spread, and understanding of architectonic ideas, as opposed to the notoriously nonvisual and literary means by which Vitruvius's ideas were spread through handwritten manuscripts (Carpo 2001). The new technology enabled a powerful and stable form of understanding in visual and formal terms that could rise above the idiosyncrasies of local understanding and, through their visualized printed forms, achieve a stability and reproducibility that would transcend local contingencies, traditions, and space and produce a more universalizing form of knowledge (Carpo 2001).

Such Enlightenment-era preoccupations with the underlying principles behind superficial form are at the heart of the project of Rousseau and his search for the *homme naturel* as Hvatuum (2004: 31) notes. As with Rousseau, the Abbé Laugier, as Hvatuum observes, attempted to find the foundations of architecture, which were so intimately linked with social order and morality: "It is the same in architecture as in all other arts; its principles are founded on simple nature, and nature's process clearly indicates its rules" (Laugier 1977: 11 quoted in Hvatuum 2004: 31). Laugier notes further, "Such is the course of simple nature; by imitating the natural process, art was born. All the splendours of architecture ever conceived have been modelled on this little rustic hut I have just described. It is by approaching the simplicity of the first model that fundamental mistakes are avoided and true perfection is achieved" (Laugier 1977: 12 quoted in Hvatuum 2004: 31). Thus, the "primitive hut" was closest to God's divine creation and order. By human mimesis, the hut was reproduced and was a means of harnessing the power and authority of the divine through what can be described as sympathetic magic—that is, the reiteration of certain forms to reproduce and re-present and harness the power of the original form.

Laugier's project was clearly to establish these origins. Hvattum (2004: 34) notes how Laugier wanted to follow in Descartes's footsteps (a century earlier) in formulating a foundation for architectural reasoning—"an axiom for architecture." As Hvattum observes, "The domain of architecture, obscured by the relativity of taste and sensation, was now to be brought into the daylight of reason" (Hvattum 2004: 34),

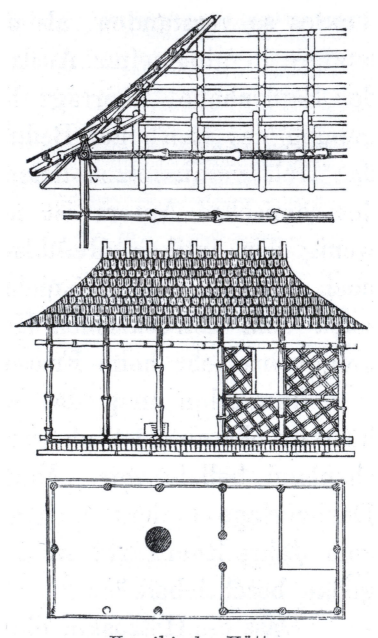

Karaibische Hütte.

Figure 4 Semper's Carib hut. *Source:* The University of Edinburgh.

thereby "to save architecture from eccentric opinions by disclosing its fixed and unchangeable laws" (Laugier quoted in Hvattum 2004: 34). Thus, rather than being the point of an obscure origin, as in Vitruvius, the "primitive hut" of Laugier, according to Hvattum, was a "Cartesian axiom" (2004: 34).

Hvattum notes how the mid-nineteenth-century theorist Gottfried Semper, though rejecting the idea of an original "primitive hut," did not see one direct prototype. Nonetheless, Semper still shared the project of finding an axiom, but in relation to a specific tradition: "[r]ather the origin and principle of architecture was to be found in the historical particularity of its inception" (Hvattum 2004: 35). Thus, anthropology provided numerous examples for how this might work across the world. Hvattum notes how Semper's supreme example was another architectural form, albeit a recent one, the "Carib hut" from the Crystal Palace at the Great Exhibition of 1851 (Figure 4). Hvatuum notes this was not an obscure abstraction like Laugier's example "but a real building"—"no phantom of the imagination, but a highly realistic exemplar of wooden construction, borrowed from ethnology" (Semper quoted in Hvattum 2004: 36). Semper went on to describe the hut thus: "all elements of ancient architecture appear in their most original and unadulterated form: the hearth as center, the mound surrounded by a framework of poles as terrace, the roof carried by columns, and mats as space enclosure or wall" (Semper quoted in Vuyosevich 1991: 6). In so doing, Semper could be seen to echo the Crystal Palace itself with its columns/"poles" framing glass/"mats" (Figure 5).

However, Semper's discussions of ornament—and, in particular, wall decoration—emerge as centrally relevant for the consideration of architectural forms. Unlike Viollet-Le-Duc, Pugin, and Ruskin (Mallgrave 1989: 40), who were preoccupied with the honesty of materials and architectural form, Semper turned the focus away from built structure to the surface of interior ornamentation. Surface and decoration were anterior to architectural form. Architectural elements such as walls were seen as merely inconsequential material supports for the decorative surface of walls. Semper argues this position from an investigation of nomadic and tent forms, arguing that woven partitions, textiles, and so on were primarily for the creation of enclosures and that walls per se as permanent architectural elements exist merely to support the surface (Semper 1989: 103–4). The veracity of the claim regarding the primal nature of textile partitioning over architectural form is not what is significant to note. What is noteworthy in Semper's analysis is a shift from form to surface as the key site for analysis. Semper posits an intriguing and productive reversal of concerns that at once opens out a more phenomenological engagement with the significance it attaches to surface. It suggests a more nuanced understanding of surface as the key site of social engagement in terms of use and maintenance of architectural forms, particularly in terms of quotidian activities that serve to reproduce social relations over the long

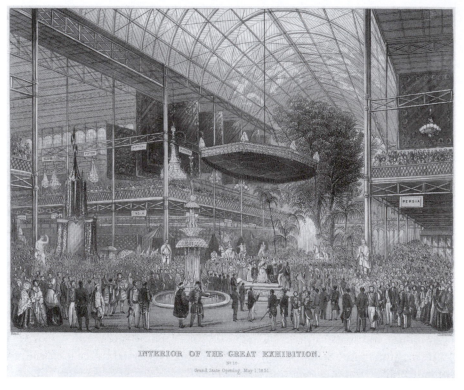

Figure 5 The Crystal Palace, 1851. *Source*: Mary Evans Picture Library.

term as opposed to the more infrequent interactions associated with the creation and maintenance of built forms per se.

Regarding Semper, Hvattum (2004: 37) argues that the possibility of a single unitary origin thesis was challenged by the proliferation of travel accounts by missionaries and others since the eighteenth century. These accounts began to contradict the notion of timelessness through their descriptions of encounters with the extraordinary diversity of built forms influenced by local conditions and circumstances. This indicated a shift to geographic particularism that Hvattum argues would later inform the notion of a *Volksgeist* and the subsequent role that notion would play in the creation of nationhood, national forms, and autochthonous national/ethnic and material culture origins. Later, these environmental concerns would be at the core of investigations into sustainability and environmental impact that dominate more recent explorations into vernacular and non-European and nonsedentary architectural forms (Amerlinck 2001; Prussin 1995; Rapoport 1969; Vellinga 2009).

Semper, Hvattum notes (2004: 42), thus rejected the idea of a unitary origin thesis and the idea of an actual originary "primitive hut"—and, along with it, the tripartite scheme of Quatremère, which described "three types of human communities: hunters and gatherers, nomadic herdsmen, and, finally agricultural peoples" (Hvatuum 2004: 39). True architecture within this scheme only emerged with the built forms of agricultural sedentary peoples (Neolithic revolution), and each architectural type referred to a particular kind of social organization and climatic condition (Hvattum 2004: 39–43).

Hvattum observes that Semper instead argued for the "poetic ideal" of architecture emerging from his study of the diverse and burgeoning anthropological sources of the nineteenth century. Hvattum notes the influence of Gustav Klemm, who was influential in exploring this diversity, which he investigated at heroic length in his *Allgemeine Kulturgeschichte der Menschheit* (2004: 43). He argued for the "human desire for representation," which resulted in the different types (*Kunsttrieb*). These forms echoed beliefs in origins through their mimesis of mythic understanding; basically, differences in material culture were differences in available techniques in effective representation (culminating in writing) (Hvattum 2004: 43–6). Keeping in mind this point of different techniques for instantiating mythic understanding, architecture and other arts represented "the urge to appropriate a world through playful imitation" (Hvattum 2004: 46). Eventually, Semper's response to the "primitive hut" was: "the constituent parts of form *that are not form itself*, but the idea, the force, the task and the means" (Semper quoted in Hvattum 2004: 65). As Hvattum notes, "It was Semper's lifelong ambition to find and define these 'constituent parts'—and he found them, not as archaeological facts but as a creative principle" (Hvattum 2004: 65). Semper argued that architecture, walls derived from woven panels, and the weaving and knots therein derived from ritual expression and dance: "The beginnings of building coincide with those of weaving" (Semper quoted in Hvattum 2004: 70). Hvattum observes that, for Semper, clothing, *Bekleidung*, was "intrinsically linked to spatial enclosure" and "preceded even the clothing of the human body" (Hvatuum 2004: 70–1), reiterating the common theme of the imbrication of body and built form and the wider phenomenological frame of this engagement.

Semper thus displaced the notion of the originary "primitive hut," as Hvatuum notes, and proposed "a composite structure composed of the four primary motifs, or elements, of architecture" (Hvatuum 2004: 71). The wall and its constituents imitate the original woven enclosure, the principle of which is encompassment. This is the principle or structure that is imitated in each age and culture. What is imitated is not the external form but the internal structure. Hvattum observes that Semper, like the comparative anatomist Cuvier, categorized built forms according to function: "not a formal but rather a functional entity, making it possible to compare functional relations rather than form" (Hvattum 2004: 130).

2

The Crystal Palace, of course, is key to understanding the context in which Semper's own insights into the origins of architectural forms emerge (see also discussions in Purbrick 2001). In reference to the Crystal Palace, Semper notes (quoted in Hermann 1984: 179): "If the slender columns had become the bearers of the "primitive" *velum*, which would have completely harmonized with the suspended draperies and figured carpets, . . . then we should have seen in this marvellous building the original type of the most primitive architecture unwittingly realised." It is at the exhibition that Semper encounters not only this new architectural form with atavistic motifs but also the model of the Caribbean hut exhibited in the colonial section (Hermann 1984: 169). It is important to note here the continued and intimate relationship drawn between clothing, dwelling, and language: the three categories of culture that traditionally distinguish humans from animals. The three act at various times as analogues for one another. In particular, the analogue of dwelling to clothing is fundamental and indicates the unstable and shifting relationship between architectural form and bodily form, where the two are often hard to distinguish meaningfully, as we shall see later (Casten and Hugh-Jones 1995).

As Rykwert (1981) asserts in *On Adam's House in Paradise*, the preoccupation with the "primitive hut" is an eternal preoccupation with the return to first principles. But the contention here is to move away from architectural form as the guarantor of these understandings, emphasizing instead the way architectural form is just one means of gathering, establishing propinquity—that is, bringing things and people in relation to one another—to effect relationships, to effectively make people. While there are other means for establishing relations of propinquity working within different material registers, these are often imbricated with architectonic ones. What is at stake in these discussions is the very essence of humanness, what sets humans apart, and the elemental categories of culture and the very terms by which these categories can be understood and at times expanded (see, for example, the work of Nold Egenter, who calls into question these distinctions and expands them outside of the human species in reference to nonhuman forms of architectural construction).

Rykwert argues that investigations into the "primitive hut" occur at times when there is a need for renewal (1981: 183). One can extend this to suggest that such speculations into original forms, be they a "primitive hut" of some sort or more recent biomimetic investigations, are all attempts at renewal in times of need. This is a theme concerning renewal and reiteration that justifies the preoccupation with the analytical category of built form from the works of Martin Heidegger in the mid-twentieth century to the developmental and reformist concerns at the heart of vernacular studies in the twenty-first century, where it is precisely the reiteration of these forms and their rearticulation and expansion that these categories of social life and the conflicts characterizing them are rehearsed, expanded, obviated, and challenged.

3

As with Gottfried Semper, the occasion of the Great Exhibition and the Crystal Palace marked an important moment not simply for the understanding of architectural form but for the development of comparative understandings of human society. The extraordinary gathering of objects and peoples under one vast glass-enclosed space made possible by the new materials and technologies of the Industrial Revolution could suggest the possibility of new forms of knowledge and their social mediation. The space itself, far grander than anything the ancient cabinets of curiosities could achieve, made possible the assembly of a vast (and decidedly less elite) public along with the enormous output of human productivity across time and space to facilitate not only the systematic understanding of the evolution of material forms and their attendant social formations but also their apprehension across a wide social scale encompassing both elite and working-class elements of British society. The production of such forms of knowledge within such radically democratic spaces and congregations could suggest Pitt Rivers's later efforts in Bethnal Green to educate and advance the wider working-class population of London and England, where such congregations simultaneously facilitated novel social reforms and forms of knowledge (Chapman 1985; Bennett 1995). The novel forms of the Crystal Palace, which suggested such new terms for renewal in the present for Semper and the underlying unitary principles of architectural form, arguably served a similar function for Pitt Rivers in his efforts to understand the unitary principles that might underlay the vast output of human technological achievement laid out in a manner theretofore inconceivable at the Crystal Palace Exhibition.

The Crystal Palace Exhibition demonstrated how the assembly of objects within a radical architectural frame could enable a systematization of knowledge unimaginable and unrealizable until that time. It is at the Crystal Palace that Pitt Rivers likely imagined a systematic and comparative setting that enabled a more rigorous and comparative science of humankind that inspired him to collect (Chapman 1985: 16). Pitt Rivers, preoccupied as he was with the rapidity of social and material change in the nineteenth century (Buchli 2004), found the means by which his "philosophy of progress" could be realized in systematic and material form. Artifacts as a comparative means for establishing knowledge had a long history since the cabinets of curiosities of Renaissance Europe that are the precursors of museums and the museological tradition familiar today (see Belk 1995; Pearce 1995; and Thomas 1997 for histories of these European collections). The emerging disciplines of archaeology and anthropology could engage with artifacts of far-flung and long-vanished societies as the primary means by which human societies could be systematically understood. Both disciplines of archaeology and anthropology relied on artifacts as their key data—the so-called object lessons described by Tylor (Buchli 2002) that were the key reference points in the development of the two allied disciplines.

This preoccupation was influenced not only by the collections of artifacts of far-flung peoples that constituted the primary means of contact with the lifeways of distant peoples and distant times, but it arose as well as part of an overwhelming sense of change that motivated figures such as Pitt Rivers himself. Initially, Pitt Rivers, as a military man, was preoccupied with the rapid change of firearms in his lifetime that necessitated a detailed understanding of those changes (Buchli 2004). Similarly, the vast and unprecedented scope of changes and differences that were experienced in the nineteenth century in the wake of the Industrial Revolution required a systematic understanding cast in terms of a "philosophy of progress" (Buchli 2004). Such comparisons enabled the articulation of emerging liberal principles of universal progress and unilineal evolution. The "psychic unity of man" could be understood in these terms, where all peoples in time and space could be seen as possessing one common humanity but in terms of varying degrees of technological progress. But this progress was tinged with a profound sense of melancholy, which fueled the anthropological effort as expressed by Pitt Rivers in 1867:

> for there can be little doubt that in a few years all the most barbarous races will have disappeared from the Earth, or will have ceased to preserve their native arts. The law which consigns to destruction all savage races when brought into contact with a civilization much higher than their own, is now operating with unrelenting fury in every part of the world. (Pitt Rivers 1867)

The racist, imperialist and ethnocentric legacies of unilineal evolutionism have been well and justly rehearsed, but it is important to remember the strong liberal and universalizing values that a philosophy of progress enabled and the object lessons that material culture served. Figures such as Tylor, according to Stocking, saw anthropology as a "liberal 'reformer's science'" (Stocking 1995: xiv).

4

With the Crystal Palace building and its wide, brightly lit expanses made possible by the industrial production of glass and cast iron, one was able—in a rather spectacular fashion—to experience what many later liberal Victorian thinkers would call the "psychic unity of mankind" attributed to the nineteenth-century German anthropologist Adolph Bastian. On a sensual and intellectual level, such a space could facilitate this sense of psychic unity on an unprecedented and decidedly embodied level. It is precisely the ability of these industrialized spaces to assemble in an extraordinary way (see Latour and Weibel 2002, on assembly and the *Ding*) new forms of community and new forms of knowledge. Thus, Semper could begin to discern the underlying principles that made sense of the bewildering diversity of human technical and artistic output that were neatly summarized in the elegant little Carib hut. Similarly, Pitt Rivers might have seen a theoretical and material way of displaying and thinking about the diverse technical outputs of various human societies that would inform the unilineal evolutionary schemes he was proposing, his first systematic studies of material culture and the evolution of human societies (Figure 6). As the cabinets of curiosities facilitated comparison and novel linkages between diverse things, so too could the Crystal Palace on an unprecedented scale and to as a wide a public as was possible. The remnants and effects of this comparison are still to be found in the

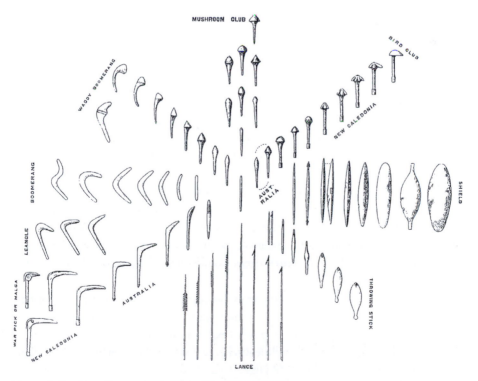

Figure 6 Pitt Rivers's weaponry. *Source:* Pitt Rivers, 1875a.

encyclopedic collections of London's Science Museum and Victoria & Albert Museum, whose foundations followed the Great Exhibition of 1851.

Artifacts constituted as material cultures were used to characterize peoples according to their level of social and technological progress. These unilineal notions of social and technological progress were best exemplified in Lewis Henry Morgan's *Ancient Society*. Morgan's work in material culture studies, along with that of other anthropologists, was instrumental in the development of the materialist philosophies of Marx and Engels. As Marx was to note: "Relics of bygone instruments of labour possess the same importance for the investigation of extinct economic forms of society, as do fossil bones for the determination of extinct species of animals" (Marx 1986: 78). With this understanding one could elucidate past and current forms and speculate as to their progress into the future. Later, feminists, in their rediscovery of Engels's writings, were to use these same insights into existing forms of domestic life, gender, and sexuality and to speculate on the development of new, socially just forms. The object lessons produced by such a philosophy of progress were to be highly influential for the development of social and historical critiques in the nineteenth and twentieth centuries as well as serving as the basis for the critical imagination of new forms of social life at the heart of progressive social movements.

Lewis Henry Morgan articulated in a manner more extensive than Pitt Rivers the relation between material form and social form, further developing a coherent and powerful theory of unilineal human and social evolution that formed the theoretical backbone of much North American anthropology and archaeology into the twentieth century as well as the basis of Soviet Marxian theories of human evolution and material culture that have shaped the anthropological understanding of architecture. Morgan similarly argued along themes laid out by Laugier, and later by Semper, in keeping with the Victorian notion of the psychic unity of man: "All the forms of this architecture sprang from a common mind, and exhibit, as a consequence, different stages of development of the same conceptions, operating upon similar necessities. . . Their houses will be seen to form one system of works, from the Long House of the Iroquois [Figure 7] to the Joint Tenement house of adobe and of stone in New Mexico, Yucatan, Chiapas and Guatemala, with such diversities as the different degrees of advancement of these several tribes would naturally produce" (Morgan 1965 [1881]: xxiii–xxiv).

For Morgan, examples such as the Iroquois represented the lower period of barbarism, and Aztecs the middle period of barbarism. Thus, when encountering such forms, one could literally go back in time to examine an earlier stage of unitary social evolution. Therefore, Morgan's unilineal scheme could be summarized in this chart from *Ancient Society* (Morgan 1978 [1877]: 12):

FIG. 12.—Ho-de'-no-sote of the Seneca-Iroquois.

Figure 7 Morgan's Iroquois longhouse. *Source:* Morgan, 1965 (1881).

I.   Lower Status of Savagery, From the Infancy of the Human Race to the commencement of the next Period.

II. Middle Status of Savagery, From the acquisition of a fish subsistence and a knowledge of the use of fire to etc.

III. Upper Status of Savagery, From the invention of the bow and arrow, to etc.

IV. Lower Status of Barbarism, From the Invention of the Art of Pottery, to etc.

V.   Middle Status of Barbarism, From the Domestication of animals on the Eastern Hemisphere, and in the Western from the cultivation of maize and plants by Irrigation, with the use of adobe-brick and stone, to etc.

VI. Upper Status of Barbarism, From the Invention of the process of Smelting Iron Ore, with the use of iron tools, to etc.

VII. Status of Civilization, From the Invention of a Phonetic Alphabet, with the use of writing, to the present time.

One particular exemplar within Morgan's work on the architecture of American Indians as part of one system of unitary evolution was his example of the Iroquois longhouse which he referred to as embodying "communism in living": "Here was communism in living carried out in practical life, but limited to the household, and an expression of the principle in the plan of the house itself" (Morgan 1965 [1881]: 127). The Iroquois longhouse also exemplified the principle of *Mutterrecht*, or "mother right," developed by Bachofen that was to lie at the heart of Engels's later assault on the nineteenth-century institutions of the family and gender in *The Origin of the Family, Private Property and the State*, which was to be the Soviet Union's primer on prehistory until the 1930s (Miller 1956) and an early text of feminist history and social theory.

Morgan's conclusion that "they practised communism in living in the household, and that this principle found expression in their house architecture and predetermined its character" (Morgan 1965 [1881]: 139) resonated with a prevailing consensus that architectonic forms created their respective forms of social life and being. The formalistic language employed by Morgan, with his focus on form, spatial arrangement, and the materials used to create these forms, tended to emphasize the abstract structural aspects of architecture (not the rich context of their daily use and experience) as the modern print tradition dictated (Carpo 2001). Drawings emphasized these abstracted structural principles, with only passing references to atmosphere, noise, smell, clutter, artifacts, human activity, and so on. These abstracted images appear in a sense cut and pasted, to use a contemporary expression, from earlier source books and, in the spirit of the synthetic endeavors of armchair anthropology, systematized according to recent developments in social theory. Print, paper, and the book form facilitated such comparative explorations, as Latour once noted in relation to the emergence of Lévi-Strauss's theories as an artifact of the card catalog of the Collège de France (Latour 1990: 19). Such images abstracted and compiled according to the underlying principles of Morgan's unilineal scheme of evolution functioned in similar manner to Thomas's (1991, 1997) observations regarding the empirically detailed images of the late eighteenth and early nineteenth centuries, whose promiscuity and formal qualities enabled them to be incorporated into and produce other forms of knowledge such as unilineal schemes and others in their attempts to describe the history and form of the psychic unity of man. Such architectural images functioned in the manner of an *épure* as described by Anthony Vidler (2000) in reference to standardized and modernist architectural drawings in the twentieth century, which evacuated the specificity of local understandings and engagement in order to produce stable, interchangeable, and more universal understandings of architectonic knowledge. In the later part of the nineteenth century, anthropology and archaeology fueled the political imaginary through these abstracted and interchangeable forms in highly significant ways, as we shall see from the profound influence Morgan had on the development of the political and historical work of Karl Marx and Friedrich Engels.

In retrospect, the Crystal Palace can be seen as a watershed, which gave full expression to the new forms of spatiality, community, and knowledge that industrialized forms enabled and facilitated a new form of universality evinced in later ideas concerning the psychic unity of man. Later figures, such as Walter Benjamin writing in the early part of the twentieth century, noted how the antecedents of the Crystal Palace found in the glass-covered arcades of Paris produced a new kind of space with new kinds of activities and social relations. The figure of the *flâneur* in Benjamin's writings exemplifies this new form of personhood. He is produced within these new and early spaces emerging with industrialization and is constituted into being within its material effects and the new kinds of spatial and social relations these materials and technologies engendered.

As public space takes on a new dimension of interiority in Benjamin's writings in response to the spaces of the arcades, the domestic interior is equally transformed, becoming a distinct and atomized, dense space that is productive of a new interiorized self.

> The 19th century, like no other century, was addicted to dwelling. It conceived the residence as a receptacle for the person, and it encased him with all his appurtenances so deeply in the dwelling's interior that one might be reminded of the inside of a compass case, where the instrument with all its accessories lies embedded in deep, usually violet folds of velvet. (Benjamin 1999: 220)

The quote reveals a certain enduring preoccupation with the lessons of natural history and the European preoccupation with visual form, where architecture and architectural spaces are seen as being fossil-like, able to be arranged and understood in terms of material and structural forms to produce "genus and species." The domestic sphere and the home take an almost anatomized form ready for description, inspection, and comparison; it becomes a kind of corpus delicti. Marx's subsequent metaphor serves to describe how architectural and domestic spaces can be interpreted as fossils, as the remains of the indwelt surfaces of living beings (see Marx 1986: 78). Such fossil metaphors have endured well into the twentieth century, as noted in the writings of Csikszentmihalyi and Rochberg-Halton: "Like some strange race of cultural gastropods, people build homes out of their own essence, shells to shelter their personality. But, then, these symbolic projections react on their creators, in turn shaping the selves they are. The envelope thus created is not just a metaphor" (1981: 138).

As a corpus delicti, these fossilizations of lifeways not only suggested alternative and progressive modes of living but specific architectural principles, as suggested in Semper's writings. Archaeology and anthropology influenced the development of architectural thinking and political imagination particularly in the later years of the nineteenth century and the first part of the twentieth century. Le Corbusier, for one, was a keen student of studies of archeological forms, which, according to Vogt, was the source of Le Corbusier's ideal of the minimal essential architectural unit, the *cellule*, which was to form the basis of his modernist vocabulary (1998: 216). Such ancient forms gave proof to the primacy of geometry and an eternal platonic preoccupation with geometric forms and the divine order these inspired, accessible to early man with "primitive" means (Vogt 1998: 215–19).

More spectacular in these regards was the discovery of the lake dwellings of Lake Zurich in Switzerland in 1854 (Figure 8). Vogt observes how Keller's visual reference by analogy to dwellings from the Pacific served to promote the idea of the psychic unity of man, which influenced the highly publicized images of these dwellings; thus, a common cultural level could be discerned through analogous technical responses to similar conditions. The seemingly improbable analogy between alpine

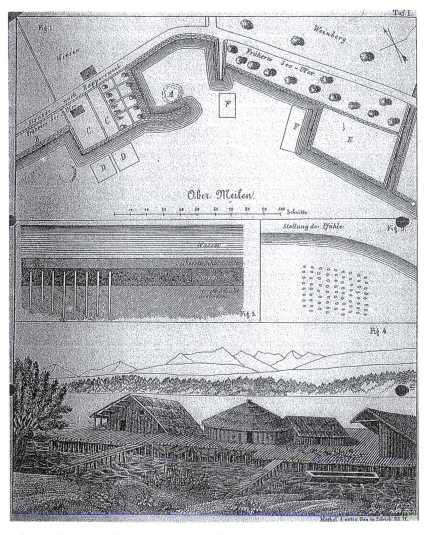

Figure 8 Lake Zurich dwellings. *Source:* Vogt, 1998.

peoples and the peoples of the Pacific could be made by reference to similar forms, technologies, and types of social organization within the spirit of the psychic unity of man and unilineal evolution.

Vogt argued that "Keller was aware that his transposition of the picture of the Doreï village to primeval Switzerland—what the schoolbook *La Patrie* called the 'analogy to Polynesia'—was a *retrograde ethnological inference*. In the middle of the nineteenth century this method of retrogressive inference was fascinating because it promised to supplant the *mythological approximation of first origins* with a *pragmatic approximation*" (Vogt 1998: 232).

Keller also noted that artifacts found at the site were similar to the artifacts discussed by Captain Cook from New Zealand (Vogt 1998: 232). The productive force of comparative empirical criteria could make a compelling material and theoretical claim for the inherent similarity of cultures and their social and material forms despite wildly different temporal, geographic, and climactic contexts.

Morgan, Keller, and others relied on such images and then, of course, used them as evidence of the categories according to which they organized them—simply reassembling images from earlier sources in addition to the ones they themselves caused to be made. Decontextualized, yet represented in great detail, the empirical quality of these images was compelling, as Nicholas Thomas asserts in regard to "curiosity." But they had a certain promiscuity, as Thomas further argues (Thomas 1991), that attached themselves more readily to their beholders, and particularly those armchair anthropologists of the nineteenth century who scoured these representations, particularly those of dwellings.

5

The Victorian legacy of systematically establishing the psychic unity of man was carried through into the unilineal evolutionary schema of Marxists, especially later Soviet Marxists. However, such schemes became increasingly disillusioning in other circles. The Boasian and subsequent Malinowskian tradition worked against this evolutionist approach within ethnology, in which architecture had an important place. Despite this waning interest, the understanding of dwelling and "house-life" as process and technique lies at the heart of the two single most important thinkers on the home within the anthropology of the middle part of the twentieth century: the French anthropologists Claude Lévi-Strauss and Pierre Bourdieu. These two followed a vein of inquiry going back to Marcel Mauss, where architecture is understood as "the archetypal art, as creation par excellence" (Mauss 2006: 130).

Mauss argued forcefully against the abstracted morphological account of housing implicated in the establishment of national traditions and the "almost comic" efforts at the Versailles Peace Conference after the First World War that "such and such nation should extend here or there, on the grounds that we can still find there such or such shape of house" (Mauss 2006: 43). These comments reveal the limits of the formal comparative method as well as the importance of such formal typologies for the establishment of vernacular studies and the consolidation of nation-states. Instead, Mauss argued for the significance of architectural forms as the key technology by which social life and reproduction are made possible. As such, within this emergent tradition, the idiosyncratic problem-solving and dynamic qualities of dwelling were emphasized. In this vein, Lévi-Strauss characterized the home as a specific problem-solving entity (Gibson 1995), as did Bourdieu with his concept of the dwelling as an *opus operatum*. Within Lévi-Strauss's concept of "house societies," he notes how the house serves as the "*objectification of a relation*: the unstable relation of alliance which, as an institution, the role of the house is to solidify, if only in an illusory form" (1987: 155). The house as such an "illusory objectification" (Carsten and Hugh-Jones 1995) serves to reconcile social tensions. Here Lévi-Strauss gives emphasis to the idea of the house as a deliberate fetishization or misrecognition of a relationship in the spirit of Marx (Carsten and Hugh-Jones 1995: 8). This misrecognition, however, as mentioned earlier, is a productive one that attempts to negotiate, relieve, and overcome existing tensions toward the creation of particular form of human life—one that is characterized by dynamic processes over static ones (Carsten and Hugh-Jones 1995: 37).

House form as analytical trope in the nineteenth century can be understood as a misrecognition, a fetishization, as Pietz (1985) describes in relation to the origins of the term and the concept of the fetish, that emerges as a result of an encounter. Here, the encounter can be understood as between colonial-era administrators, agents of the nation-state, surveyors, missionaries, and anthropologists and the subjects of governance, be they the inhabitants of consolidating nation-states or indigenous non-Western peoples in the colonial sphere, and within this encounter the house as an analytical category and instrument of governance emerges. These architectural typologies and their attributes are some of the first things constituted and noted within the colonial and administrative encounter, serving as means of surveying, classifying, and administering a population rather than being understood according to its own local terms. Yet despite its violence, this is also a productive misrecognition, rather like an *opus operatum*, according to Bourdieu, or the "illusory objectification" (Carsten and Hugh-Jones 1995) suggested by Lévi-Strauss, that resolves difference and tensions toward the constitution of a new, or novel moral collectivity—on the one hand, the house society of Lévi-Strauss; on the other, the universal humanism embodied by the concept of the psychic unity of man in the nineteenth-century context or the governed and enfranchised "citizens" of a nation-state.

6

Within the context of Anglo-American anthropology, this disillusionment with house form and unilineal schemas was notably signaled in the work of Franz Boas. Stocking notes how Boas questioned evolutionary classifications of "genera and species" and the preoccupation with form as a basis for analyses that "were not instead superficially similar instances of phenomena with quite different cultural meanings" (Stocking 1995: 12). However, this disillusionment was most pronounced in the wake of 1922, the annus mirabilis, which, according to Stocking (1995), was when Malinowski's *Argonauts of the Western Pacific* was written as well as Radcliffe-Brown's *The Andaman Islanders*. These works consolidated a mandate for fieldwork-based anthropology. Additionally, the stress on the importance of direct contact and representation must be understood in light of rapidly vanishing cultures in the face of colonial administration and contact. Societies were disappearing too quickly to merely collect objects and classify them.

Frazer's introduction to *Argonauts of the Western Pacific* praised Malinowski for seeking "to penetrate the motives" of behavior. This signaled a shift to psychological life and mind. As Frazer noted, "sociology cannot fulfill its task without calling in at every turn the aid of psychology" (Frazer in Malinowski 1961 [1922]: viii–ix). The way of looking moved beyond appearances and typologies, with a slight but crucial shift toward emphasizing mind. In another vein, in Malinowski's equally complimentary "Frazer Lecture," Stocking notes how Malinowski called on the anthropologist to " 'relinquish his comfortable position in the long chair on the veranda of the missionary compound, Government station, or planters bungalow' and go out into the village and the garden, where information would flow 'full-flavoured from his own observations of native life, and not be squeezed out of reluctant informants as a trickle of talk' " (Malinowski cited in Stocking 1995: 234). This was his appeal according to Stocking for an "open-air anthropology" (Stocking 1995: 234).

This announced a spatial shift in the way anthropological knowledge was to be constituted. In his text, Stocking notes how Malinowski places "the Ethnographer's tent" at the start and finish of his narrative (Stocking 1995: 272; also Stocking 1999).

Stocking refers to similar photographs (Figure 9) as representing "ethnographic authority: 'The Ethnographer' at work" (Stocking 1995: 262; Rosaldo 1986). This placement indicates a significant shift from what might be called, in more modern terms, an "anthropology of space" signaled by the evolutionary works of Morgan, Pitt Rivers, and others to a methodologically innovative reconfiguration of the "space of anthropology." Thus, Stocking notes, "As 'the ethnographer' Malinowski was not only capable of sharing their vision of the their world, but knew things about it that they would never know, bringing to light 'phenomena of human nature' which 'had remained hidden even from those in whom they happened'" (Stocking 1995: 272). Authority in Malinowski's account was derived from the representation of an experience that could penetrate the inner lives and motives of his informants—a vast methodological and epistemic shift away from the object lessons of nineteenth-century material culture studies.

At the same time, the emphasis on mind evinced a renewed preoccupation with the universality of underlying structures. Stocking notes that Radcliffe-Brown had a "structuralist" inclination because of his earlier study of anatomy (Stocking 1995: 304). Similarly influenced by the radicalism of the Russian anarchist Prince Kropotkin, Radcliffe-Brown stated that "Kropotkin, revolutionary, but still a scientist, pointed

Figure 9 Field tent. *Source:* The Library of the London School of Economics & Political Science, reference Malinowski/3/18/7.

out how important for any attempt to improve society was a scientific understanding of it, and the importance in this respect of what our friend Elie Reclus called 'primitive folk'" (Radcliffe-Brown cited in Stocking 1995: 305).

Within this emergent new vein of social anthropology, Radcliffe-Brown noted that which was significant was found "not in native explanations but in its 'interrelation with other elements' and its place 'in the whole life of the people'" (Stocking 1995: 351). Thus, cultural features could be related to "known sociological laws" that could be uncovered through the "comparative method"—that is, the "synchronic study of 'many diverse types of culture' and of the 'variations of a single culture type'" (Stocking 1995: 351). Since "simple societies" were rapidly disappearing, it was more urgent to study them before any diachronic study could be meaningfully possible (as would be warranted in an archaeological or material culture context [Stocking 1995: 351]).

Stocking notes how, in the early 1930s, "Radcliffe-Brown looked forward to the 'task of the twentieth and succeeding centuries' as 'that of uniting all the peoples of the world in some sort of ordered community'" (Stocking quoting Radcliffe Brown 1995: 352)—which proved attractive to people with socially progressive ambitions (Stocking 1995: 352). As such, Radcliffe-Brown arguably shared some common purpose with Marxian schema of unilineal evolution and the foundation of the Soviet Union and Soviet theories of language indebted to Nikolai Marr, which advocated the merging of peoples and languages into new unitary forms with the advance of socialism into communism.

Of course, as Stocking notes, understanding such structures was effective not only for realizing social progress but for more effective colonial management. As colonial management shifted to local government structures and rule through local elites, social anthropology's functionalism served these administrative colonial goals well, even if this was a double-edged sword: "Whereas evolutionism had served primarily as the ideological legitimation of the initial conquest of 'savage races' by 'civilized' Europeans, the 'function of functionalism' was to sustain an established and routinized colonial order by clarifying the principles of traditional native systems through which 'indirect rule' could be carried on" (Stocking 1995: 368). Similarly, more recently, the late-twentieth-century postmodern concern with identity and diversity in the face of essentialism has been criticized by figures such as the art historian Boris Groys (2008), who sees the articulation of diversity and identity as the driving force of late capitalist market economies. This is a concern echoing sociologist Nicholas Rose's (1990, 1996) discussions of identity and lifestyle production as the cornerstone of the political and social contract that produces the forms of governance characterizing late capitalist neoliberalist societies. The ambivalent legacy of universalism in the twentieth century can be seen in the preoccupation with mind—in particular, the structures of mind and cognitive processes in the light of the development of linguistic thought. It is here that we see the beginnings of the linguistic turn and the rise of structuralism. The Vitruvian passage cited earlier stakes out the intimate connection between architectural form and language as being forged in relation to one another. With the rise of linguistics in the early twentieth century, the structural analysis of language provided a means by which to consider architectural forms in terms of underlying cognitive structure. Later twentieth-century figures in American folklore such as Henry Glassie along with the historical archaeologist James Deetz were instrumental in the development of linguistics-based models of structuralism applied to material culture. This linguistic turn in the wake of structuralism echoed the linguistic analogies employed by earlier Victorian figures such as Pitt Rivers toward the study of material culture, "that by studying their grammar, we may be able to conjugate their forms" (Pitt Rivers 1875b: 300). The question of why such a renewed focus should emerge will be later asked in regard to changes in postwar social life.

7

While the study of architectural forms and material culture waned with the rise of British social anthropology, the case was very different for Soviet archaeologists who were preoccupied with them because of the importance of evolutionary frameworks for the development of Marxist thought (Buchli 2000). Similarly, folklore and museum studies within nationalist traditions retained an interest in vernacular architectural forms that constituted understandings of national culture and nation-building enterprises. The role of architecture as a source of renewal remained in national folkloric traditions; similarly, it remained in the Soviet context, where it continued in the reformist vein of nineteenth-century philosophies of progress.

With the postwar period, the positions of such studies of architectural forms and other analytical categories of material culture take on a different and renewed significance. Within the anglophone tradition, certain investigators occupy a particularly important position—namely, E. T. Hall, Amos Rapoport, and Henry Glassie, who revived the significance of architectural form for the study of human society. The postwar period saw a particular emphasis placed on the understanding of architecture and housing form. As Heidegger observed in relation to the postwar period, dwelling takes on a particular importance in the wake of the devastation of the Second

World War and the subsequent housing boom in Europe and America in the years after: "The proper dwelling plight lies in this, that mortals ever search anew for the essence of dwelling, that they *must ever learn to dwell*" (Heidegger 1993: 363; see Heynen 1999).

The architectural historian Amos Rapoport, in particular, plays a pivotal role in reestablishing the importance of vernacular studies toward the renewal of mid-twentieth-century housing and social problems, invoking indirectly the trope of the "primitive hut" as source for renewal as posited by Rykwert. The preoccupation with underlying forms—and, in particular, the emphasis on the psychic unit of man—continues to maintain its hold on postwar thinkers. Rapoport reiterates Morgan's point that "primitive" architecture is "primitive" in means, not concept. Rapoport notes the dearth of interest in architecture, asks why such interest should develop now, and answers that there is much that we can learn from the past. At first glimpse, this might seem a rather unsatisfactory answer, but upon closer examination, writing in the United States in 1969, one must keep in mind the postwar boom in economy and population. Rapoport (1969: 12) asks: "Why study primitive and pre-industrial house form in the space age, with its rapid tempo of change?"—a question that was perfectly self-evident in 1851 at the time of the Crystal Palace Exhibition (see essays in Purbrick 2001). In the first part of the answer, Rapoport posits that we need to study such forms to understand the complexities of our increasingly diverse cities and environments, but secondly he argues that "comparisons of this type can offer an insight into the basic nature of shelter and 'dwelling,' of the design process and the meaning of 'basic needs'" (Rapoport 1969: 12).

Here the echo of Laugier and the Cartesian axioms of architecture are felt again almost two centuries later. There is the persistent idea that such "primitive" buildings and vernaculars are closer to nature and in fact productive of mid-twentieth-century Euro-American notions of nature: "Building of this type tends toward a state of balance with nature rather than dominating it, which further reinforces its superiority over the grand design tradition as a topic of study for the relation of the built environment to man and nature" (Rapoport 1969: 13). Similarly, the belief is expressed that since the vernacular is tradition and not subject to fashion and technological change, "such societies extend from the dim past to the present day" (Rapoport 1969: 14), suggesting in a manner familiar to most nineteenth-century unilineal thinkers that one can directly access earlier periods of time in relation to the formal complexity of architectural and technical forms. One can say that Rapoport in these writings might have believed in the nineteenth-century commonality of form and mind that would suggest Oceania in the Alps: "European Neolithic lake dwellings on stilts seem identical to some in New Guinea" (1969: 14). In the manner of Morgan, Rapoport investigates a whole array of types that "seem identical" to others, citing drawings within manuscripts and bringing attention to similar formal typological attributes: "In all of these examples, the existence of an accepted model with few major innovations has resulted in the very strong persistence of form" (1969: 14).

It is important to note that Morgan's *Houses and House-Life of the American Aborigines* (1881) was republished in 1965, a few years before Rapoport's key 1969 text. Morgan's *House-Life* had been separated out from *Ancient Society* of which it was supposed to have been the fifth part. But because the final volume would have been too large to publish, the section on architecture was published separately by the U.S. Government Printing Office in Contributions to North American Ethnology (volume 4, 1881) (see Morgan's original preface: 1965 [1881]: xxiii).

8

The arc described here from Morgan to Rapoport shows an enduring concern with the constitution of the universality of human forms of habitation and their implications for our understanding of mind, body, environment, and history. At a higher level of analysis, this arc can be understood in terms of an abiding concern with constituting the contours and extent of what is universally human—in short, these investigations at the level of discourse make up human being, just as the dwellings themselves make and constitute the various forms of human biological and social life. As Rapoport claims to want to identify those "which seem most universal, and to examine them in different contexts so that we can best understand what it is that affects the forms taken" (Rapoport 1969: 17). However, the key distinction to earlier universalist approaches to mind and cultural evolution is the concern Rapoport and others, such as Susan Kent within archaeology, have for developmental issues—a major concern in the postwar era, along with the rise of developmental anthropology. Similarly, it is the excess of diversity that motivates such investigations into the universality of human forms, such as the problem of diversity in choice in house form and furnishings fueled by the postwar boom: "The result is the problem of excessive choice, the difficulty of selecting or finding constraints which arose naturally in the past and which are necessary for the creation of meaningful house form" (Rapoport 1969: 135).

It is worth considering why these ideas reappear regarding mind, language, and structure. It is not just that one is reinventing the wheel every time; the fact is, one needs to build always again and again, so the social project of building requires its reconsideration each time. This is the continuous process by which human life and its novel forms are made, as Heidegger noted earlier: "The proper dwelling plight lies in this, that mortals ever search anew for the essence of dwelling, that they *must ever learn to dwell*" (Heidegger 1993: 363). The continuous reiteration of the task is the productive and creative force that sustains the task of making people in the face of eternally shifting contingencies.

2 ARCHITECTURE AND ARCHAEOLOGY

I

Anthropological archaeology has traditionally been the subfield of anthropology that has concerned itself most emphatically with the study of material culture, and architecture in particular. As Ross Samson puts it, archaeology is the study of "the dead, the dross and the domicile" (1990: 1). Traditionally, archaeology has almost invariably been preoccupied with architectural remains. However, within archaeology, a particular subfield of research—ethno-archaeology—emerged with the New Archaeology of the postwar period with particular significance for the anthropological study of architecture. At this time the interface between people, material culture, and architecture assumed a renewed methodological and theoretical significance for the study of society. This chapter will examine this tradition along with postprocessual responses to the New Archaeology and the similarities and differences of these approaches toward the study of architecture. In turn the different ways in which the materiality of built form has been dealt with will be discussed. In short, this chapter is about archaeology and the perspectives enabled by its preoccupation with long temporal frames. This has enabled an extraordinarily rich perspective on the anthropology of architecture. It has facilitated, as we shall see, the development of evolutionist forms of thought, Marxism, and the promise of political renewal in the present. In addition, the preoccupation with the structures of the mind and language with the development of linguistic analogies and structuralism, along with the performative nature of architectural engagements, have more recently enabled discussions of architecture as extended forms within multiple material registers across varying dimensions of time, space, and embodied engagement.

Anthropological archaeology's preoccupation with architecture is really a consequence of the specific material conditions constituting the archaeological record—quite simply, the remains and footprints of buildings are some of the most enduring artifacts. But within this context it is mostly a particular material register that is engaged with: the monumental and materially durable remains are the focus of analysis, as opposed to more ephemeral forms of building, which often do not endure and are otherwise invisible in the archaeological record except through the use more recently of highly sophisticated excavation and laboratory techniques.

For these reasons, archaeology as a discipline has probably developed some of the more sophisticated attempts within anthropology to address the issues surrounding architectural form, from describing the primary material contexts of human social evolution through time to constituting the debates surrounding heritage and the production of communities and nation-states in the present. Archaeology has paid particular attention to the materiality of built forms to engage with these issues— a preoccupation that arises from the inherently empirical and material nature of the data archaeologists have traditionally dealt with.

Archaeology's inherently historical approach—working in scales of diachronic time as opposed to the synchronic scales of the ethnographic moment characterizing ethnographic research—has meant that archaeology has naturally lent itself to various diachronic, and notably evolutionary, approaches since the nineteenth century. The unilineal evolutionism of Lewis Henry Morgan, with its distinctive emphasis on the development of architectural form, held a particular appeal to archaeologists. Looking closely at nineteenth-century and mid-twentieth-century texts, there is often little to distinguish, fundamentally, the kinds of evolutionary approaches being proposed over the span of a century.

What is important to bear in mind in relation to archaeological engagements with architecture is the profound preoccupation with form, the principles that structure a given form, and the capacity of these structures to enable comparison across time, space, and cultures. More important, archaeology provides a deep temporal perspective at once amenable to evolutionary perspectives of various kinds from Marxist to environmental, and more recently to an understanding of architecture as process over different scales of time and material registers.

2

In another, yet connected relation, the architectural forms encountered in archaeology— notably those provided by prehistory—could provide evidence of the earliest stages of human social evolution and their social formations that would capture the imagination of radical political thinkers. The discovery of Upper Paleolithic sites in the nineteenth century influenced the development of the political imagination in other ways, such as the parallel rise of interest in the Paleolithic in radical Russian political circles (Buchli 2000).

One of the great investigators into the Paleolithic as it emerged in the late nineteenth century was Feodor Kondrat'evich Volkov. An ardent Narodnik, he trained his student, Petr Petrovich Efimenko, who became a preeminent archaeologist of Soviet times (Buchli 2000). The Paleolithic and its dwellings were virtually ignored in the West but were the subject of intensive research among Soviet archaeologists (Childe 1950: 4). Notably, these structures offered evidence of the forms of life that corresponded with Morgan's stage of savagery and matriarchy, particularly because of the discovery of female figurines (Figure 10).

As such, archaeological and anthropological forms served as a means of imagining what the next of stage of social and political evolution would look like for Russian and

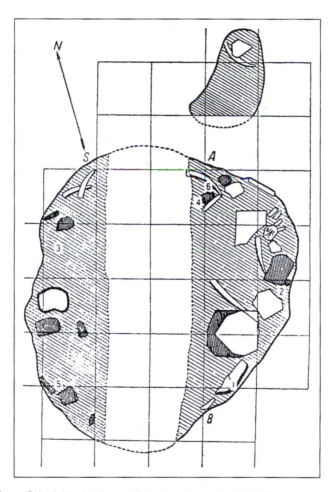

Figure 10 Upper Paleolithic dwelling at Gagarino. *Source*: Buchli, 2000.

later Soviet social reformers. Soviet Marxists updated the unilineal schema outlined by Morgan, introducing further socialist and final communist phases whose material culture and social organization might echo the earlier egalitarian forms found in prehistory. Much of the debate in late-1920s Soviet planning between urbanist and disurbanist forms was a question of what one might otherwise call a competition between huts and longhouses as to which of the two egalitarian structural forms would be appropriate for the realization of socialism (see debates in Buchli 1999). Morgan's Iroquois longhouse would emerge later in Soviet planning literature as the historical precursor to mid-twentieth-century Soviet modernist housing proposals, as can be seen in references to the Iroquois longhouse in Gradov's primer on Soviet planning (see discussion in Buchli 1999: 196).

As mentioned earlier, with the rise of British social anthropology in the wake of the disillusionment with unilinealism, architecture as an analytical category started to lose its immediate appeal along with other material culture approaches in the face of the detailed and intimate encounters of ethnographic fieldwork. However, there is a continuity between the evolutionism of Lewis Henry Morgan and British social anthropology in terms of the importance placed on kinship, despite the tendency for material culture—and architecture in particular—to move to the periphery of anthropological analysis. The underlying preoccupation with social structure within this emphasis on kinship meant that certain resonances were still maintained, especially as regards wider political agenda. This is certainly the case with Radcliffe-Brown and his political beliefs as they related to the decidedly unilineal approaches of Marxist archaeologists and later neo-Marxist approaches in the twentieth century. There were common underlying currents despite the apparent lack of direct engagement. It was certainly the case that nationalist archaeological traditions in the area of folklore studies continued to maintain a significant engagement with the study of architectural forms as a means by which to constitute a common national past and thereby forge a common national future. In addition, the Marxist-inspired Russian Revolution meant that emerging Soviet archaeology retained an interest in the study of the origins of architectural forms as part of a wider political and social agenda sustained by Marxian notions of unilineal evolutionism.

3

The rise of geology, paleontology, and archaeological prehistory went hand in hand in the nineteenth century (see Lucas 2000; Schnapp 1996; Trigger 1989). Within this context, the fossil metaphor emerged as a dominant trope for understanding architectural form and material culture more widely, as Marx himself was to note: "Relics of bygone instruments of labour possess the same importance for the investigation of extinct economic forms of society, as do fossil bones for the determination of extinct species of animals" (Marx 1986: 78). The fossil as dominant analogical trope (see Stafford 1999) enabled a wide range of interpretive possibilities from evolutionism, Marxism, processualism, and structuralism. Nowhere was this notion of analogy more developed than with the rise of processualism in the postwar period and the development of ethnographic analogy within ethno-archaeology. Both structuralism and processualism were characterized by a certain "systemness" (Hodder 1986: 34–5) that the fossil analogy permitted.

In terms of architecture, 1965 saw Morgan's 1881 work on architecture emerge from obscurity into a fully reprinted volume. The new introduction to the volume, authored by Bohannan, was keen to note the significance the work had for neo-evolutionary perspectives (such as those of Leslie White and Elman Service) important for the processualism of the New Archaeology and postwar concern with proxemics in the study of space fueled by the writings of Edward T. Hall. The search for analogues and the theoretical innovations of the New Archaeology saw the advent of methodological developments that had an enormous theoretical impact on the New Archaeology and responses to it, primarily in the form of postprocessual archaeology and the subsequent rise of material culture studies more widely within archaeology and anthropology. This innovation, of course, was ethno-archaeology, which prefigured contemporary material culture studies and whose primary aim was to ethnographically examine contemporary societies and their material practices. Human societies could be studied in the present to discern material analogues with which to understand societies in the past. Present-day hunter-gatherers such as the Nunamiut famously studied by Lewis Binford, the key theorist for the New Archaeology, could be used as material analogues for similar societies existing under similar material and environmental conditions in the past. So-called middle-range theory could provide the structural explanations with which to render present-day societies and their activities comparable with similarly structured materials in the distant archaeological past. Within this new school of ethno-archaeology, the minute details of everyday behaviors are meticulously detailed (see Binford 1978a, 1978b). Inventories of objects, their spatial distributions and flows are scrupulously recorded and accounted for in their overall spatial context. Here, however, architectural form, architectural techniques, and so on are subservient to an overall interest in environmental adaptation and wider evolutionary process. As Binford famously suggested following White, culture is "an extrasomatic means of adaptation": the totality of "people, places and things" in relation to one another (Binford 1972: 205). Material culture and architectural form could be seen as means toward wider environmental adaptation in the tradition of neo-evolutionary research while the earlier work of Daryll Forde, the founder of the department of anthropology at University College London (UCL), stressed the importance and diversity of architectural form and material culture in relation to the environment (see Daryll Forde 1934). It was here, at UCL, that material culture studies within anthropology were to enjoy a resurgence in later years.

This reengagement had a number of significant consequences—namely, a close interest with ethnography by archaeologists and, with that, a growing appreciation for the significance of contemporary material culture for the study of human societies and a growing importance for the study of architecture in particular. This also facilitated a more nuanced and finely observed understanding of human behavior in its engagement with the material world, resulting in what would then be known as the postprocessual critique of the New Archaeology. For these archaeologists the desire to establish positivist analogues with which to secure meaningful material bases for comparison met with the criticism of more interpretive approaches that warned of the limitation of these analogues in the face of the wider social and cultural contexts in which ethno-archaeological phenomena were examined in the present. Archaeology was seen to be more of an interpretive than positivistic practice, attuned to the wider context of human and cognitive material behavior—hence the emphasis on context in the moniker "contextual archaeology" advocated by postprocessualists such as Ian Hodder, his students, and others.

The emphasis on neo-evolutionary approaches discussed by Bohannan suggests a renewed preoccupation with the systems of cultural processes, well in keeping with the concerns of the New Archaeology. More widely, the comparative approach toward architectural forms as discussed by Rapoport, Goffman, and others suggests a form of cross-cultural and cross-temporal systemic theory that lent itself to modernizing developmental agenda. As Rapoport (1969: 12) states in his foundational postwar text: "comparisons of this type can offer an insight into the basic nature of shelter and 'dwelling,' of the design process and the meaning of 'basics needs.'" Rapoport's statements echo those of a century earlier expressed by Lewis Henry Morgan: "All the forms of this architecture sprang from a common mind, and exhibit, as a consequence, different stages of development of the same conceptions, operating upon similar necessities" (Morgan 1965 [1881]: xxiii).

With this developmental agenda in mind, the analytical space of the anthropology of architecture shifts to a familiar nineteenth-century one, where field research is synthesized into larger schemata suited to a universalizing modernist developmental agenda. Susan Kent's (1984) seminal work on the ethno-archaeology of space replicates much of the evolutionary systemness of Morgan a hundred years earlier. She recreates a similar spatial context for the creation of knowledge where the Human Relations Area Files, not unlike the many reports Morgan likely availed himself of, served as the empirical framework from which to identify cross-cultural and cross-temporal formal characteristics based on architecture data. In the spirit of middle-range theorizing that characterized New Archaeological approaches, Kent could posit "That as a society becomes more socio-politically complex, its culture, behavior or use of space, and cultural material or architecture become more segmented. This occurs particularly with respect to increasing segregation or partitions" (1990a: 127). And furthermore, through the application of this analytical method: "It is possible to factor out universal processes, thereby elucidating culture-specific variables . . . which are influential on the cross-cultural level" (Kent 1990a: 128).

Using data used from Human Relations Area Files, other ethnographic sources, and her own fieldwork, Kent could establish a scale of homologous architectural and social/cultural complexity according to five categories along a scale of increasing complexity and spatial segmentation of "little" to "much," down from the seven categories in Morgan's schema (see Kent 1990a: 142–3). Underlying this categorization and production of homologies was an acknowledgement that "[t]he understanding of such relationships and the development of reliable, predictive models will aid us in our understanding not only of present uses of space and built environments, but those of the past and future as well" (Kent 1990a: 151). Kent reasserts an old binary unity of archaeology and architecture: "how a group organises its culture determines how it organizes its use of space and its built environment" (Kent 1990a: 129)—a direct equation and attribution of causality (see Yaneva 2012 for a cogent critique of these and other forms of causality in relation to architectural form). Furthermore, this categorization works to suggest a form of management and planning:

> By elucidating the inter-relationship between culture, the use of space and architecture, we not only can formulate models that enhance our understanding of architecture and activity areas, but can actually predict past and present uses of space and the built environment. We can thus begin to develop a spatial theory of society which can then guide future architectural form to better fit people's needs, as well as help us to understand past architectural forms. (Kent 1990a: 129)

Kent's emphasis on degrees of complexity in terms of segmentation has resonances with the even more avowed systemic rationalism of "space syntax" developed by the planning and ethnographic team Hillier and Hanson. Their *Social Logic of Space* (1984), which promoted the founding principles of space syntax, was to emerge later as a significant planning and managerial tool in the control and development of spatial systems from city planning to retail store layout. Hillier and Hanson provided a generalized and quantifiable theory of spatial use that could effectively be used in cross-temporal and cross-cultural contexts within archaeology (see also Hillier and Vaughan 2007). Preziosi's (1983) study of Minoan palace architecture, similarly, is a classic example of how formal analysis applied to the remaining outlines of architectural walls could describe formal patterns toward the interpretation of architectural forms in the distant past.

It is worth pointing out the importance of line drawing and print culture for enabling these theoretical engagements. Quite simply, the emphasis on line drawing that characterizes the segmentation of space represented by durable walls (be they flimsy or monumental) as opposed to the other forms of spatial bodily and sensorial engagements and distinctions enables a certain stability of information and a stable and extensive understanding of architectural form (see Alder 1998; Carpo 2001; Latour 1990; Vidler 2000) by virtue of the extensive distribution of paper and print forms. This stability assures that knowledge is the same everywhere at all times and in all places as extensively as print culture enables, but also that stability of form not only produces a community of universal knowledge and scholarship but can enable comparison of widely divergent contexts over time and space. Once the complex sensual experience of space can be reduced to line, then universal forms of spatiality, and architectural experience can be stabilized. The stable line of print culture produces the means of comparability and, with that, the means by which universality of form and function can be surmised and, with that, universal needs.

4

As linguistics helped to establish nation-states, this long-held preoccupation with language played a significant role in in the development of archaeological theory about architecture. With developments in linguistics and the subsequent rise of structuralism within anthropology there arose a renewed interest in linguistic analogies with which to understand material culture—and, in particular, architectural forms. The postwar period saw a reprise of Pitt Rivers's observation in the middle of the previous century, "that by studying their grammar, we may be able to conjugate their forms" (Pitt Rivers 1875b: 300). Notably, the structuralism of Lévi-Strauss and the linguistic developments of Noam Chomsky had a significant influence on folklorists such as Henry Glassie and archaeologists such as James Deetz. Glassie in particular developed a very detailed and highly pronounced linguistic analytical technique with which to study the development of the vernacular architecture of Virginia (Glassie 1975). Glassie's magisterial efforts attempted to discern the underlying grammatical competences of architectural form and then describe their evolution and development over time. In these respects Glassie was particularly indebted to the work of the linguist Noam Chomsky. Mind and building had language-like competences deriving from the same cognitive structures and served to establish what would later be described as the Georgian order and worldview within architectural forms characterizing mature colonial society in North America (Hicks and Horning 2006). Archaeologists such as James Deetz would develop this even more fully for diverse categories of historical material culture (Deetz 1977) as well as Mark Leone.

Henry Glassie (1975), writing in *Folk Housing in Middle Virginia*, observed: "The building provides the context for its parts, the farm or lot is the context for the building, the community is the context for the lot, the landscape is the context for the community, the political division is the context for the landscape and so on and on until the universe gathers its own into order" (1975: 114). Thus, the analysis of built form served not only to explain the immediate household in which it was understood but could more widely provide a critical insight into larger scales of political and cosmological importance. Moreover, built form in Glassie's scheme linked the dwelling to the wider world and linked that wider world to the very inner workings of the mind: "The structure of the abstracted context is internal, in mind, but it binds the object to such external variables as the materials available in nature or the expectations of the maker's group" (1975: 116).

Analyzing seemingly visually unrelatable elements, upon deeper inspection one could thus discern how changes within something like the arrangement of rooms could provide evidence of a cultural unconscious, and this unconscious serves to structure the wider environment through the material medium of built form. "[T]he artifact is the medium of transfer within the ecological system" (Glassie 1975: 122), but it is a transfer where mind was primary over the landscape: "But the middle Virginia house was not modified to fit its site; the type was extended into space without regard for the particulars of topography" (1975: 144).

Overall the focus relies upon a distrust of surfaces, but an "excavation" or "dissection" reminiscent of Semper nonetheless of the observed phenomenal world to uncover the underlying cognitive structures that give shape to the phenomenal world. The impulse is Durkheimian in terms of how one can methodologically get at the forms of such collective consciousness:

> Our method has not been complicated. It begins with the recognition of a pattern of relationships at the phenomenal surface and leads through the search for explanations to the discovery of patterns in logic. I described these patterns in terms of the mediation of binary oppositions. This was due of course, to the attractiveness of the discourse of Claude Lévi-Strauss. However, while the application of the method to unconscious cultural logic is primarily his gift, as an

> explanatory technique it is antique and widely employed. It has been used by
> old philosophers and modern scientists, by anthropologists, artists and learned
> pedagogues. If binary sets seem too simple or too pat to be the real structures of
> unconscious logic, their reality is not beyond good possibility, and they do pro-
> vide us with a rigorous means for travelling toward a larger truth—that thought
> is structured and systematically so. (Glassie 1975: 160)

All these built forms teleologically move toward increasing order and symmetry,
hence the eventual rise of the so-called Georgian order. More relevant to our discussions here, Glassie speaks of the effects certain structures of thought and related
material form have on one another. Paraphrasing the sculptor Henry Moore, Glassie
finds that "symmetrical form may not be easier to make, but it is easier to think"
(Glassie 1975: 163) and thereby enable the wider uptake and spread of ideas such as
the Georgian order.

5

Matthew Johnson's (1993, 1996) subsequent study of English post-medieval architectural forms that were the historical precedents to those colonial forms discussed by
Glassie built on this structuralist tradition to propose in a postprocessualist manner
the contextual recursive processes by which architectural forms, culture, and behavior
could be understood. Rather than seeing architecture and behavior in the more static
structuralist terms proposed by Glassie, Johnson, proposed that: "[m]eaning is vari-
able: it is produced by individual people working within a given cultural structure,
by renegotiating and transforming that structure by creatively manipulating existing
meanings to produce new combinations" (1993: 31).

Hodder and the work of his students is associated with this postprocessual turn
in archaeology and its preoccupation with the recovery of meaning relating to social
and material processes. He emphasizes the different forms of material signification
in the past and the importance of immediate context (hence contextual archaeology)
rather than the establishment of universalizing principles. A good case study is Hodder's analysis of European Neolithic houses. Hodder argues that, as the Neolithic pro-
gressed, there was a move from houses to tombs as settlements became more dispersed:

> In this less stable, more varied system, houses and villages could not provide a
> long-term community focus. Daily settlement practices did not form the basis
> of long-term social structures. The latter were, however, set up in the practices
> of death and the veneration of ancestors. It was the tomb, especially as it began
> to be used over many generations, which could become the "home" of dispersed
> local units. (Hodder 1994: 77)

Such archaeological approaches, focused on long-term development over time, are able to move away from a preoccupation with the analytical unit of the dwelling per se to—in respects—consider the relative unimportance of the physical dwelling. These approaches demonstrate what Hodder describes as "how to create continuity out of discontinuity" (1994: 80), where tombs built on top of houses, create a spatial proximity and link to earlier settlements within apparently unrelated architectural idioms at least to modern sensibilities (tombs and houses). In addition, Hodder draws attention to how continuity is expressed through actions of redecoration as well as superpositioning. This continuity of practice is what he refers to as the principle of the domus that is enacted over time. Alternatively, continuity could be achieved by the use of "tectomorphs," or through the rebuilding of houses on older houses (Hodder 1994: 81).

Hodder notes: "Both houses and tombs, then, are concerned with continuity and both have similar rituals to deal with the end of use, to close off. But the tombs also introduce new ways of creating renewal in the face of discontinuity or death" (Hodder 1994: 83). Hodder continues to observe, "After abandonment, the house or tomb came to 'stand for', refer to or represent the long-term ancestry of the group" (Hodder 1994: 84). The tomb thus becomes important for regulating inheritance rights and of course the economic continuity of the community: "society and economy are indeed actively constructed in the events associated with the tomb" (Hodder 1994: 84).

Hodder argued for the active agency of these forms for maintaining social order that is continuity. But what is highly significant in his analysis is that their meaning and materiality can change: "But after the tombs had been closed off, they often came to act as reference points on the landscape . . . now being meaningful less through direct experience and more through reference to the past. Thus the meaning of tomb material culture may have shifted through time from referential to experiential to referential again" (Hodder 1994: 85). What is important to note here is the importance of the shifts in material register these processes entail and the different forms of social life they enable.

6

Postprocessualist approaches were heavily indebted to the work of Pierre Bourdieu and Anthony Giddens. With Giddens, the notion of structuration theory elaborated a more dynamic understanding of structuring principles that emphasize the open-ended nature by which structuring principles could be seen to be in evidence to explain the development of architectural forms not in a deterministic fashion but in a nonarbitrary open-ended way.

More significantly, the work of Pierre Bourdieu—in particular, his work on the Kabyle house—elaborated a theoretical framework within which to understand architectural forms in terms of a habitus—those "structuring structures" or underlying dispositions that structure social and material life. In a similar manner to Giddens's structuration theory, they could provide a unified analytical frame with which to describe regularities without foreclosing open-ended, albeit nonarbitrary, yet non-deterministic development and social change. Both approaches, despite their expressed distinctions from structuralist approaches, nonetheless hold to a system of understanding that presupposes underlying principles with which to explain the regularity and dynamics of cultural and architectural forms.

In the wake of structuralism, poststructuralism influenced by the writings of Derrida, Foucault, Lyotard, and others, responded to the perceived rigidity of such structuralist interpretations and the hardwiring of human actions with an emphasis on the multiplicity of interpretations one can bring to any given text or item of material culture and the social conditions and effects of such multiplicities. The works of Michael Shanks and Christopher Tilley in particular stand out here. Architecture as a central analytical category emerges and can be seen as being textlike that can be read off subject to the multiplicities of different readings in poststructuralist approaches.

However, a certain dissatisfaction with the textual analogy emerged, notably with the phenomenologically inspired work of figures such as Chris Tilley (and others). Text gives way to the phenomenological experience of space focused on the body, where the engagement of the body with space and architectural form becomes more complicated and difficult to disentangle, unlike the rather firm separation of architectural form and perceiving subject implied by linguistic and textual metaphors. The work of Susan Preston Blier was of particular importance for establishing a phenomenological sensibility that privileged the embodied relation of bodies, metaphor, and built form. The Batammaliba structures of her analysis demonstrate Carsten and Hugh-Jones's (1995: 43) observation of how difficult it is to meaningfully understand the difference between bodies and buildings. The Batammaliba example shows how dwellings exist as a multiply gendered genealogical entity within which individual bodies, both male and female, are variously subsumed—gender being merely an "aspect" of the multiply gendered and multiply bodied generative capacities of the lineage (Blier 1987).

Such an emphasis on the embodied aspect of one's engagement with architectural form owes a particular debt of influence to the rise of the work of Michel Foucault and the importance of space and architectural form as a disciplining entity that establishes sites for the production of knowledge and certain kinds of bodies, following in a tradition of the analysis of body techniques established by Marcel Mauss. In particular, Foucault's emphasis on governmentality and "micro-physics" established a framework for analysis that could explain how small changes in material and bodily behavior could be implicated in higher-order changes in social life. For archaeologists, this provided a theoretical frame with which to examine small-scale material changes evident in the archaeological record that, when viewed over time, could explain the nature of culture change more broadly. Again, the emphasis on space and architecture provided the analytical categories with which to engage these issues.

Mark Leone, in his historical archaeological work on Annapolis, speaks in structural Marxist terms about the means by which power and inequality are inscribed in the landscape and the material terms by which this is achieved. He describes the William Paca Garden in Annapolis, Maryland, with its uses of bilateral symmetry, landscaping, and control of nature and visuality, which created hierarchies in spatial and visual terms that inscribed in a seemingly natural fashion the decidedly contingent orders of inequality and power in eighteenth-century Annapolis (Leone 1984; Figure 11). This masking of inequality was achieved through the naturalizing effects of a visualist material register derived from perspectival drawing forms that geometrically subdivided and ordered space in regular intervals to produce a visual effect of universal order and progression within the landscape. In this way, it naturalized the hierarchies of space and time that characterized eighteenth-century American society. This visualist mode was produced by widely available printed handbooks that could reproduce such a universal order uniformly in divergent settings geographically and culturally through this visualist register. Thus, by recourse to this perspectively produced and visualist mode—made stable and extensive through eighteenth-century colonial trade networks and print culture—a common object could be created that was uniformly perceived within the landscape and that naturalized the contingency of a given social hierarchy and order, both in the colonies and the British homeland. It was precisely the genericness of this segmentary geometric visuality that could sustain such a notion of universality and order across wildly divergent contexts (British homeland to American Colonies). Leone's analysis suggests the extraordinarily productive nature of generic forms in certain stable material registers that produce a very specific perception of space and form in the political economy of eighteenth-century British colonialism. In a Marxian vein, Leone further notes how the fetishization of such forms masks the inherent objective social and economic tensions and inequalities of eighteenth-century colonial society. Thus, the seemingly banal nature of such generic forms serves to mask through their forms complex inequalities and opposing claims that are obviated through the naturalizing effects of such generic visualist conventions structuring the perception of spatial and architectural forms.

The emphasis on small-scale material changes established a certain sensitivity to the very specific effects of empirically evident material qualities, such as the generic qualities of space, and their naturalizing effects that in more recent years has resulted in a very specific attentiveness to what is frequently referred to as the materiality of things (see Ingold 2007; Miller 2005). Figures such as Gibson, with his notion of affordances, and the influence of philosophers of science such as Bruno Latour and others, as well as anthropologists of art such as Alfred Gell, have all directed attention to the specific material capacities of things, forms, and their effects, directing attention to what in fact material things *do* rather than *represent* within earlier linguistically preoccupied analyses.

This emphasis on doing builds on earlier preoccupations with phenomenology and the embodied nature of built forms, which focus on the way in which material forms—and, in particular, architectural forms and materials—enable and constitute certain forms of social life and, with that, certain forms of social being and personhood, building on earlier preoccupations with the material in terms established since Marx by which certain forms of life and consciousness are made materially possible.

More significantly, in line with the rise of heritage as a national resource and means for establishing social and cultural inclusion, archaeologists whose primary

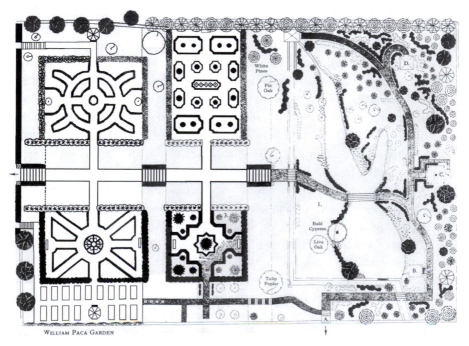

Figure 11 William Paca Garden, Annapolis, Maryland. *Source*: Plan of the restored William Paca Garden by Laurence S. Brigham, ASLA, ca. 1976. © Historic Annapolis.

analytical context is architectural find themselves actively producing the objects of such claims for heritage through their constitution of the archaeological record—and, in particular, the architectural objects of that record: buildings move from being dwellings and functional and ritual objects to objects of heritage, which require certain forms and technologies of preservation, which in turn require an attentiveness to material, surface, and material integrity with which to facilitate heritage claims and discourses. Archaeologists are called to constitute these entities and, as such, are more deeply involved than ever in the political life such highly inflected and deeply politicized architectures enable (see contributions in Skeates, McDavid, and Carman 2012, and in Meskell 1998 and Mark Leone's work).

The rise of phenomenological approaches emphasizing the embodied aspect of architectural form suggested the significance of the performative dimension, not only in terms of gender but also of the very process by which research and writing itself is conducted and how such archaeological investigations are immediately situated within contemporary political contexts. This would lead to a more emphatic engagement with the archaeology of the present or contemporary past (see Buchli and Lucas 2001; Harrison and Schofield 2010). Archaeology was about creating relations in the present: describing a more ethnographic focus to the work of creating archaeological objects. Michael Shanks's Three Rooms project (Shanks 2004) focuses on the archaeological investigation of three rooms: one in ancient Corinth, another in late-twentieth-century East London, and one in nineteenth-century Wales. The existing data (stories, reports, excavation reports, relevant artworks, etc.) are presented side by side in succession. Each entry relates to an abstract concept such as death, the body, documentation, and memory, whose proximity side by side along with their empirical data, ordered by these structuring abstract concepts, produce associations and the possibility of other narratives. They become assimilable into other systems of knowledge as a result of this experimental rhetorical device and thereby an intervention into the wider fabric of political life in the present.

With such a more direct engagement with publics and with the shift to a more performative dimension also comes a shift in the analytical space in which the archaeology of architecture is performed. The site-specific dimension of performance over a limited duration, in limited locales produces a new set of knowledge, sociality, and political aims. Here, an immediate and interactive process of knowledge production emerges that engages immediately with a wide audience while employing more embodied and more sensorially diverse forms of knowledge rather than those produced within conventional discursive and textual forms. The practice of a much earlier generation of archaeologists unexpectedly is invoked here—notably Pitt Rivers. It was the clear ambition of Pitt Rivers to present the material culture of the archaeological past and ethnographic present and recent past into a specific architectural context, such as his museum for the benefit of working men in nineteenth-century Bethnal Green in London. If the field site and archaeological intervention is performative within a specific landscape (the site) placed within a wider community in which it engages as an unexpected intervention to suggest new interpretive practices and, with that, political configurations, then this impulse can be seen already long before here. Pitt Rivers, as Bennett notes, was very keen that the working man could apprehend both in a visually discursive format and an embodied manner through his negotiation of the successive spaces of the museum whereby the Bethnal Green spaces literally encode physically and in embodied performative fashion the spread of unilineal evolutionary knowledge (see Bennett 1995: 183, 199–201). The field site where knowledge is produced, the museum where knowledge is interpreted are all part of a highly complex, contextual, and politicized sphere of engagement where new forms of social life are negotiated and contested.

7

The waning of the fossil metaphor with the rise of poststructuralism and its emphasis on citation, embodied action, appropriation, and recontextualization created an opportunity to look at architectural form in extended, distributed, and, what is suggested here, palimpsest form. The performative dimensions that are suggested by the palimpsest, whereby the embodied practices of the past are sustained in the embodied practices of archaeology, are at once performative in the present but coincident with the phenomenological practices within the archaeological record in the past. And as these "palimpsestuous" practices demonstrate (to borrow the literary historian Sarah Dillon's (2007) neologism), they create a new series of connected relations through their interactions, whose authenticity lies not in their segregated elements but in their situated and contingent relationship to each other, which is constantly open to reinscription and rearticulation (see Dillon 2007).

Dušan Borić (2002) explores citationality and the workings of palimpsests toward the production of sustained memory in prehistory and provides insights into how one is interpellated within the same phenomenological frames of the palimpsest to provide a meaningful and enduring account of prehistoric forms and memory. He explores a Mesolithic and early Neolithic context where one can discern Hodder's notion of the domus at Lepenski Vir. Borić addresses the issue of citationality in the archaeological record and, by extension, implicates the archaeologist and the reader in the phenomenological effect of this citationality to provide a situated interpretive truth to the architectural forms he encounters through: "retrospective actions of the collectivity, through the 'citation' of material traces of the past or through repeating ingrained actions and forms" (Borić 2002: 48). He describes the superpositioning of houses involving the "citation" of the earlier occupation: the hearths of earlier buildings are "cited," reproduced in the rectangular hearths of later trapezoidal buildings. As Borić argues, this introduces a new dimension to the materiality of the sequences of dwellings at Lepenski Vir—that is, a specifically contingent notion of time. "Previous buildings are physically 'touched upon' by partial or full overlapping or cutting through old buildings by new ones" (2002: 56).

Borić argues that the trapezoidal shape of the buildings reflects the trapezoidal shape of a prominent local mountain peak and that, through the mimesis thereof, the inhabitants of the site acquired the power of the mountain itself: "Applied to Lepenski Vir, the process of recapitulation—via the abandonment of an old house and its sequential replacement with a new floor following the previous outline—might have been a way of repositioning of individuals grouped through a lineage or 'house' in relation to both the past and the future" (Borić 2002: 60). Why do this? Borić answers: for protection—that is, protection of the ancestors. "Thus architectural parts of a house can be seen as parts of a collective or ancestral body, which embodies genealogical and social links to the past. These accumulated biographies enrich and enhance the potency of a house's physicality" (2002: 61). He adds, "Furthermore it seems that the potency of the past was embodied not only in the accompanying heirlooms, but also in the physicality of overlapping houses delimiting the protective arena. After this burial, the whole location, which might have been used for over a century or longer, was finally abandoned" (2002: 66).

Ruth Tringham (2000), in another analogous context, provides a good example of how the materiality of built form as understood through a deep temporal perspective facilitates continuity and memory, and, in particular, how a sensitivity to the specific material qualities of architectural forms enables a certain phenomenological truth in terms of what sorts of social effects are enabled through the embodied citationality of multiply layered palimpsests.

Tringham examines house forms and settlements in Neolithic southeast Europe and the Near East—specifically Opovo, a late Neolithic village in former Yugoslavia. She notes in particular the ubiquity of clay as a material used for everything, from ceramics to furniture, and, of course, houses.

What is unusual here is the "universal firing of the houses at the end of their uselives," which "has led to this period also being dubbed the Burned House Horizon" (2000: 116). Tringham asks why they were built of clay and why they were burned. She argues for a particular understanding of continuity that is distinctive from the accretions of structures within tells, as they characterize Anatolian contexts. Rather, clay, she argues, is a difficult material to move, but it is highly malleable and abundant, literally underfoot and ready for use: "It can be made into an infinite number of portable and non-portable artefacts. When clay is burned, it is transformed chemically into an indestructible material . . . It is difficult to burn clay walls, but when they are burned they are preserved forever" (2000: 123).

Previously, these burned houses were understood in terms of accidents or set on fire intentionally as a result of social conflicts. Tringham has determined that the house fires at Opovo were individual and intentional: "set on fire intentionally to signify the death of the household head as a symbolic end to the household cycle, in effect to 'kill' the house" (2000: 124). Furthermore, she suggests, following Stevanović, that "burning the wattle-and-daub houses at high temperatures vitrified the clay, thus ensuring that the physical house and its place would be identifiable and remembered forever—modern farmers can attest to that!" (2000: 124). As she notes further,

> Even though there was no obvious sign on the landscape, however, the farmers who ploughed the field were just as aware of these sites as prehistoric places, if not more so. In coming into contact every day with burned rubble, ceramic sherds, stone tools, in the regular daily and seasonal cycle of cultivation in their fields, it seemed that the villagers had incorporated these places into their village's social memory. (2000: 133)

Tringham notes that while monumental tells in Anatolia interest archaeologists, they are not of interest to local villagers, who do not engage with them in any direct embodied way. Rather, Tringham argues that the cycle of burning, preservation, fertile fields, memory, and the recession into a constantly emergent series of palimpsests about the past produce a local form of material knowledge, as attested to by the example of the farmers' deep awareness of the prehistory of their site. There is a material rhythm over time in terms of the constant referencing to these remains through the plowing of fields that produces memory in enduring form, unlike the monumental forms of tells, at least for the local inhabitants. Tringham notes that, while they excavated at Opovo, villagers took a keen interest. "These places were not something 'other' to them like a mound, they were not their link to 'the past', they were just part of their enduring memories that had been gossiped about through many generations and made part of their village's experience" (2000: 134).

More recent archaeological approaches actively participate themselves in the materiality of their sites. This constitutes a form of phenomenological engagement that not only produces a guarded truth about the nature of the material to sustain relations and social engagements in the present—such as the trapezoidal forms mentioned by Borić or the affordances of clay described by Tringham—but, more importantly, becomes a means of direct engagement with the present as illustrated by those farmers, who are intimately aware of the past in their daily lives. In a more contemporary, British context, Gabriel Moshenska's (2008) work on the archaeology of the Second World War and children's shrapnel collections engages with the ubiquity of shrapnel at bomb sites and shows the highly fragmented nature of shrapnel: dispersed, unmarked, culturally unremarkable from a heritage perspective but extraordinarily remarkable from the perspective of amateur collectors and children coping with war. Shrapnel was collected as souvenirs and thereby formed a specific engagement with the past and the sites of conflict surrounding the Second World War, producing intimate and unofficial histories. This could not be done in any other way except through the kinds of material engagements that modest shrapnel affords, which are then the focus of an archaeology producing novel forms of community and historical knowledge.

Archaeology's focus on diachronic time in relation to architectural forms suggests the limits of established analytical categories and how they can be expanded more meaningfully. The focus on the diachronic enables a view of the repetitive and iterative dimension of architectural forms that only a deep temporal perspective can yield. As Alfred Gell (1998) concluded in *Art and Agency*, it is the Maori meeting house in its multiple and varied iterative form that is the relevant category of analysis, as the house is a continuous iteration and extension and incorporation through time of the higher-order collectives it constitutes (see Figure 1 in Introduction). The familiar ethnographic snapshot is literally just that—a photographic snapshot of this entity in its becoming through time; it is not the static architectural form presented. As we shall see in later chapters, architectural from—to paraphrase Rivière's (1995) Kantian terms—is almost like a phenomenal manifestation of a higher and more obscure (from the standpoint of an individual's observation) noumenal expression. The dwelling, set aside from these extensions that characterize its lived reality, actually then pales into insignificance in terms of our empirically based commonsensical understandings. It is the process of iteration and extension through time and space in its open-endedness and temporal indefiniteness that is significant here, while the architectural footprint—the dwelling per se in its given empirical form—is relatively insignificant.

In another vein, Douglass Bailey (2005) discusses the extension of architectural forms not diachronically but extensively and the interactive effects of architectural forms in the prehistoric landscape as a means of establishing presence. Bailey eschews traditional interpretive perspectives and suggests instead an experiential approach derived from an analysis of 1960s serial minimalism in modern sculpture (Donald Judd, Carl Andre, Robert Morris, and others). He argues for an extensive environmentally based phenomenological experience of the serial. The Neolithic landscape of southeast and central Europe, according to Bailey, was characterized by a serial landscape of nearly identical houses. What he argues for is not the specific house itself, not its agglomeration into a community or village, its meaning or structure, but the more generic, expandable, and repeatable quality of the serial—extending into the landscape and over time—as key toward understanding the experience of the Neolithic house. That is, their generic seriality situated people in space and time: "it is just one specific object within a longer serial order of villages across a landscape, up a river valley, across a region, and through a sequence running for hundreds and sometimes thousands of years" (Bailey 2005: 96). Its genericness and its serial repeatability were the material qualities that were important for the experience of the landscape across time and space, an experience that is distinctly exteriorized rather than interiorized in more conventional accounts.

Archaeology, in its engagement with the empirically evident, only confirms the truth of discrete architectural form's relative insignificance in light of the multiple interactions of architectonic dwelling space through time—hence Bailey's frustration with the "meaning" of Neolithic dwellings. Here, archaeology demonstrates, through its simultaneous attention to temporal depth and the materially empirical, the scales that are significant for understanding the workings of architectonic space (as Gell's understanding of the Maori meeting house over time does so well). These different temporal scales have everything to do with how one understands the materiality of architectural space. As Buck-Morss (2002) notes in relation to the different temporal scales of bourgeois national space and Marxist space, very different scales are negotiated with very different materialities and political contexts.

Earlier formal analysis based on built form enabled a comparative frame with which to produce the psychic unity of man, while nation-building enterprises to this day focus on vernacular studies, where archaeology—and, in particular, historical archaeology—are often complicit. Archaeology enables the constitution of these highly visible and potent material forms that at once affirm political settlements as they are, but are also able to challenge them and suggest others. As with Leone, the works of Habermas inspire these investigations into architectural forms to create forums for dialogue and reconciliation within settings that create "ideal speech situations" for communication across disputed histories and conflicted and marginalized groups. Thus, the performative and community-based archaeological work focused on architectural forms facilitates an extension of the understanding of human being through marginalization, rupture, and difference in a manner that is quite distinct from the synthetic scales of the nineteenth century. But as the nineteenth-century believers in the psychic unity of man segregated out specific characteristics of the built environment to facilitate this unity, so too do more recent practitioners facilitate this unity through its critical extension by the incorporation of difference and alterity. The marginal and the abject are segregated out so as to be considered in relation and inclusion through the expansion of the universal human. The work of archaeology continues to challenge the boundaries of exclusion and inclusion in relation to architectural forms through these more recent performative turns—affirming the philosopher Judith Butler's (2000) call for the continuous expansion of the boundaries of the universal as a never-ending process. In this sense, the often-noted destructive nature of archaeological techniques functions in its generally constitutive nature to build, but in reverse; to reconstruct rather than construct. But while engaging in the putative fiction of reconstructing, constructing in distinctly nonfictional terms, new conditions within which communities are made and unmade, expanded and dwelt.

8

These themes emerge in the archaeologist Barbara Bender's (1998) work, which addresses the inherently contested nature of built forms within archaeology—in particular, the archetypal architectural monument of Stonehenge (Figure 12). Her work provides not only an archaeological account of this iconic monument of British prehistory and heritage but also a genealogy of its emergence. She describes its status at various times and the different and contested histories, meanings, and attachments this monument has had. More important, she addresses the collision of commitments to this form and the varying material registers they have engendered over time. Like other poststructuralist approaches, Bender's analysis is keenly aware of the multiplicity of interpretations and meanings associated with the site, but more in keeping with Bender's empiricist predilections as an archaeologist, her analysis is acutely aware of the material means by which this meaning is able to articulate across time and across different groups of people. For a long period of its existence, the stones existed in a manner that might seem paradoxical to modern sensibilities: at once powerful stones as well as decidedly nonmonumental forms, despite what might be imputed to the durability of stone and monumentality more generally. For certain periods, similar sites, such as Avebury, were seen as mere rocks, remains of pagan practices that to Christian sensibilities were suspect and better handled as raw materials to be used in new building contexts. It was not until the early modern period that Stonehenge was recognized as a monument and became set on its path as a supreme object of national heritage. Bender goes on to describe how Stonehenge emerges as a monument and assumes a variety of different material registers in reference to the various groups that lay claim to it. The so-called Battle of the Beanfield of 1985 epitomizes the extent to which different groups could lay claim and, through those claims, constitute the site within different material registers. Like the Druids, New Age travellers, who emphasize the importance of the monument in

Figure 12 Stonehenge. *Source:* Guylaycock, Dreamstime.com.

terms of their intimate embodied interaction with the site, come into conflict with Thatcher-era heritage officials who seek to "preserve" the site against its perceived vandalization and deterioration in relation to these embodied engagements. As a result, the National Trust and English Heritage preserve Stonehenge within a mode that downplays direct embodied interaction with the site in preference to one that is highly controlled, visualist, and disembodied.

Eleana Yalouri (2001), in a similar vein to Bender, addresses another iconic architectural monument, the Acropolis, and the multiplicities of materialities in effect from pagan stone remnants to be appropriated toward Christian ends, to the use of the Acropolis as a munitions dump by Ottoman forces that was then blown up by the Venetians in 1687 (Figure 13). In the late eighteenth century, with the rise of classical studies and the assertion of a common European classical heritage, the Acropolis emerged as the architectural context par excellence for the revival of this classical tradition within eighteenth-century northern European centers and the subsequent removal of the controversial Parthenon marbles by Lord Elgin. As Yalouri notes, it is only with the rise of Greek nationalism that the Acropolis becomes the focus for nation building, where the idea of the ethnic nation-state and the

Acropolis become coterminous with the national body—a body that at times has been described as violated, dispersed (as with the Parthenon marbles), and in need of reconstitution in order to consolidate the nation-state itself (Yalouri 2001). The site assumes a wild variety of conflicting registers from meaningless stones to national body and then distributed body, through stolen marbles to a wide and heterogeneous variety of visual representations in images, models, and other material forms whereby Greekness, ethnic identity, and nationhood are consolidated across vastly different time scales, spaces, media, and material registers. As a result, the Parthenon marbles exist within an exquisite state of distributed tension (following Gell), while the new Acropolis Museum designed by Bernard Tschumi displaced down the side of the Acropolis itself "waits" for the marbles to be reunited. The inherently conflicted nature of the Acropolis, in its multiplicity of dimensions, media, and registers, are myriad and conflicting but by no means arbitrary whose excesses produce an implacable materiality that can never be contained—which is the effect of these conflicted commitments.

Figure 13 The Acropolis. *Source:* The Mary Evans Picture Library.

9

The archaeological preoccupation with deep temporal scales reveals the varied nature of material registers and how they shift over time as regards architectural form and the differing social projects these registers enable. The preoccupation with form based on visualist ideologies of observation and documentation enables a comparative discipline toward the establishment of unities such as the nineteenth-century psychic unity of man or the universalist aspirations of twentieth-century developmental agendas. With a shift from fossil-based metaphors to palimpsests, the performative, embodied, and shifting material registers over time could be evinced through the study of the archaeological record. Thus, whether a form is experiential or referential in Hodder's words produces two distinct material registers with two distinct social effects in relation to one another over time and in different registers. Similarly, the register in which a given form works also informs how one can understand the relative significance of built form—with its generic replaceable and repeatable character, as suggested in Bailey's work—and how this register downplays the importance of certain empirical qualities that in another context would be paramount, such as in traditional vernacular approaches or heritage-based approaches. Built form per se as it might conventionally be understood is relatively unimportant as opposed to its generic, serial, and repeatable qualities. In the next chapter, a number of examples of architectural studies within social anthropology provide further insights into the socially productive power of seemingly insignificant material forms that resist traditional vernacular and heritage concerns and the social relations those forms engender, while attending to the wider ways built forms regulate "generative substances," following Strathern, and their flows.

3 SOCIAL ANTHROPOLOGY AND THE HOUSE SOCIETIES OF LÉVI-STRAUSS

I

With the influence of the work of Claude Lévi-Strauss, architecture begins to reassume a central significance in the understanding of human societies through his concept of "house societies." This chapter will examine Lévi-Strauss's contribution and the way it has turned anthropological inquiry toward the architectural and the different responses and innovations that have resulted. In particular, this chapter will address the specific material qualities at play, such as partibility, genericism, stillness, and inversion and how these relate to the processual nature of the house within Lévi-Strauss's concept of the house society.

Probably the single most important concept regarding the anthropological analysis of architectural form is Lévi-Strauss's notion of a house society (*sociétés à maison*). It has had a profound impact on how anthropologists and archaeologists have understood dwellings and the role of architectural form in the reproduction of human societies (see Carsten and Hugh-Jones 1995; Joyce and Gillespie 2000). Lévi-Strauss's understanding of house societies comes primarily from the concept of a house as an institution, as found in medieval European contexts and those of the Pacific northwest coast. As Lévi-Strauss notes, the house is primarily a "moral person holding an estate made up of material and immaterial wealth which perpetuates itself through the transmission of its name down a real or imaginary line, considered legitimate as long as this continuity can express itself in the language of kinship or of affinity, and most often of both" (Lévi-Strauss cited in Carsten and Hugh-Jones 1995: 6–7).

One of its key attributes besides that of being an extrasomatic collective form of moral personhood to which concepts of honor, integrity, and longevity are attributed is the "processual" nature (as noted by Carsten and Hugh-Jones 1995: 36) of what the house society does in relation to the reproduction of social relations, as Carsten and Hugh-Jones note: "Transfixing an unstable union, transcending the opposition between wife-givers and wife-takers and between descent and alliance, *the house as an institution is an illusory objectification of the unstable relation of alliance to which it lends solidity*" (Carsten and Hugh-Jones 1995: 8, my italics). This "illusory objectification" thus performs the key task of inversion: "By putting, so to speak 'two in one', the house accomplishes a sort of inside-out topological reversal, it replaces an internal duality with an external unity" (Lévi-Strauss 1982: 184–5), one that inverses the preexisting conflicts between women and men, "wife-takers and wife-givers," and their respective conflicted views. As such, the institutions of the house society perform a number of key inversions necessary for the production and maintenance of social relations into the future (as developed further by Bourdieu [1977, 1990] in his discussions of the inversions facilitated by the Kabyle house). In these respects, the illusory nature of the house approximates Althusser's notion of a "material ideology," which sees ideology not as representation—or more precisely as a misrepresentation—of reality but as the actual means by which a given reality is apprehended, produced, and constitutive of human relations.

The house as illusory objectification thus becomes a means by which tensions of social reproduction are resolved (Carsten and Hugh-Jones 1995: 8). When two distinct groups with distinctive interests are thus united in marriage toward procreation (Janowski 1995: 85), it is this "illusory objectification" that enables the reproduction of the family unity within its purview. Thus, the house is inherently a problem-solving entity (as Gibson [1995: 129] notes) that enables this resolution through its institutions, practices, and, more importantly, its material context, as we shall discuss here further. The house is in many respects a fetishization (Carsten and Hugh-Jones 1995: 8), but a necessary and productive fetishization and misrecognition of relationships in order to forge a new set of relations that ensure continuity over time. More importantly, it is the element of time that archaeologists have identified that makes this concept so powerful for both archaeology and social anthropology (see Joyce and Gillespie 2000). Lévi-Strauss notes that "in order to recognise the house, it would have been necessary for ethnologists to look towards history" (quoted in Carsten and Hugh-Jones 1995: 6). Memory and history are therefore important ways of dealing with the house, as the house reckons memory, which is essentially the memory of a lineage—that is, the terms by which kinship is forged.

But the notion of the house as an "illusory objectification" is more than a mere metaphor (as Carsten and Hugh-Jones note in reference to Fox; 1995: 22). In all its institutions—material in terms of built form and immaterial in terms of moral imperatives—it is not a metaphor of these relations but literally productive of them in both material and immaterial ways, as the case studies presented here will show and as suggested by Althusser's notion of a material ideology. This is a constant project of work, maintenance, and innovation across different registers of experience both material and immaterial that helps sustain and reproduce human relations into the future. As Carsten and Hugh-Jones assert in terms of the relation of houses to kinship: "'Kinship' has several different sources. It is not just about sleeping together, but also living together, eating together and dying together, not just about bed but also about house, hearth and tomb, the last sometimes a monumental hypostasis of the house itself" (1995: 19).

The structuralism of Lévi-Strauss had enormous significance for anthropological and archaeological understandings of architectural form, as seen in the work of Henry Glassie and other structuralists discussed earlier. Within British social anthropology, Caroline Humphrey's (1974) short but highly influential article on the Mongol yurt provided a succinct structuralist analysis of the deportment of interior space in the Mongol setting, describing the structured use of space in pre-socialist and socialist times and the impact of socialist industrialist society on the transformation of cognitive and material elements structuring Mongol interior space. Humphrey's work signaled more widely the emerging reengagement with the anthropology of architectural form (Humphrey 1988 in Carsten and Hugh-Jones 1995: 3) that came into particular force with the publication of *About the House*, edited by Janet Carsten and Stephen Hugh-Jones (1995) following a workshop on the relevance of Lévi-Strauss's concept of the house society and the importance of architecture as a key locus for the study of human societies emerging within anthropology more widely.

Lévi-Strauss's key contribution, according to Carsten and Hugh-Jones, is the recognition of the importance of native categories (1995: 20). If people think in terms of house, then the house is significant, and, as most societies do, it provides an opportunity for cross-cultural analysis. As such, Carsten and Hugh-Jones note, Lévi-Strauss's concept of house societies heralds a key foundation for anthropological inquiry. As a concept and metaphor, it has a translatability that enables it to be the context par excellence for comparative work on how social relations are reproduced and the role that architectural form takes in that reproduction. Notably, it is its fluid and processual nature that sees architectural form as a momentary context in which the work of the house is done and that, more significantly, the house, as this "illusory objectification," serves to regulate more than shelter and food but the very terms both material and immaterial by which social and biological life can be reproduced. This is especially relevant when one considers the observation made by Carsten and Hugh-Jones that the body and the house are very difficult to disentangle: "Because both body and house constitute the most intimate everyday environment and often serve as analogies for each other, it may sometimes seem unclear which is serving as metaphor for which—the house for body or body for house" (1995: 43).

This emphasis on the interrelatedness of bodies and built form focuses attention on the importance of how the house regulates substances, both prosaic and sublime, from foodstuffs such as rice to semen and other powerful sublime substances in human reproductive processes. The house regulates these through its material forms and its practices, but these forms and their material registers often change and shift to enable the reproduction of social and human life in different conditions. What is important to note in advance, though, is the significance this category of analysis holds. The awareness of the house and what it does comes into being only in a crisis, or, as Carsten and Hugh-Jones note, "under exceptional circumstances—house-moving, wars, fires, family rows, lost jobs or no money" (Carsten and Hugh-Jones 1995: 4). More widely, the analytical trope of dwelling as identified by Heidegger (1993) is the sign of a crisis in the terms by which "dwelling" takes place, it functions "house-like" in the sense proposed by Lévi-Strauss to negotiate these inherent conflicts toward the more successful reproduction of social relations into the future. The wider discourse of the house is a discourse on enabling dwelling within changing contingencies. The house in this respect is the site where these conflicts are assembled, focused, negotiated, and obviated through the integrative work of the institution of the house (Carsten and Hugh-Jones 1995). Thus, as Heidegger notes, we must forever learn to dwell. And because dwelling is the primary circumstance in which social life proceeds, it is central to the anthropological endeavor, as Carsten and Hugh-Jones note. The following case studies will highlight the dynamics of this process and importance of the materiality of built forms in various registers to facilitate the reproduction of human social life.

2

Janet Carsten's (1995) discussion of Langkawi houses illustrates how the resolution of opposing interests is negotiated with the materiality of Malay Langkawi houses. Two principles are important in her discussion: that of commensality and the means by which kinship is created through consubstantiation and the mobility of architectural forms for the production of kinship that emphasize lateral relations over relations of descent.

Carsten is at pains to note how the houses of the Langkawi are rather unremarkable compared to other Indonesian examples: "the symbolism seems curiously flat, the architecture unexceptional, the units themselves impermanent and mobile" (1995: 107). These are highly flexible forms whose unmarked qualities, in their relative banality, make them easily enlarged and moved. It is, in fact, their unremarkable and rather interchangeable and generic qualities that are at the heart of their productive power. It is this flexibility that is at the center of the material processes by which these houses work to make up Langkawi society. Carsten notes that little new construction occurs, that existing houses are added onto, reworked, and moved about in their entirety, "creating the impression that the village is under continuous construction" (1995: 107). This flexibility and fluidity is part of the productive work of kinship—whose relations are constantly being forged, adapted, augmented, and enhanced within a field that emphasizes lateral relations based on sibling pairs as opposed to vertical relations of descent and, with that, an entirely different materiality and material register. The emphasis on siblingship as the primary means by which kinship is expressed emphasizes lateral relations over others and has a flexibility that can produce greater degrees of attenuated and horizontal connections. Married couples are subsumed within this and ideally should refer to one another in sibling terms; similarly, extended relations are understood in terms of siblingship in relation to previous generations, and non-kin can be incorporated within this ethos of siblingship (1995: 115). Carsten notes (1995: 116) how children are believed to be born with a symbolic sibling in the guise of the placenta, which is always buried by the father near the house. The making of siblings is what anchors people and forges them within houses.

As Carsten notes, actual biological siblings and affines are problematic and can produce conflict, hence the need to keep them apart. This is less of an issue until children are born. It is with the birth of children, and especially grandchildren, that any conflicts that might arise because of sibling and affinal rivalries are obviated by the birth of the grandchild whose symbolic sibling pairing reiterates the primacy of that relationship (1995: 119). As siblingship is understood in terms of its coincidence with the house, commensality, the sharing of food and substances, produces kinship and incorporation in this lateral manner as well. Women as affines become incorporated through the sharing of substances both sexual and commensal. Sexual relations are understood in terms of cooking and eating together (1995: 120). Wider community and sociality is realized in the guise of grandchildren: "For it is these grandchildren that represent the culmination of the process of transformation in both directions: at once the product of affinity as it is cooked in the house, and also the result of household consanguinity as it dissolves into shared affinity in the community at large" (Carsten 1995: 121). It is the process of the sharing of vital life-giving substances that produces kinship based on the sibling principle that is then able to be expanded laterally through the incorporation of affines, through communitywide feasting, especially during marriage ceremonies, and the general extension of relations laterally along fictive sibling lines (1995: 121). The relative banality of house form and its high degree of malleability and mobility is precisely what produces these more extensive and attenuated forms of community within this principle of lateral siblingship. Hence, "houses are often mobile and impermanent structures, and what is important is their lateral continuity. This process is materialized when new houses are established which ensure the expansion of the compound, neighbourhood and village" (Carsten 1995: 126).

In Carsten and Hugh-Jones's edited volume, the discussion by Rivière (1995) stands out for its even greater emphasis on the relative "insignificance" and immateriality of architectural forms and materials. His study of the Ye'cuana among the Carib-speaking peoples of "Guiana," South America, discusses how the physical fact of the dwelling is irrelevant in relation to the immaterial context of its emergence. To be more precise, the actual enduring dwelling in this context refers to the mythological first house built by the culture hero Wanadi when he built a house and created the Ye'cuana people. This mythical house is visible as the form of the cone-shaped mountain in the center of the Ye'cuana homeland. The dwellings themselves are a representation of the universe, with the sea and earth inscribed in its spaces, and the conical roof indexes the sky, with its upper and lower parts picked out in different kinds of thatch. The transverse roof beams represent the Milky Way and other beams "sky trees" (Rivière 1995: 194–5). The skylight above is believed, according to Rivière citing Wilbert (Rivière 1995: 195), to be an astronomical device, making the dwelling serve as an astronomical calendar. However, Rivière is at pains to note that each ephemeral visible house, including the mythical house of the culture hero indexed by the conical mountain, has an enduring invisible double: "If this is so it suggests that the visible house with its transient existence is less important in terms of societal continuity than the invisible counterpart" (Rivière 1995: 201).

Rivière notes that settlements are short-lived in the region; not more than ten years and usually six. According to Rivière, this could be explained by the depletion of local resources. One could dismantle the beams and reassemble them after the thatch decays or rethatch, as he notes. But the entire house is rebuilt elsewhere. An oft-cited reason for abandonment, Rivière notes, is a misfortune—the death of children or an illness, but more typically the death of the village leader. When a leader dies, his house also dies, which initiates the abandonment of the village, which is intimately associated with the figure of the village leader (Rivière 1995: 197–8).

The "visible house" is "no more than a fleeting phenomenon in a noumenal world" as Rivière explains in Kantian terms (Rivière 1995: 202). "Settlements are spatial and temporal discontinuities in a visible world that is, in a sense, contingent on an invisible reality. Settlements are the visible but ephemeral evidence of an invisible continuity" (Rivière 1995: 202). In contrast to the traditional requirements of anthropological analysis that places overwhelming emphasis on the constituted empirically evident material forms of dwelling, the dwelling in its empirical static form here is irrelevant; what is significant are the actions within the built environment whereby the community's resources are marshaled every six years or so to reinvigorate it through what might only be called purposeful destruction—from an otherwise empiricist perspective—of their dwellings on a regular basis. It is this "processual" nature by which the manipulation of material forms produces the relations of Ye'cuana society and their origin myths. As Carsten and Hugh-Jones, in relation to such "processes," argue: "It is also to stress that such architectural processes are made to coincide, in various ways, with important events and processes in the lives of their occupants and are thought of in terms of them" (1995: 39). These activities *are* the relationship; the two are indissoluble.

Another example within this house society paradigm in social anthropology comes from Maurice Bloch and his discussion of house building and wood carving among the Malagasy in Madagascar. Here, house form and materiality produce a more recognizable monumentality in a Euro-American sense, in terms of duration and material elaboration. Homes here, Bloch notes (1995a: 77), are only properly and permanently established when a couple has a certain number of children. It is only at this time that the relationship is believed to take root and emerge in enduring material form. Bloch notes how the sexual relations of the young are considered erratic and impermanent; it is only with time that they take on a permanence through the successful birth of a certain number of children and through the gradual emergence of a solidifying material dwelling. The first structure built is relatively insubstantial. However, with time, the individual architectural elements are strengthened and consolidated in keeping with the enduring solidity of the relationship. Thus, the Malagasy, according to Bloch, speak of the dwelling getting "bones" (Bloch 1995b: 78). Elaborate carvings on the well-chosen hardwoods, which at first confounded the ethnographer in terms of their intended meaning, do not represent anything. Linguistic analogies here failed the ethnographer. The carvings, as his informants told him, "honour the wood" (see Bloch 1995a: 214). The use of a hardwood, which is difficult to carve, through this very action produces and articulates the "hardness" of the relationship of the couple that has been housed there with their expanding family for many years. It is through these acts of carving that the hardness and enduring quality of the relationship and house—as a single, indivisible entity—is produced. Over time, when the original couple that founded the houses dies, their descendants build other houses in accordance with these principles. But it is the original house of the founding couple that then becomes the "holy house" within the community in relation to this lineage and which indexes the continuity of that lineage over time. Literally, the founding ancestors transfer their generative potency to the enduring architectural forms simultaneously with their progeny that are at once the expression and means by which generational continuity and the continuity of architectural forms are produced. Very poignantly, Bloch (1995b: 70) describes how French colonial forces on a retaliatory mission burned down such houses in the late 1940s; the agony that this destruction produced was far more profound than the loss of shelter. The lineage itself and its enduring legacy and the blessings of ancestors were destroyed—an act of destruction that was more an act of murder in relation to the greater "moral person" that this manifestation of a house society suggested. This was a distinct form of urbicide before the emergence of this late-twentieth-century concept in modern warfare (see Coward 2009).

3

The specific material registers of form are discussed in detail by Helliwell (1992, 1996) in the context of another Southeast Asian tradition associated with the Dayak longhouse in Borneo. The Dayak longhouse comprises a number of households; Helliwell's study concerned two longhouses, with fourteen and nine apartments, respectively, while the majority of other households (eighty-three of them) occupied individual segregated family dwellings favored by younger families (Helliwell 1992). Within this more traditional arrangement, Helliwell describes how a number of households occupy the segregated apartments along one longitudinal half of the longhouse, while the other longitudinal half is an unpartitioned area where people can come and go and engage in activities without the permission of the householder on the other side of the longhouse. This arrangement, she notes, produces a division not of "private and public" but of "we and other," inside and outside, the elements of the outside world such as Muslim Malays, who are associated with this unpartitioned area of the longhouse (1992: 182). Helliwell rejects the prevailing hypothesis that these are highly individualized households segregated from one another within the partitions of the longhouse (1992: 182). Rather, she attends to the specific material properties of the architectural forms to describe how Dayak/Malay and individual family/wider community relations are produced and sustained in tension, echoing the principle of house societies as problem-solving entities suggested by Gibson (1995). What might seem like the very strict segregation of individual households from each other according to a restricted and empiricist understanding of partitioning is made more complicated and nuanced in her discussion of the materiality of these partitions and the specific sensorial register in which they function. The physical movement of bodies might seem to be delimited by these partitions, but Helliwell notes (1996: 138–9) voice and light permeate these spaces, producing a very specific kind of materially embodied sociality that negotiates the range of social relations and their—at times—conflicting demands. Helliwell notes how voices carry and are overheard, enabling individuals to be aurally aware in a collective fashion within the longhouse of the presence and activities of otherwise segregated households. She provides the example of a husband and wife about to quarrel physically (Helliwell 1992: 188), whose raised voices call other members inhabiting the longhouse to intervene. Similarly, the light of the hearths in the household signal that an individual apartment is occupied and all is well with its occupants (1992: 185). The flimsy partitions, which let light shine through and voices carry, literally produce this collectivity and its collective ethos, socializing individualizing tendencies or alienating conflicts such as those of a quarrelling couple, or signaling mutual aid, as in the case of Helliwell herself falling ill and not lighting her lamp, thereby eliciting the concern and care of her neighbors (1992: 185–6). Helliwell describes her efforts to thwart the sensorial effects of this materiality—to fill in the gaps of the walls (1992: 186), which were big enough for small animals to squeeze in and objects to be passed through—to produce her Western sense of desired privacy, which is aurally and visually segregated. These attempts would be casually sabotaged by her Dayak cohabitants who would remove fillings, enforcing this visual and aural sphere of communality that these material forms facilitated (1996: 140). As Helliwell notes (1996: 140), the proscription to keep the hearth lights burning at some regular intervals is paramount for assuring the cohesiveness of the community. What might appear to previous researchers as highly compartmentalized and segregated is, in fact, highly social and communal in terms of the aural and visual sensorium that these flimsy material forms with their gaps enable.

Paradoxically, Helliwell is at pains to note that this constant ambient awareness produced aurally and visually by the flimsiness of partitions also assures a certain privacy, in that unless individual behaviors are particularly egregious (such as the mistreatment of a child or a spouse), accepted rules of propriety regarding when to linger, when to enter an apartment, and when to intervene are strictly observed, assuring a guarded privacy within this highly communal space (1992: 189). The unremarked background noise, Helliwell notes (1992: 185), at once assures the contingent everyday privacy of individuals while simultaneously producing the assurance of comfort and proximity through these enveloping aural and visual effects. "Flimsy walls" produce a complex sensorium enabling the negotiation of individualizing and communalizing needs through their materializing effects.

The theme of house societies was taken further in the edited volume by Joyce and Gillespie (2000), *Beyond Kinship*. One of the work's significant accomplishments is to highlight the importance of the diachronic dimension for the understanding of architectural forms in the reproduction of social relationships. This is a dimension noted by Lévi-Strauss, but which the synchronic technique of ethnographic fieldwork is often at a disadvantage to capture, unlike archaeology.

Susan Gillespie (2000) discusses the phenomenon of the "nested houses" of the Maya. Gillespie's study focused on ethnographic and ethnohistorical materials and describes the significance of concepts of movement in relation to the materiality of built forms, offering a novel understanding of the nature of monumentality that is counterintuitive to dominant Western concepts, where the monumental is seen in terms of empirically solid, enduring material forms. In this context, monumentality is produced by stasis and immobility, and it is precisely this quality that the domestic architectural forms of the Maya produce. Gillespie notes:

> Among the Maya, passive behaviours—sitting, resting and sleeping—are intimately connected to houses; one who is seated in his house is in his place, representing a microcenter. Spirits and ancestors are also petitioned once they have been immobilised, usually in their own houses. But creating a house as a still and stable centre requires the actions of people, around its periphery, often enacted as a counterclockwise movement in ritual that simultaneously identifies the persons who engage in it, or on whose behalf it is undertaken, as a specific social group localised to that space. (2000: 139)

Thus, passivity, stillness creates a center and focus—an immobility, in effect, that is a defining characteristic of monumentality more conventionally—about which everything else revolves. The Maya house, therefore, serves to immobilize and create a center about which the cosmology of the world emerges. This cosmology is inherent in the way in which the house immobilizes and produces a center in relation to the cardinal points, an immobility and center that focuses on the immobilizing and centering qualities of square shapes. As Gillespie notes:

> More frequently, the horizontal segmentation of the cosmos into four cardinal directions or quadrants is signified by the form and structure of houses and certain analogous phenomena, especially the table altar and the maize field (*milpa*). Evon Vogt (1976: 11) cited a Tzotzil Maya informant's statement that the universe is "like a house, like a table" and concluded that "all pre-eminent cultural symbols are square." (2000: 143)

As such an immobilizing center, the house serves to focus on not only cardinal points but the relation of the body to this centering device, not simply in terms of spatial comportment but in terms of the embodied connections between built forms and bodies, referring to Vogt:

> The Tzotzil also place their own bodily detritus—the hair that is combed from their heads—into the cracks of the house walls each day to further materially mark their co-identification with their houses (1969: 465). The same body part names are also given to other phenomena, including mountains, maize fields, and tables. In more general terms, a mountain, a field, a house, a table, and a human body are oriented to a single spatial model (1969: 580). (Gillespie 2000: 144)

Gillespie noted, referring to Vogt, how the dead used to be buried in the house, but "Now the dead are buried in cemeteries rather than under house floors, but their graves are topped with roof thatch (or pine needles to represent thatch) in order to make the grave a replica of a house for the dead" (2000: 146). Thus, a shift in register from embodiment to synecdoche is produced and with it a very specific materiality: "In this respect, the house does seem to be privileged as an exemplary architectural model, a man-made container for both the living and the deceased, and the altar as a miniature house is a material point of contact between the living and the revered dead, denizens of the spirit world" (2000: 146).

Within this schema, beds and benches have particular importance, as the locations where those passive activities that produce stillness, place, and monumental power around which other actions revolve. Spirits rest on benches as people do in ordinary life. Gillespie notes, referring to Hanks, how at the beginning of the twentieth century "the dead were still being buried under their own beds in their own houses" (Gillespie 2000: 147).

Gillespie notes from ethnohistorical sources that "Immobility was a valued quality associated with centrality and ruling power in Mesoamerica" (2000: 149). Quoting Waterson, Gillespie observes, "Immobility and fertility seem frequently associated with the centre; the idea of rulers or ritual specialists 'staying put' often actually in a house, recurs with noticeable regularity . . . Immobility thus is utilized as a way of representing a concentration of creative, supernatural or political power" (Waterson in Gillespie 2000: 149). The archaeological evidence presented of miniature house models at Copan as well as small shrines at Palenque showed how models and "these small shrines are considered the place of specific divinity linked to the ruling house, whose claims to legitimacy and identity necessitated the objectification of the houses of these spirits as a medium for localising and possibly immobilizing them" (Gillespie 2000: 150). Gillespie notes, referring to Hanks, how "a Yucatec Maya shaman 'activates' his altar, converting a table into a sacred locus. He does so by invoking specific animate spirits in turn and metaphysically tying each one down, in sequence, to a corner of his altar, thereby immobilizing them and allowing him to interact with them" (2000: 155). In sum, Gillespie notes that the archaeological, ethnographic, and ethnohistorical evidence points to a Maya cosmology of "nested houses"; the universe is composed of series of nested containers

> reflecting the concentric principle of Mesoamerican socio-cosmology that orga-
> nizes all space (Sandstrom 1996). These houses, great and small, are analogous
> not simply because their material form is based on a single rectilinear pattern, but
> because all are ritually created via a circumambulating motion that defines their
> perimeter (and hence encloses their center)—walking around a village, cornfield,

or house, or calling upon spirits to move around an altar. They are interconnected by their mutual encompassment on a gradual scale as the container in turn becomes the contained, and movement between these boundaries requires certain ritual prescriptions; hence, each invokes the others. (Gillespie 2000: 159)

McKinnon (2000), in another context, writes about the dynamic processes of the house in a different manner, focusing instead on the different material registers in which dwelling and genealogical continuity take place. The focus of her discussion is the elaborately carved house altar, the *tavu* (Figure 14): "A hard, enduring object that abstracts the human form, the *tavu* further indicates the ability of the noble house to generalize and objectify their relations with allied houses that ensure their noble standing, something that commoners are unable to accomplish" (in McKinnon 2000: 161).

Thus, the *tavu* works to transform three different material registers in which genealogical continuity and human life are expressed and transformed: "between the anchoring stability of roots and the effervescence of growth, and between the objectification and concentration of value in hard, immovable objects and the extension of value in the softness and fluidity of living beings" (McKinnon 2000: 162). The *tavu* thus manipulates and transforms the key metaphor of social and

Figure 14 A *tavu* house altar. *Source:* Tropenmuseum, Amsterdam. Object number: 10000871.

genealogical life, the "metaphor of plant growth": the "unmovable root or trunk" (the general lineage), "mobile, branching tips" (the particular individual) (2000: 162), and the forests noble families claim as the source of their rank and productive capacities.

As McKinnon notes, the *tavu* itself is anthropomorphic, appearing to support the main beam upon which rest skulls and bones of ancestors. In addition, other artifacts reckoning descent such as heirlooms are stored above (2000: 165). At the bench in front of the panel sat the head of the household during household rituals. Thus, as McKinnnon notes, "an heirloom extracts value from circulation and concentrates it in a particular house, where it also then becomes a pathway that links that house back to ancestral sources of power and life. Although valuables circulate through both named and unnamed houses, only named houses are able to immobilize named valuables as heirlooms" (2000: 173). Just as the heirloom transmits and sustains the potency of the lineage, the name also functions to similarly transform and transmit it: "A name also signifies an entity that has concentrated and immobilized value as opposed to those entities that are more dispersed, mobile, and transient. Finally, a name signals the ability to transcend the personal and individual and to objectify relations in a more abstract and generalized form" (2000: 173). Thus, named houses are associated with land and trees, thus a permanent relation to land and trees; unnamed houses are associated only with trees, whereas "By contrast, the character of unnamed houses is manifest in their dispersal of value, their lightness and mobility at their periphery, their particularization of relations in terms of blood, bodies, people, and trees and their mediated relation to the founding ancestors" (2000: 173–4). As named houses fixed the generative potentiality of ancestral forests and land, so too did named heirloom valuables as extended embodiments of that generative capacity. Even in the absence of a named valuable that may have been stolen and sold, its representation in name as a carved decoration could index that generative force (McKinnon 2000: 223n13).

The specific mode of representation is necessary to produce the desired transformation: "This nonreferential abstraction produces a powerfully synthetic representation: generations of individual forebears are condensed and abstracted into a generalized image of ancestral potentiality" (2000: 175). Though quasi-anthropomorphic, they are nonreferential, as one might consider the carvings of the Malagasy house in Bloch's analysis discussed earlier: "While the image of the ancestor was abstracted to the point where it was almost submerged into the structure of the house, at the same time the structure of the house was such that it seemed to emerge out of the image of the ancestor" (McKinnon 2000: 175).

Ancestors are literally the solid "root" of the house, their descendants as particularized in the individual household head are the ephemeral "tip" of that lineage that is eventually subsumed in the larger-order entity. Ancestors were not located in any particular location, but the *tavu* and the artifacts associated with it "were the points of contact between the living and the dead" (McKinnon 2000: 169). In relation to the *tavu*, the present and the past were related, not in a representational manner but in terms of a "point of contact" and transformation not unlike the kinds of anaphoric slippages in terms of contact and association discussed earlier.

Returning to the significance of the yurt, Empson (2007) examines the arrangement of objects in the Mongolian yurt (*ger*) and home and the question of partibility and contact to examine how "a part, when separated from a whole, is essential for the maintenance of different kin relations. Furthermore the invitation to 'see' kin relations through these things elicits the realisation of different relations at a single moment of time" (Empson 2007: 113). Empson is attentive to the manner in which the dwelling—as in a number of the other examples discussed—performs an inversion. It inverts relations to indicate the competing and conflicted claims the house as an institution supports. In particular, her focus is on display and concealment and the different material registers in which agnatic and other kin relations and wider cosmological associations are negotiated. She is especially attentive to the way absences and their differential material modes are presenced: "I suggest that things, placed on top of and inside the household chest, together act as a site that absorbs aspects of people's relations and draws attention to the relations in the absence of people" (2007: 114). Thus, Empson notes: "They allow for the continuation of certain relations that cannot be enacted in shared place" (2007: 114).

This continuity despite geographic dislocation in the Mongolian landscape is facilitated by an understanding of material contagion and partibility: "When something is separated, be it an animal, a family member, or some thing, precautions that involve keeping a piece back ensure that the essence, or fortune, is retained to support the whole" (2007: 115). Empson notes, how selling an animal, for example, will involve a woman rubbing her coat over its muzzle or a snippet of tail hair to be kept in the house. These actions evince a particular strategy whereby "It is imperative for Mongolians, who are nomadic herders, that people are able to manifest themselves via things, in different spatio-temporal locations, beyond the confines of a single bodily form. In this way, people are not just where their bodies are, but in many different places simultaneously" (2007: 117). Therefore,

> Instead of people constituting a home, in Mongolia, valued things inside the house remain in place and stand for relations that are attached to it. This idea is also extended to the landscape surrounding the house, which is marked with stone cairns, sacred trees, buried placentas and tethering posts that invoke a sense of inhabited space in the absence of houses and people. (Empson 2007: 118–19)

Empson draws particular attention to a prominent item of furniture, the chest, and the way it draws together visual and invisible relations, agnatic and other kin relations, male and female networks, and different scales of social connection, vertical patrilineal relations in time, and other horizontal relations over space. She notes that things displayed on the top of the chest are there for preserving agnatic kin relations. But "Inside the chest, concealed from general view are hidden things that have been detached from people at various moments of separation and transformation" (Empson 2007: 123). These are hidden resources outside of dominant sets of relations that are invoked through "things hidden at the bottom of chests that . . . comprise of actual parts of people's bodies, such as pieces of umbilical cords and children's hair from the first hair cutting ceremony" (2007: 123).

These items constitute relations based not on vertical agnatic relations through genealogical time, but horizontal synchronic relations. They enable premonitions and other intuitions that bind people across time space synchronically. "By creating a physical distance and by giving a part of oneself away, a liveable version of the relation is formed. It is because of this that, when people are physically separated from each other, a part is produced during the act of separation" (Empson 2007: 124). Inherently partible, by "retaining a piece of umbilical cord at their natal home, relations between a woman, her children, and between siblings, all of whom may later disperse, are maintained. It allows women, who move between groups and never fully belong to their groom's or father's agnatic kin, to maintain a partial connection with their natal home" (2007: 124).

Though more conventional accounts focus on the terms by which certain dominant and enduring sets of relations are maintained through material form, Empson highlights the seemingly inconsequential: "In this way, the contained and hidden parts become visible manifestations of relations that are concealed from general view and are not displayed openly in daily life or through communal rituals" (2007: 125). She provides the example of a Rubin's figure-ground reversal to schematically indicate how these complementary material registers and kin relations at both intensive and extensive spatial scales might function

> and allow us to switch perspectives between different ways of imagining kinship in Mongolia. When first viewed agnatic relations are foregrounded on top of a chest, and the actual chest, as well as its contents, serve as a physical as well as relational background for these relations. When we switch perspective to the parts contained inside the chest, however, we see that people have to transform and separate so that agnatic kin relations can continue. Through the Rubin's figure-ground reversal we can see how Mongolians alternate between a set of relational perspectives that are dependent on each other. (Empson 2007: 130)

Empson notes how the mirror at the center of the chest creates a kind of ideal person composed of all these complementary relations. As such, this arrangement provides an idealized representation of social relations. The chest and its elements so configured "provides a vehicle for recognizing a type of exemplary personhood" (2007: 132). But it does so by bringing together divergent elements, distinctive material registers that in a hybrid fashion reveal the totality of relations that produce the dominant one: "through the use of photographic montages, far-reaching kin terms, and spatial layout of the house Mongolians construct flexible ways in which to incorporate outsiders" (2007: 134). This act of montage also produces the relation of the visitor in relation to the displayed assemblage, for "The display allows the viewer to respect their host while at the same time to imagine themselves as placed, albeit fleetingly, within this web of relations as a potential part of the network that they are honouring" (2007: 121).

Buchli (2006) describes a different dimension of the Kazakh yurt, in terms of another manipulation of material register—here, in relation to its key structural and symbolic component: the *shanyrak*. The *shanyrak* is a circular bent wood aperture found on the top of the yurt. It forms the opening of the structure to allow light in and smoke out and structurally is the key element holding together the other elements of the yurt structure. Symbolically, the *shanyrak* can also be said to be a representation of the male lineage, which is passed down from youngest son to youngest son. It is said that a *shanyrak* as such does not come into existence really until it is successfully passed down, indexing the momentary successful continuity of the lineage. When the male lineage dies out, the *shanyrak* of that lineage traditionally marks the grave of that last member, and in contemporary cemeteries the *shanyrak*, as a decorative element, makes an appropriate grave marker. As such, the *shanyrak* regulates the anticipated continuity of the lineage both backward and forward in time, as an old and honored *shanyrak* is referred to as a *kara shanyrak*, blackened by the soot of many generations. It is also referred to as *kwok*, beautiful or sky blue, because it frames the blue sky above. More recently, the *shanyrak* has emerged as the primarily decorative emblem of the seal of the Kazakhstani nation state after the collapse of the Soviet Union. Buchli argues that its slippage from an index of agnatic continuity to symbol of the nation-state is due to a profound shift in the way that historical continuity is reckoned in the postsocialist period. If before the *shanyrak* functioned in the material register of an index of agnatic lineal continuity, then its adoption as the metonym of the nation-state as decorative element and not as an architectonic one (though it is now being expressed as a decorative element in various contemporary building projects, too) is part of a shift by which national space is being consolidated in the postsocialist period. Here, the material registers in which they function are key, and the sensorial dimension in which those registers work is vital to understanding their social effects.

The question of substance, both sublime and prosaic, and its regulation in the production of persons and life are at the heart of Goodfellow's (2008) analysis of the imbrication of sex, moral personhood, and addiction, where social relations and moral personhood are forged within the conditions of addiction, notably to methamphetamine, among others. Here, dwelling and the conditions of moral personhood are regulated by a drug. Though Goodfellow does not address the question of built form directly, he draws attention to the question of substance and its regulation that has been central to the case studies presented here. However, the generative substance discussed here is not that of the conventionally life-enhancing substances of foodstuffs, at the heart of commensality and social reproduction and the forging of kin ties examined so far, wherein the architectural frame is the means by which these substances and their social work are regulated. Rather, in Goodfellow, what might be rice in another context is supplanted with crack cocaine and methamphetamines as the sublime life-sustaining and reproductive substance. As the key informant in Goodfellow's study notes, his paternity is crack cocaine, as he was the result of one of his mother's sexual encounters to pay for the crack cocaine that sustained her addiction. As his mother's need for crack remained, he grew up, matured sexually, and then was able to engage in sex work to provide food for himself and for the general maintenance of the family and its affective ties in more prosaic terms. Within such a setting, it is the contention here that the street and temporary lodgings were the primary spatial and architectonic context in which these exchanges and the regulation of these substances took place. They were not important as static spaces as such, except in as much as moving between them was part of the means by which these life-sustaining substances were regulated, enhanced, and partaken in the maintenance of the guarded, vulnerable, and frequently chaotic terms by which the relationships of family, love, mutual assistance, and nurturance were assured (and at times undone). Considered here from the perspective of substance, a very different material landscape seems to emerge that cannot be reduced to one thing or the other, one house, one street, one community, except in terms by which various spatial and architectonic settings are marshaled to sustain these regulations and life-sustaining relations, even though these forms of life are not easily recognized from the point of view of conventional biomedicine or normative frames of reference. However, the central role of substance and its capacities to sustain and maintain life in Goodfellow's analysis suggests a view of an otherwise unstable, conflicted, and agonistic spatial and architectonic setting that offers a different means of understanding architectures and their configurations otherwise indiscernible, except in reference to substance, its regulation, and its architectonic, material, and social effects.

In another manner, Goodfellow's analysis is suggestive of a process long noted by Lévi-Strauss in relation to house societies, "they originated in a structural state where political and economic interests tending to invade the social field did not yet have distinct languages at their disposal and, being obliged to express themselves in the only language available, which is that of kinship, inevitably subverted it" (Lévi-Strauss 1987: 152 cited in McKinnon 1995: 173). This is the process by which the relations of the house become a site of appropriation and subversion toward the articulation of larger-order interests—in this case, the biomedical imperative for sustaining a viable life within the logic of neoliberal societies. Kinship, substance, and the terms of habitation are the site in which alliances, subversions, and control are brought into a critical and at times agonistic relation to one another, as Goodfellow's example suggests and which theorists such as Nikolas Rose (1990) in a related manner discuss in terms of governmentality and where the "psy disciplines" and the alliances of lifestyle, individual determination, and state interests are set in an agonistic relation to one another.

4

Within the tradition of research established by Lévi-Strauss's concept, the house and built form emerge as a key context for the regulation of generative substances and the regulation of social conflict that this "illusory objectification" productively facilitates. As such, the emphasis on the architectural context of the house enables a perspective that moves away from more conventional static empiricist approaches and suggests how the house serves as a specific and transformative register that facilitates these flows, social and reproductive life, employing a variety of material registers to do so. The numerous examples presented here attest to the extraordinary diversity of scales and material registers in which such flows can be regulated, from movement to commensality, to immobility, backgrounding and foregrounding, and naming and dematerializing, which attest to the subtle and original ways in which people in different times and different places manipulate the wide range of material registers available in the architectonic context of the home. Often it is the unremarkable aspects of built forms in terms of genericism, unmarkedness, immateriality, and instability that in fact enable the regulation of such flows of prosaic and sublime forms, following Munn (1977) or the "elementary" and "obscene" associations, following Bataille (1987 [1928]). It is through such anaphoric chains of transformation that such flows enable dwelling and social life in diverse and productive ways over divergent scales of time and space.

4 INSTITUTIONS AND COMMUNITY

I

While anthropologists have primarily been interested in domestic architecture in all its various forms, the intimacy of face-to-face ethnographic research extended in the second half of the twentieth century to encompass larger contexts of human interaction within wider communities, villages, neighborhoods, and cities and other architectural contexts, such as meeting houses, plazas, markets, places of worship, prisons, hospitals, schools, offices, waiting rooms, public transportation, and airports, encompassing the wider spheres where people gather and socialize with one another and where novel forms of personhood and sociality are forged alongside those associated with dwellings.

Again, we come back to the Crystal Palace and its innovative use of industrialized glass and iron that has been implicated as the site for so many innovations in nineteenth-century thought, as we have seen in the works of Semper, Pitt Rivers, and others. The structure itself was an architectural wonder, and it is precisely the new materials deployed that produced this sense of the wondrous in the people who visited it and commented on it. And in this respect, despite its short life at Hyde Park (1851–1854 in the original Hyde Park location; 1854–1936 at Sydenham), it inaugurated a radical reconfiguration of how people socialized and assembled in public. Connected as it was with the expanding railway system of the time, it attracted people who until then could never visit the capital, now in reach from the provinces and abroad more readily and with greater ease. Similarly, never before had an enclosed space been created that could accommodate so many people from so many diverse locations and such diverse social backgrounds, allowing an albeit regulated yet unprecedented comingling of people, classes, and accents in relation to one another under one roof. From a social point of view, a new kind of space was suggested that broke down traditional linguistic, class, and regional boundaries, which had apparently been permanently fixed within the established spatial, geographic, and class hierarchies of the time and which these new material forms could displace. People who would never encounter each other so freely might do so in one space. It challenged conventional spatial hierarchies and the social relations they sustained.

However, just as the materiality of glass and iron could facilitate new forms of comparative knowledge, as evinced in the work of Pitt Rivers and Semper, from which disciplines such as archaeology and anthropology could emerge in more mature form, these materialities of glass and iron also suggested new forms of sociality.

It is within such a historical moment that Marx and Engels developed their materialist philosophies from an earlier Hegelianism that problematized processes of objectification (see Miller 1987). It is also in this climate that Marx could formulate his ideas regarding the material basis of social life: "It is not the consciousness of men that determines their being, but, on the contrary, their social being that determines their consciousness" (Marx 1977: 389). It was the general sense that material conditions produced not only certain forms of society but certain forms of thought and consciousness. And it is this understanding of the intimate relation between the materiality of life and consciousness that was at the heart of subsequent Marxian analysis and the empirical social sciences. Thus, if one could change an aspect of the material world, then its effects on society and consciousness were altered as well: the base determines the superstructure. This intimate understanding of the materiality of life with human consciousness was developed in Marx's *The Eighteenth Brumaire of Louis Bonaparte* (1954), where he was at pains to diagnose why social revolution failed and a bourgeois emperor was installed. How could the French masses go against their own better interests? One of the key observations in *The Eighteenth Brumaire* is Marx's own analysis of the material conditions of the time, not so much in strict economic terms but in terms of what the materiality of social life enabled. He bitterly complained about French peasants being unable to mobilize as a group to pursue their own interests, atomized in segregated, individual households in the countryside, separated over long distances with no means of being brought into proximity with one another to produce a collective consciousness and political will—hence his "sack of potatoes" metaphor to describe this incoherent collective. One could observe that the situation was the opposite in the cities, such as Paris, where the proletariat squeezed into cramped apartments, and poor proletarian districts were forced to interact, engage, congregate, and thereby forge a collective identity—and, with that, a collective consciousness. The forced proximity of poverty and overcrowding produced a collective political consciousness, and the materiality of urban forms was therefore intimately implicated with new forms of sociality and thought. Under these conditions, the senses become theoreticians, as Marx formulated elsewhere, and the theoreticians of a new way of thinking and behaving in the world. Similarly, these same cramped, impoverished conditions also provided the physical means to resist both bodily and mentally. The narrow streets paved with cobblestones became emblematic of this process, immediately becoming available for revolutionaries to barricade (Figure 15). The easily dislodged stones placed by a skilled individual workman could be displaced by an individual revolutionary and used to form a barricade against the police and the army and claim sections of Paris against the state (see Traugott 2010). Interestingly, Traugott notes that not only cobblestones

Figure 15 Paris barricades. *Source:* Jean-Louis Ernest Meissonier (1849), *Barricade, rue de la Mortellerie, June 1848* (Remembrance of Civil War). Oil on canvas. Louvre / Giraudon / The Bridgeman Art Library.

were used to form barricades but also other mobile and easily handled objects such as furniture from dwellings. Thus, elements of the domestic interior and public space were reconfigured in radically new and revolutionary ways to alter social and spatial relations. Later, Baron Haussmann razed these quarters with their narrow streets and replaced them with the broad boulevards that are so admired today for their grandeur, but that could bring troops in to quell any revolutionary attempts in the future and, in fact, make those revolutionary attempts impossible through the very materiality of the streets and their broad prospects, disabling a certain form of collective consciousness and action through their consciously developed material and political effects.

It is a later Marxian theorist, Walter Benjamin, who, armed with these insights, would speculate on these nineteenth-century forms in his retrospective study of Paris and its arcades, written in the early twentieth century (Figure 16). Taking this point seriously—that material conditions determine consciousness—and the fossil metaphor at the heart of these nineteenth-century ruminations, Benjamin examined, in effect, the material culture and materiality of Paris, notably the formerly novel arcades. At the time of his writing, they were falling into disrepair, and as a result of their disappearance, the historical truth of their existence, through his method, would come into focus. He described how the covering of narrow streets with new industrial materials such as glass and iron created new architectural forms and, with them, new forms of social life and sociality. These were embodied in his figure of the *flâneur* who inhabited these previously exteriorized spaces that became new interiorized ones, where new forms of sociality, bodily comportment, dress, and gendered behaviors could emerge. In short, a new form of social life was created within which a new set of sensual behaviors and dispositions emerged.

Michel Foucault problematized this Marxian principle of the material determining consciousness in his seminal work on the utilitarian philosopher Jeremy Bentham's panopticon—a new kind of structure, albeit using traditional materials, that reconfigured space to discipline prison populations and produce a new form of consciousness. The panopticon was originally envisioned by Bentham for the estates of Prince Potemkin in Catherinian Russia to effectively mobilize, rationalize, and oversee the productivity of serfs (Werrett 1999). However, it is best known for its subsequent use as an innovation in the creation of an architectural space to discipline and reform prisoners. If the principle of proximity produces sociality and specific forms of consciousness, then the panopticon produced socially atomized individual prisoners, sequestered in individual cells surrounding a single watchtower. As Bentham himself described it:

> A building circular . . . The prisoners in their cells, occupying the circumference—
> The officers in the centre. By blinds and other contrivances, the Inspectors

Figure 16 Paris arcade. *Source*: Rene Drouyer, Dreamstime.com.

concealed . . . from the observation of the prisoners: hence the sentiment of a sort of omnipresence—The whole circuit reviewable with little, or . . . without any, change of place. One station in the inspection part affording the most perfect view of every cell. (quoted in Werrett 1999: 1)

The architectural innovation produced a new sensorial dimension with profound effects. It produced a new form of visuality wherein a single watchtower in the center produced an omniscient, "Godlike," all-seeing eye peering into each individual cell (Werrett 1999: 17). The prisoners did not know whether they were actually being watched but could only presume they were. Enclosed within a cell observed by an all-seeing eye, prisons were designed not so much to punish as to produce a sense of conscious interiority—in short, a "conscience" or, as Foucault phrased it, produced the idea of the modern soul. This was the solitary self-reflective and self-regulating self, and thus a prison population could be controlled without producing a collective, but instead by producing an individualized consciousness that would self-regulate and self-reform in relation to this innovative reconfiguration of visuality within architectural space. As Foucault interpreted it: "The history of this 'micro-physics' of the punitive power would then be a genealogy or an element in a genealogy of the modern 'soul'. Rather than seeing this soul as the reactivated remains of an ideology, one would see it as the present correlative of a certain technology of power over the body" (1977: 29). And he concluded: "The soul is the effect and instrument of a political anatomy; the soul is the prison of the body" (1977: 30).

Foucault's writing presents the means by which such subtle, powerful reconfigurations of space produced new forms of power and control and, more significantly, how these forms of power pervaded every level, not just from the top down but from the bottom up, and could be employed subtly and with equal tactical effect to subvert power—whereby power is seen by Foucault as pervasive, not just hierarchical (see also Foucault 1986, 1991).

In the terms of an anthropology of architectures of communities and institutions, it is the insight of power being all-pervasive and the ability to diagnose new configurations and tactics of resistance and with it new forms of social life, agency, and personhood that provided the analytical tools with which to consider changes in the material conditions of social life and architectural form and new forms of being (consider the work of Markus 1993). In the mid-twentieth century, two Marxian theoreticians, Lefebvre (1991) and de Certeau (1998), stand out for their insights into how these spatial and material processes would work in the postwar capitalist West and, in particular, for our understandings of cities. Both privileged the spheres of daily life in these urban contexts where the effects of power could be both felt and resisted. It is within these contexts that the notion of spatial "tactics" (de Certeau 1998) emerged, which described the workings of local resistances to dominant practices that attempted to momentarily and contingently rework the dominant forms of power and hierarchy within capitalist economies and cities.

The "Situationists" (see also Sadler 1998), along with the student riots in 1968 in Paris, adopted these insights to pursue such tactics to use the capitalist city against itself through ludic practices that denied the rationality and hierarchies of capitalist (and, by implication, Soviet socialist) cities. The situationist slogan of the student riots echoing the rebellions of mid-nineteenth-century Paris expressed this succinctly: "*sous les pavés, la plage*"—"underneath the cobblestones, the beach." It is the attention to the specific materiality of built forms enabling new forms of consciousness and action that this situationist slogan refers to—how the now iconic cobblestone that an individual can dislodge within a collective action against what would appear to be the overbearing and immovable structures of capitalist rationality and order and suggest an utterly new collective one, a mode of being that the ludic reference to the beach suggests. It is, in short, a very poetic expression of a tactic and how a Foucauldian "micro-physics" might work.

This Foucauldian and, ultimately, Marxian tradition is exemplified in the work of the anthropologist Paul Rabinow, *French Modern* (1989), on the emergence of urban planning as a form of governance in nineteenth- and early-twentieth-century France and in its colonies. He discusses the role of architecture, architectural style, and planning as an emerging modernizing bureaucratic and colonial technology of control. He discusses how French authorities used planning instruments to govern colonial cities, notably those in North Africa. Rabinow worked in an avowedly Foucauldian vein, focusing on the genealogy of philosophical currents that informed French bureaucratic practice on the ground. In particular, Rabinow focused on what he refers to as the emergence of "middling modernism," the evolution of a modernizing, ahistorical, abstracted notion of planning that produces abstracted space in aid of bureaucratic management, privileging this over the more diverse, historically inflected, and contradictory and heterogeneous forms of lived practices on the ground. Rabinow reflects on the beginnings of the colonial control of Morocco and how new European settlements were built alongside traditional Moroccan ones, segregating the French from the Moroccans, Christian from Muslim, and the modern from the nonmodern. However, the early part of the twentieth century saw a manner of spatial control through "association" and "segregation" facilitated by the incorporation of decorative Arab elements within European forms: "Morocco's public buildings would present Moroccan forms in the service of modern norms of technology and administration" (Rabinow 1989: 312). Rabinow notes how the French preoccupation with the production of traditional Moroccan forms, their analysis, and preservations served as a mode of domination and governance:

> The reconstitution of Morocco's architectural patrimony (for example, the pres-
> ervation of the *décor artistique*) was more than a question of attracting tour-
> ists (although the economic and political interest in tourism was considered).
> Lyautey believed, in a last whisper of the Baroque, that appearance was at least
> functionally equivalent to being. Reconstruction was thus an essential compo-
> nent of pacification, including the pacification of the French. (Rabinow 1989:
> 284)

The key was to govern both the French and their colonial aspirations and the indigenous Moroccans through the orchestration of these spatial and decorative forms
in the early part of the twentieth century. And Rabinow is at pains to note that this
strategy served to co-opt and satisfy the needs of indigenous elites who also desired
segregation from "Christian invaders" (1989: 287). This would eventually give way
to a more avowedly rationalized and universal modernism in subsequent planning
by French authorities in the region, notably in the guise of the Corbusian planner
Michel Ecochard's work in postwar Morocco, moving from what Rabinow describes
as this earlier "historico-natural milieu into a socio-technical one" (1989: 13)—
especially in the postwar period, which sought to recast Moroccan cities according
to high-modernist principles and the universality of human needs. In effect, this was
a genealogy of what was to become twentieth-century French urban modernism.

Against the modernist logic of town planning and control, the works of situationists exemplified the means by which modernist planning could be subverted (see
Sadler 1998). But it is under conditions of postmodernism—when consumerism,
spectacle, and play become implicated in their complicity with the maintenance of
late modern institutions—that the issue of the materiality of built forms takes on a
more problematic role. Fredric Jameson's (1984) discussion of the Westin Bonaventure Hotel in Los Angeles exemplifies the issues at stake when confronting the new
rationalities of postmodernism (Figure 17).

Jameson famously refers to the Bonaventure Hotel, designed by the architect John
Portman, as "a mutation in object, unaccompanied as yet by any equivalent mutation in the subject" (1984: 80). It poses a direct challenge to conventional modes
of perceiving the built environment and "an imperative, to grow new organs, to
expand our sensorium" (1984: 80). It is not, as Jameson notes, a utopian attempt
to insert itself within a "tawdry and commercial sign-system" (1984: 80–1); rather,
it embraces this "sign-system" and speaks its language (as the postmodern theorists
of architecture Venturi, Scott Brown, and Izenour elaborated in *Learning from Las
Vegas* [2000], Jameson notes). Jameson observes that the hotel's entrances are not like
those in any traditional hotel. They are indirect. What might seem to be the main
entrance only goes to the second floor; only thereafter one needs to take an escalator
to registration. It is a self-contained and segregated space, a "miniature city," as he

Figure 17 Bonaventure Hotel, Los Angeles. *Source*: James Feliciano, Dreamstime.com.

describes it. That is why there is no real entry, as the entry is what connects it to the world outside, and the building is resolutely not to be connected.

Jameson's "diagnosis" is confirmed by the materiality of the building's surfaces, the reflective glass that rejects the city outside and makes the Bonaventure "placeless." One does not see a building, just the distorted reflection of everything around it. This disorientation is further confounded upon entering the building. Once inside the lobby, with its soaring atrium and vertical elevators, the

> space makes it impossible for us to use the language of volume or volumes any longer, since these last are impossible to seize. Hanging streamers indeed suffuse this empty space in such a way as to distract systematically and deliberately from whatever form it might be supposed to have; while a constant busyness gives the feeling that emptiness is here absolutely packed, that it is an element within which you yourself are immersed, without any of that distance that formerly enabled the perception or volume. (Jameson 1984: 82–3)

Despite the overt symmetry of the towers from the outside, nothing corresponds to the fragmentation and juxtaposition of the experience of space and the city within. It subverts modernist rationality: nobody can actually find the stores, directions are impossible, and the commercial spaces cannot attract their customers. Jameson here describes a situation where a "post modern hyper-space—has finally succeeded in transcending the capacities of the individual human body to locate itself, to organise its immediate surroundings perceptually, and cognitively to map its position in a mapable world" (Jameson 1984: 83). Furthermore, he notes: "[this] can itself stand as the symbol and analogue of that even sharper dilemma which is the incapacity of our minds, at least at present, to map the great global multinational and decentred communicational network in which we find ourselves caught as individual subjects" (Jameson 1984: 84). And, finally, "We are submerged in its henceforth filled and suffused volumes to the point where our now postmodern bodies are bereft of spatial coordinates and practically (let alone theoretically) incapable of distantiation" (Jameson 1984: 87).

However, Jameson is at pains to note that the Bonaventure Hotel, despite all this, is a popular building whose visitors are delighted and transported by the disorienting effects of its forms. It is a decidedly ludic space in the service of postmodern capitalist economy, where the precise ludic working against the modernist grain is co-opted to serve the logic of a consumerist postmodern economy (de Certeau, Lefebvre). Thus, Jameson warns that such circumstances require "a breakthrough to some as yet un-imaginable new mode of representing this last, in which we may again begin to grasp our positioning as individual and collective subjects and regain a capacity to act and struggle which is at present neutralised by our spatial as well as our social confusion" (Jameson 1984: 92).

The ethnographer James Holston (1989) takes on these themes of the subver-sion of modernist spatial logics when addressing the Brazilian capital, Brasília, under the conditions of postmodernism described by Jameson (see also Epstein's [1973] earlier ethnography of Brasília). Here, modernist forms are unable to accommodate the intended effects of their builders and users; they begin to be appropriated in unexpected ways against the conditions of their inherent logic and thereby re-create many of the conditions and inequalities of the Brazilian cities these modernist forms attempted to reform and eradicate (just as the Bonaventure reproduces the inequali-ties of postmodern capitalism) while inculcating new ones. Modernist rationality is subverted, and a very different postmodern space emerges within its heterogeneous spaces, forms of sociality, and unstable forms. Holston (1989) argues that it is the traditional modes of city life that are legible and coherent and that enable Brazilian forms of sociality to occur, which are disabled by these rationalizing forms that the spontaneous subversion of these principles by immigrants, residents, workers, and bureaucrats attempt to rework. The plan of Brasília produces a visual and material regime that is at odds with the workings of Brazilian life, unsustainable in material form and thus inevitably subverted through the various spatial tactics that transpire at all levels of social life.

In particular, Holston comments upon the unintended formal effects of modernist planning that inhibit traditional forms of Brazilian sociality. He describes the "reversal of figure and ground" that is produced by the massing of modernist forms on the urban landscape in Brasília and makes a claim for the ethnographic effects of this reversal (Holston 1989: 127). Traditional Brazilian cities create a spatial understanding of private and public space whereby the solid masses of buildings within the cityscape indicate private areas as ground, while the voids of streets and plazas create figural areas against the ground of private areas, indicating public areas and public life (Holston 1989: 129). In Brasília, Holston notes, this relation of "ground/ solid/private and figure/void/public" is reversed. Thus, the traditional means of being able to cognize private and public realms of action are disabled (Holston 1989: 134). Instead, everything becomes figural in terms of the monumental architectural forms and their function. "Each competes for attention, each immortalizes its creator, and each celebrates the 'beauty of the speedway' leading people and machines to apparently limitless horizons" (Holston 1989: 135; Figure 18). Urban lifeways, which were structured according to legible private and public domains and the forms of moral and social life these domains described, are disabled. Hence, a series of appropriations occurs to redress the disabling effects of this monumental modernism, with limited effect. Holston notes how the *flâneur* of street culture is extinguished (1989: 141) in favor of the driver in an automobile, a machine-based sociality of rational flows and movements whose speed realize the "beauty of the speedway" that these forms are meant to produce. An entirely different phenomenology and a disembodied and automotivally enabled mode of personhood and perception are thereby produced at the expense of traditional nonmechanistic modes of habitation in the streetscapes of Brazil. Thus, the kinds of intermediary spaces of urban encounter and sociality are disabled, and "social life oscillates unremittingly between work and residence" (Holston 1989: 163). Holston's claim for the formal qualities of these spaces argues less for the significance of the materiality of modernist forms as their authors would have them (in terms of architectonic details, programs, plans, partitions, colors, textures, and surfaces) and more for the unintended consequences of the massing of these forms according to modernist logics—a massing that produces "figure/ground inversions" with unintended yet profound effects.

Astana, the new capital of Kazakhstan, is another, more recent context where urban planning is used to create a new exemplary capital for the emergence of a nation-state and the creation of a new Kazakhstani identity for its inhabitants and the wider nation. Here, the spectacle of postmodernism with its play of surfaces and ludic spaces of leisure, pleasure, and living are designed to create this new nationalist subjectivity as opposed to a universalist Soviet one. As Buchli (2006) notes, the surfaces of buildings become the focus of social engagement and social critique under the

Figure 18 Brasília. *Source*: Bevanward, Dreamstime.com.

conditions of an authoritarian democracy. Their instabilities are the means by which the stability of the emergence of the nation-state and Kazakhstani identity are literally forged in relation to them. Laszczkowski (2011), working at Astana several years later, describes these maturing forms that create a gleaming vision of futurity—one that not only seduces immigrants to the capital but also disappoints because of the harsh economic conditions of postsocialist life. Here, the contradictions indexed by these new forms, rather than creating the conditions for new forms of social engagement that might challenge the status quo, are so internally linked with the individual aspirations of inhabitants and immigrants he describes, that the failure of these conditions to produce the desired forms of life are seen as individual failures rather than the result of the systemic contradictions inherent within an authoritarian democratic state based on neoliberal values. The co-option is complete, and the seemingly faltering power of these forms prevails. The logic of the spectacle is utterly complete (Figure 19). It is precisely for the "camera-readiness" of postmodern forms (see Adamson and Pavitt 2011), their amenability to various digitized platforms for engagement (e.g., video screens, mobile phones, etc.), that the ubiquity of this digitally mediated and visualist experience of the city produces the sense in which inhabitants are unable to actually inhabit in an integrated and meaningful way despite being an actual resident (Laszczkowski 2011; see also Buchli 2013).

Figure 19 Astana skyline. *Source:* Author.

McGuire (1991), in his discussion of the landscape of inequality in Broome County, New York, explains how two different forms of materiality in the urban environment produce two different forms of political consciousness and forms of inequality. In one context, the aspirations of nonelites are harnessed materially through the mimicry of architectural forms—namely, an architectural style that is differentially accessible to everyone and that purports an ideology of equality in the urban landscape through the use of neocolonial and "craft-style" architectural elements that masks the profound inequalities in evidence within this company town. The other urban context sees workers segregated into worker housing not given access to material forms and housing aping elite aspirations. Here is a setting where individualizing and governable aspirations that might be otherwise co-opted, work to promote a collective consciousness through overcrowding and proximity within the distinctive forms of worker housing vastly different from company town elites. But these conditions offer the possibility of an alternative form of political consciousness that challenge the hierarchies of the capitalist town. What McGuire's analysis shows is that the same economic realities are materialized in different ways to produce two different common objects. In one instance, the manifest differences between capitalist and worker are differentiated spatially and architectonically, with the result that the lack of a common architectonic object results in the emergence of two distinct social identifications—one elite- and one worker-produced within the confines of distinctive worker housing and crowded conditions. The other attempts to overcome the inherent class conflicts of worker and capitalist by producing a common metaphor of democratic architectonic objects, similar housing, similar massing, and similar decorative motives, interspersed within a common landscape, seemingly equal despite degrees of perceived inequality within this common, yet differentially (and at times antagonistically) experienced landscape. Here, the common object of decorative motifs and a generally unsegregated and uniform landscape constitute materially a distinctly different consciousness and body of political action, despite identical economic hierarchies and inequalities. What McGuire identifies as the consumer culture of democratic forms produces a common object and fetishism (or misrecognition) that belies the inherent conflicted interests that converge on this produced common landscape sustained by these material forms.

It is within the conditions of capitalist cities that new forms of collectivity and consciousness can emerge, as these examples have shown. However, these new forms of being are not always felicitous and can be dystopic, as seen in the work of Setha Low (1997, 2003) on the gated communities of North America (Figure 20). Here, the materiality of suburban forms, through gates of varying degrees of permeability and impermeability, creates boundaries both hard and soft that enforce segregated communities that are further enforced by strict internal controls regarding the arrangement of driveways, front spaces, landscape, the color schemes of housing, and strict covenants of what can and cannot be changed. The ideology of American free expression and self-determination is here traded for the security of uniformity and boundedness in varying degrees, for "fortresses of fear," as Low describes them (Low 1997). The materiality of these forms not only exaggerates and exacerbates such fears but produces new forms of disjointed, fragmented life and fragmented forms of citizenship that, through the material effects of these interventions, disable the possibility of collective forms of democracy and citizenship. The superficial architectural style of these communities—be it Spanish colonial, modern, or some other pastiche—is irrelevant; what is relevant is their uniformity and the enforcement of that uniformity to fragment the urban environment visually, spatially, and socially. It is the process of conforming to these material requirements that produces and enforces the segregation that is so desired. These manipulations of space and the materiality of built form "encode fear"—as Low notes "not just metaphorically" (1997: 53)—into the way these forms materially regulate life. As a response to the increasing disparity between rich and poor, people are increasingly segregated by class, ethnicity, and also gender. Low notes how public spaces will shrink and privatized spaces will expand, consequences of the restructuring of a global economy and migration. "The city of the future," according to Low, "will be partitioned into gated enclaves segregated by race and class" (1997: 54), which will endure. Low (1997: 56) cites Fainshtein: "This built environment forms contours which structure social relations, causing commonalities of gender, sexual orientation, race, ethnicity, and class to assume spatial identities. Social groups, in turn, imprint themselves physically on the urban structure through the formation of communities, competition for territory, and segregation—in other words, through clustering, the erection of boundaries and establishing distance." Zoning laws, Low observes (citing Merry, 1997: 56), are developed to further aid this trend.

Residents trade "a sense of community for increased security" (1997: 63) and other amenities such as maintenance. Residents, Low describes, are not overly "concerned about making friends in these new communities." They agree with the strict "rules and regulations" and like not having to take responsibility for maintenance (1997: 67). The structures facilitate a certain kind of detachment—a "retreat from society, from neighborhood, and from responsibility" (1997: 67) (their general uniformity produces this "retreat" and detachment). The regulated materials, colors, landscaping, and gates in this produced uniformity become proxies for face-to-face community engagement. In the end, the style is not so important as the "retreat" that the regulated materials of these interchangeable generic styles facilitate. Like the carvings in wood on the Malagasy house in the earlier example by Maurice Bloch, these decorative elements should not be "read"; they are not signifying, but they produce a material

Figure 20 A gated community. *Source*: Mark Winfrey, Dreamstime.com.

disposition that enables retreat through their stylistic uniformity and genericism, however arbitrary, and through the deployment of these forms.

Daisy Froud (2004), on the other hand, looks at a similar phenomenon and examines how such planned communities in an English context work to forge very different identifications through the effects of their material forms. She describes how planned communities like the Great Notley Garden Village and Beaulieu Park estates intentionally produce the material and spatial peculiarities of historical forms as a means of providing narratives to anchor social and private life in a fluid economy. In effect, overtly fake English villages are created, with seemingly irregular and irrational architectural and decorative elements, such as "built-in nooks and crannies" (Froud 2004: 219) and the like, to provide a setting within which a community of otherwise unrelated families and individuals can narrate immediately a sense of space and place through these architectural elements and even the subtle appropriation of preexisting old trees and views onto preexisting historic buildings (Froud 2004: 218). Froud is keen to note that no one is duped by these forms. They are "authentic" in that they enable authentic new narratives of place and connection within a fluid population and labor market for the households that live there.

Michelle Murphy (2006), in a different vein, considers the materiality of built form and the production of new forms of embodied consciousness in what would be the otherwise distinctly unhomely setting of the office environment. She considers the emergence of sick building syndrome and how various material effects converge to produce a new coherent subject through its consolidation of effects, the feminist office worker.

She discusses how masculinist and rationalist planning and machine metaphors gave way to metabolist ones and open-plan flexibility and the use of increasing control and mechanization of air and artificial substances that segregated women, racial minorities, and outsourced labor in these new office settings built on cybernetic principles of feedback and flexibility but in the service of increasingly flexible and fluid needs of business: "The successor office building was a rejection of static and centralized ventilation systems in favor of more "flexible" arrangements made of mass-produced parts that could be arranged to adapt to different markets" (Murphy 2006: 33).

The dystopic result was sick building syndrome and what Murphy refers to as the "regimes of perceptibility" that enabled such a syndrome to emerge. These are "the regular and sedimented contours of perception and imperception produced within a disciplinary or epistemological tradition, its 'regimes of perceptibility'" (2006: 24). As she notes, "The building-machine presupposed a body-machine, which, like itself, had an optimal level of function. In this way a machined apprehension of the human body was constructed into buildings. All bodies, no matter how different, strove toward the same ideal of efficiency. Comfort could be universalised" (2006: 25).

She notes furthermore that "The mechanical production of comfort—an odorless, sweatless, privileged environment—in office buildings was predicated on a relatively straightforward assemblage of building and body" (Murphy 2006: 34). Yet how was this universalized and according to which criteria? Murphy suggests the "ASHRAE Standard 62 (1938), a minimum ventilation of 15cfm," which was derived from the laboratory study of young, middle-class male bodies (2006: 27).

But Murphy notes that the rise of feminism created a mode of political consciousness, focused on a heightened awareness of the female body in particular. Lower-paid office staff, primarily women, pooled into large, flexible, open-plan offices, could organize into collectives. What was once dismissed as a "hysterical" response to the toxins prevalent in office environments—Murphy argues—was countered by a heightened awareness of women's bodies by themselves. Murphy shows how diverse material registers come to interpellate the body and its relation with the materiality of built forms. In her example, the materiality of built form produces a dysfunctional relation that results in the biomedical disorder of sick building syndrome.

The materiality of built form has long held the power to heal, such as the "hygienic" gleaming, reflective, transparent, and brilliant white surfaces of modernism that ward off illness and heal. Fiona Parrott (2005) looks at the limits of these attempts to heal bodies and souls through the materiality of built forms in psychoanalytic hospital settings. Parrott notes how most of the inhabitants of these units have been convicted of various violent offences in addition to being mentally ill. The interior décor is one of produced domesticity: "sofas, tables, a widescreen television, bowls of fruit and plants" along with "Soft lighting and pastel paints are thought to have a 'calming effect'" (Parrott 2005: 249). Patients are encouraged to bring their own objects (screened for security) to make their rooms more homelike. However, a number of patients tended not to decorate—hence the claim "it's not forever" (Parrott 2005: 250). As Parrott notes: "Fixing objects to the walls of these rooms metaphorically fixed them in the institution" (2005: 250). One woman kept a picture of a dog, but did not display it: "this is not my property. If it was my home I would put it on my wall" (2005: 250). Individual rooms were distinctly barren compared to the produced coziness of the common areas: "By rejecting 'home' decoration in the institution, patients maintain their hopes of an imminent exit" (2005: 250). In the words of one of her informants: "Posters would be good but I don't wanna make it look like I'm here for a long time. I wanna make it look like . . . I dunno, it's my home for the meantime. Until I get a flat" (2005: 251). Decisions about the use and decoration of these spaces was justified in terms of necessity and function. Things would be propped up, not fixed to the wall: "leave it as it comes, it's not my home" (Parrott 2005: 252).

Parrott noted that people liked to talk about having soft furnishings and other home-related objects, but only when they were released imagining their future homes outside. For women in particular, home was lost at times as a result of their incarceration, and this was a very painful and at times tearful subject: "It's not my home or my room, it's just somewhere to stay. Home's at home with my daughter and partner. I put a lot of work into my home. Bought quite a lot of bits. It was my home. It won't be anymore" (2005: 253). Patients were allowed to keep their council flats. But Parrot notes that staff advised against this, seeing it as wasteful of public monies. One woman "regularly used her escorted leave . . . to return to clean the flat. She was careful not to bring objects from the flat back into the unit" (2005: 253). Parrott notes that more emphasis was placed on clothing, which affirmed ties with an outside life and existence and connections with family and friends. Clothing did not serve to signify an ethnic or other social identification; it primarily expressed connection outside the institution and against it.

This resistance to the material and its social effects emerges in more compelling dimensions in Merry's (2001) discussion of "spatial governmentality" in Hawaii. Merry discusses control through the "management" of space, "creating spaces that appeared safe to urbanites by removing people who looked dangerous" (Merry 2001: 16). This includes the use of restraining orders as legal instruments to order populations, structuring space in novel, decidedly less material ways than might be seen from the tradition of the highly material panoptic contexts of Foucauldian approaches. Merry instead emphasizes a distinctly "immaterial" and post-Foucauldian discipline of social and spatial control—one that avowedly focuses on the movement and flow of individuals through space through the innovative use of legal instruments. The evident and empirically stable materiality of built form is here profoundly reconfigured within the relatively immaterial register of this legal and bureaucratic instrument of governance: that sheet of paper that is the temporary restraining order. Merry describes the wider effects of this innovation thus:

> Disciplinary regulation focuses on the regulation of persons through incarceration or treatment, while spatial mechanisms concentrate on the regulation of space through excluding offensive behaviour. Spatial forms of regulation focus on concealing or displacing offensive activities rather than eliminating them. Their target is a population rather than individuals . . . The individual offender is not treated or reformed, but a particular public is protected. The logic is that of zoning rather than correcting. (Merry 2001: 17)

In particular, it is poor men that are subjected to the curfews and restraining orders (Merry 2001: 26), the same men that gated communities are designed to be protected from in a decidedly different material register which Setha Low describes (Merry 2001: 18).

In Merry's analysis, following Simon (1988), spatial governmentality has evolved from the Foucauldian, panoptic kind "to a late-twentieth-century, postmodern form of social control that targets categories of people using actuarial techniques" (Merry 2001: 18). As Merry notes further (2001: 20) it creates self-regulating individuals, people being made aware of choice and encouraged to act accordingly rather than disciplining and regulating directly. Here, "consumption as a mode of identity formation" (Merry 2001: 19) dovetails with the needs to govern more inexpensively. Merry notes that "Citizen subjects are educated and solicited into an alliance between personal objectives and institutional goals, creating the phenomenon Rose calls 'government at a distance' " (Merry 2001: 20).

This is a move to "discipline and self-management" (Merry 2001: 21) reminiscent of earlier forms but in novel, immaterial ways: legal instruments in place of "bricks and mortar." Security is concerned with minimizing risk as Merry notes (see Simon 1988), not reform, as with the prisoner in Foucault's panopticon (Merry 2001: 20). In terms of gender violence, Merry notes that security protects the victim temporarily, and does not reform the offender (Merry 2001: 23). This is what temporary restraining orders do. This innovative bureaucratic and material technology works both ways: it controls the poor but it also protects women (Merry 2001: 26). It is part of a hybrid form of governance that is backed up with punishment as well as a novel form of spatial control. As Merry notes: "This is not an evolutionary relationship, but an intersecting one. Spatialized control technologies focused on security and risk management are intimately linked to forms of punishment and discipline" (Merry 2001: 26). As Merry observes these practices spread to Hawaii from other parts of the world through the processes of globalization and the needs of neoliberal governance to appear effective to electorates and to cut costs. In Hawaii, the control of sex offenders shifted the terms of control from traditional Foucauldian notions of space and the power of material forms toward a hybrid and very uncertain configuration of bodies, materials, and space (Merry 2001: 26).

2

Institutional contexts such as those described by Parrott (2005) and Merry (2001) suggest a certain failure of the materiality of architectural forms in late capitalist contexts. This failure of materiality has been noted by the legal scholar Jonathan Simon (1988) as discussed in Merry (2001) in his studies of new actuarial practices where, as he notes, the Foucauldian preoccupation with the material and spatial aspects of social discipline forming subjectivities is rendered increasingly irrelevant by the redistribution of social risk in social policy and law. This marks a change from the way power is exerted over and constitutive of subjects, from the highly intensive and extensive disciplinary regimes of Foucault—requiring great material and economic inputs (prisons, town planning, etc.) to discipline and form new subjectivities—to a new "actuarial regime" where behavior is predicted and accommodated and can be regulated by legal instruments such as temporary restraining orders (Simon 1988: 773–4; Merry 2001). Simon argues that this represents a shift from bodies to populations (Simon 1988: 774), a much less fixed and considerably more immaterial entity. Simon notes how the incorporeal, despatialized, and immaterial nature of these new social "aggregates" according to which society is increasingly organized (Simon 1988: 789), makes it extremely difficult for individuals to form common goals and purposes (Simon 1988: 774), as traditional Marxian approaches have described in the past. The disciplines that produced new subjectivities of resistance to the exertion of state power are unable to cohere (Simon 1988: 793). The "plenary" and situated authentic and coherent identities of strategic essentialism are challenged by these actuarial practices (Simon 1988: 787). Simon argues that "the representations produced by actuarial practices, e.g. insurance cells, place us in a cultural space even more alienating and disempowering than the disciplinary bureaucratic practices we have occupied for most of the last century" (1988: 787). These new actuarial categories are extremely easy to manipulate by agents of state power (Simon 1988: 789). As Simon notes, the sort of "moral density" (Durkheim) created by the weight of tradition materializes certain forms of materiality that are "attenuated" within new actuarial regimes (Simon 1988: 793–4): we move from the highly material, densely sedimented, and "solid" panopticon to the rather immaterial and "liquid" actuarial table. In short, to echo E. P. Thompson and quote Simon: "Rather than making people up, actuarial practices unmake them" (1988: 792). The terms whereby subjectivities are dematerialized means that the study of the material effects of architectural forms requires greater attention to the nuances of materiality and the registers in which it functions and its imbrication with other immaterial technologies, such as temporary restraining orders (Merry 2001), and their constitutive effects more than ever before.

Such a state of affairs requires a shift in the way we consider the registers in which material forms operate. Melanie Van der Hoorn (2005, 2009), in her analysis of Viennese *Flaktürme*, provides an example of how conventional notions of the seeming implacability of solid monumental forms operate, echoing the observations of Bender concerning Stonehenge and Yalouri regarding the Acropolis earlier. These massive concrete bunkers were built by Nazi forces during the Second World War (Figure 21). They accommodated equipment, ammunition, artwork, hospitals, workshops, and bunkers for high-ranking Nazi officials as well as civilian shelters (Van der Hoorn 2005: 116). They were entirely independent, with their own electricity and water supplies. In the postwar period, these buildings were generally hated by the population as rather painful and monstrous reminders of Austria's occupation and collaboration with the Nazi regime. At the war's end, they were emptied, and everything that could be sold for scrap was, but the buildings were too massive and solid to be dismantled, and thus they remained. Their material presence was a constant reminder of a period of violence and destruction, occupation and collaboration. Van der Hoorn notes that, through most of their history, there has been hardly any public discussion about them. They are not noted on maps of the city, there are no postcards showing them. Photographers crop them out, avoid them in their views, or retouch them out. The term *Flaktürme* does not even exist as a category in the search system of the Austrian National Library (2005: 119). Neither is the Office of Listed Buildings interested in them. The head of the Monument Registry Department "suggested that they do not need to be protected since they cannot be demolished anyway: 'They are really edifices which persist due to their monumentality; they cannot be destroyed, and therefore it makes no difference at all whether they are listed or not' " (Van der Hoorn 2005: 120). There is not even a consensus among architectural historians or heritage professionals as to how many of them there are or even what they were used for precisely. As one architect noted, "These towers are taboo. People don't see them; people drive past them, and they do not exist, they are not noticed anymore" (Van der Hoorn 2005: 120). They are like a stain that cannot be removed, seemingly indestructible, assuming an almost "primitive," primeval quality. Van der Hoorn quotes Tabor et al.: "People do not like them—yet hardly anyone demands their demolition. People do not use them—yet do not want to do without them either. People do not appreciate them—yet any conversion is considered even worse" (2005: 122). Despite numerous proposals to convert them, surround them with other buildings, turn them into museums, or use them as platforms for large monumental sculptures or even as huge advertising billboards, nothing gets done. There are some exceptions, such as one *Flakturm* right in the midst of other buildings in Vienna's urban fabric, which has been converted into a climbing wall (2005: 120). Affirming its primitiveness as a geological feature and erasing its manmade, Nazi-era connotations, it is literally covered in bright climbing grips, turning it, to some limited degree, into a cliff for extreme sports enthusiasts (2005: 121). Through a sleight of hand, the monumentally manmade comes to appear naturelike, a cliff for climbing enthusiasts.

Van der Hoorn argues that their persistence, however "attenuated," is a means of considering alternatives—alternatives to the past, to history (2005: 130), a certain open-ended utopian thinking, she observes, that needs to seem suspended in their attenuated form between destruction, ignorance, oblivion, and complete alteration; suspended in a vaguely recognized and partially and inconclusively materialized way. Thereby they always offer a means of thinking about alternative histories and futures in Austrian society. In the postwar period, they were an alibi for the victim status of the Austrian nation during Nazi occupation (2005: 123), but in recent scholarship

Figure 21 Viennese *Flakturm*. *Source*: Lucaderoma, Dreamstime.com.

they are a means for Austrian society to confront its wartime collaboration. Van der Hoorn notes there has been more discussion since the 1980s to consider different proposals to deal with the structures that engage them, but these proposals tend to erase the structures' historic significance by associating them to lighthearted, ludic concepts (art platforms, rock climbing, commercial advertisements, casinos, coffee museums, etc.) (2005: 129). Again, through a movement akin to the détournement of the situatonists, the seemingly implacable nature of their material forms, immovable concrete is subtly refigured from the monstrous to the ludic, from manmade to quasi-nature. The implacable and excessive materiality of these forms—that might render them so enduring and immovable as an effect and consequence of their inherently conflicted investments—could be subtly shifted from an inherently produced empirical solidity to be then constituted and refigured as quasi-nature on the basis of its produced monumentality and recede from and relieve those painful and conflicted investments that have characterized the experience of these immovable forms.

3

The urban sociologist Saskia Sassen has remarked upon the extraordinary impact of new technologies within urban environments of the late twentieth and early twenty-first centuries (Sassen 2006: 344–7) and how we might understand conventional understandings of the materiality of architectural forms under the conditions of digitization. She offers an analysis of how we might begin to conceive something like a nineteenth-century office building, purpose-built for conducting commerce in its time, which is now radically reconfigured in relation to notions of urban, national, and globalized space when such a building is "networked" (Sassen 2006: 346). "Bricks and mortar," in one context, become something entirely different within a digitized economy (Sassen 2006: 345). On the surface they are very difficult to disentangle. A nineteenth-century office building erected at the height of an earlier globalized colonial economy based in the City of London might appear to be a rather stable entity—but looks are very deceiving. We are rather familiar with the effects segregated work spaces in the nineteenth century had for the production of class and gender and the hierarchies of spatial domains, forms of knowledge, and the wider colonial and economic inequalities that were sustained within such settings—such as those suggested by Murphy in relation to sick building syndrome. However, if we were to consider this in the terms Sassen proposes in the present circumstances of globalization, then digitization radically transforms the material capacities that are so intuitively straightforward in this context. Twenty-four-hour financial markets, instantaneous communication, and new financial transactions and instruments extend "bricks and mortar," and the conventional hierarchies of people and space forged within them, into something very dynamic and entirely uncontained and unforeseen by the original builders of such spaces (Sassen 2006: 375). Similarly, Sassen notes, the seeming solidity of these forms within globalized and digitized financial markets are, in a sense, further "liquefied" (Sassen 2006: 345), rendering something solid in time and space into something, one might call, "partible" within the instantaneous and compressed time-space of digitized global financial markets. As Sassen notes the building itself is a fluid real estate asset, at once fixed in time and space in a conventional material manner we can visit and enter and even work within; and yet this entity of bricks and mortar is further extended and circulated globally as a liquid asset within hyper-mobile financial markets (Sassen 2006: 345)—whose fortunes, nearby or far afield, have everything to do with the immediate, materially bound future of this assemblage of "bricks and mortar." We have only to consider the recent crisis in the mortgage markets in the United States and the holes that crisis created in the market for derivatives in Europe to see how the hyperephemeral and liquid effects of the derivative markets that have emerged within these new digitized global economies are intimately bound with seemingly stable "bricks and mortar" and the physical collapse and deterioration of communities through the United States and other parts of the world. Similarly, within this space, office workers are constantly in communication with colleagues around the world via the Internet, phones, and computer screens, whose activities are only restricted by time zones, while simultaneously interacting in more conventional, embodied face-to-face contacts with colleagues within the office and immediate neighborhood (Sassen 2006: 346; see Nigel Thrift [2005] on "screeness"). Conventional boundaries of building, city, and nation-state that initially shaped this assemblage of "bricks and mortar" are profoundly destabilized and uncertain: at once very local as well as global, confounding what the terms themselves mean and what it means to exist within such a setting (Sassen 2006: 375). More significantly, how we interact and perceive the environment visually and tactilely through computer screens and keyboards, aurally through phone conversations and face-to-face contacts on the street corner or in the lobby, or more virtually in the video conferencing room radically refigures the many different sensorial ways and hybrid combinations whereby we perceive and interact within urban settings, invoking the earlier anxieties noted by Jameson in relation to the material forms of the postmodern. The interaction of such topographies, as Sassen notes, is very difficult to map (2006: 346); in fact, it resists most conventional attempts of such a mapping (though the recent work of Albena Yaneva [2012] suggests an alternative).

What is often overlooked is that within such novel settings our bodily engagements with our various senses and the ways in which we have variously been constituted as sentient, knowledgeable beings are profoundly challenged, suggesting the emergence of a new sensorium, as Jameson points out. Our embodied sensory capacities have always been shown historically and anthropologically to be radically configured with the development of new technologies, as Marx had commented regarding the theoretical and critical capacities of the senses. Anthropologists of the senses have long noted how contact between different groups and the introduction of new technologies create new capacities while disabling others, producing new and often disempowering sentient forms of knowledge (see Howes 2004; Classen and Howes 2006; Edwards et al. 2006). Such anthropologists speak of emergent cosmopolitan sensoria (Edwards et al. 2006: 15); they speak of diverse, competing, and shifting hierarchies of sensoria that gradually accumulate, shift, and sediment, and in which we constitute ourselves and our lives within an increasingly extended and cosmopolitan sensorium—such as the often-described shift from the more embodied, aural-oral sensorium in the medieval West to our more disembodied, ocular-centric visual one in the recent past (see Ong 1967; Crary 1992). Thus, one can speak of cities themselves as being highly cosmopolitan concatenations of such diverse sensoria and their various differential capacities that are actually produced, extended, and enabled within them.

Sassen describes an imbrication of technologies (2006: 345) with significant implications for what one might understand as a novel and expanding urban sensorium. This notion of a material imbrication assumes a priori the existence of certain material entities where "Each maintains its distinct irreducible character" (Sassen 2006: 345). However, instead of seeing such entities as the imbrication of "irreducible" elements, the philosopher of science Karen Barad might suggest quite different understandings of such a setting. She might describe this as the intra-action of various entities, which are variously material, immaterial, human, and nonhuman and which constitute this new setting. Barad offers another view on this kind of urban space but from a different perspective, a so-called nonplace (Augé 1995)—in this case from 35,000 feet in the air (Barad 2007: 223). She describes, paraphrased here, a setting where a passenger on a plane somewhere between New York and London is able to communicate from a computer on a tray folding out from another passenger's seat in front, with a computer in Sydney (probably another nineteenth-century office building), and transfer money from a Swiss bank to a commercial venture for a mill in China. As Barad notes: "With the click of a mouse, space, time and matter are mutually reconfigured in this cyborg 'trans-action' that transgresses and reworks the boundaries between human and machine, nature and culture, and economic and discursive practices" (Barad 2007: 223)—and, as one might imagine, variably impacting upon the family of a textile worker in Zhejiang and the rattling seat of the airline passenger sitting in front. Barad's notion of "intra-action" (Barad 2007: 33) is quite helpful in explaining how such phenomena arise and how, contrary to Sassen, how they variably emerge within these "intra-active" settings and the capacities they afford rather than seeing them as the hybridization of preexisting entities. With each shift in this complex concatenation of entities, Barad suggests how all elements are refigured and are very different from what they were before in terms of their new emergent capacities, such as our nineteenth-century city office building. Barad argues that things such as material artifacts, scientific facts, gender, and social institutions emerge within "material-discursive" and "intra-active" settings. Entities such as ethnicity or gender do not precede such settings, but are in fact produced within them. Furthermore, she observes such entities (like an office building, a neighborhood, a sexuality, an ethnicity, or an atom) are the result of complex "material-discursive" phenomena encompassing a range from ephemeral discourse to otherwise material "stubborn facts," to paraphrase Alfred North Whitehead (Barad 2007: 224). Barad shows neither the material nor the discursive preexist; both are produced "intra-actively"—they arise into being in relation to one another (Barad 2003: 802). What we commonly refer to as "things" or discrete entities—such as, commonsensically, a building or, less evidently, a community or gender identification—are diverse, complex phenomena that emerge "intra-actively," materially, and discursively within asymmetrical relations of power (Barad 2007: 224). Thus, what we understand as a given materiality is the outcome of a particular material and discursive "intra-action," where "discursive" and "material" practices mutually constitute one another (Barad 2003: 820) as part of novel emergent phenomena and whose implacable materiality and excess, as discussed earlier, emerge as an "effect" of conflicted and compounded commitments (following Rouse 2002).

However, Barad's notion of "intra-action" takes place in what might usually be described as rather fixed, specific settings and in relation to specific entities and does not quite help to explain the relation of many different "intra-active" settings and entities in relation to one another. Her purview is to understand the "intra-actions" that constitute a particular phenomenon—say, quantum physics or emergent identities of class or gender (Barad 2007: 224–30). It does not address multiple, apparently incommensurable and diverse phenomena, entities and cosmopolitan sensoria addressed by anthropologists of the senses—though her insights can be very profitably extended to do so.

Rather, what I would like to suggest here is an emergent cosmopolitanism of an unruly and expanding sensorium of "material-discursive" "intra-activity" to use Barad's terms in which such aspects of diversity as gender, class, ethnicity, and nationhood are being forged. That is, gender, ethnicity, class, and so on are what one is constrained or enabled to "do" within certain "material-discursive" sensorial configurations; such "intra-activity" is not representative, it is "constitutive" (Barad 2003: 817, 2007: 146–7). I use the word *diverse* intentionally here, keeping in mind its ideological inflections (following Groys 2008). When one talks about the frequently observed diversity within cities, one does not just mean the different migrant and ethnic groups or "diversity" of cultures—which neoliberal forms of governmentality understand in terms of resources to be husbanded, waiting to be rationalized and exploited (Groys 2008)—but also the diverse and cosmopolitan sensoria in which such identifications are "materially-discursively" and "intra-actively" sustained following Barad.

We avail ourselves of the capacities and affordances of these expanding sensoria in novel and unrecognizable ways, as in the examples that Sassen and Barad provide. One cannot resolve one to the other or even speak of the a priori integrity of any one element, as Sassen implies in her definition of the term *imbrication*. What we have is a cosmopolitan "intra-active" setting of many shifting, emerging, competing, stabilizing, and, at times, failing "intra-active" sensoria within these material settings that are at once very complex, yet increasingly this is the way we understand and negotiate the extended, diverse, and fragmented spaces of urban life. This is not, however, quite so open-ended and chaotic as one might imagine. The "bricks and mortar" of the nineteenth-century office building remain, but its "intra-active" setting is in terms of its materiality and complex sensorium—cosmopolitan and divergent. One needs to speak of cosmopolitan "intra-active" material sensoria that move, evolve, and shift in different but nonetheless coherent and nonarbitrary ways, in terms of the capacities they enable as well as the capacities they disable. This is similar to what Edwards, Gosden, and Phillips (2006: 15) refer to as "the cosmopolitan education of the senses that has shaped us all" in the wake of colonialism and capitalist expansion.

Keeping the examples of Sassen and Barad in mind, what needs to be rethought, then, in relation to the material conditions of institutions such as office buildings, neighborhoods, and whole cities? Such cosmopolitan sensoria converging on one urban setting, shaped within divergent and emerging "material-discursive" "intra-active" contexts occur almost everywhere, but not uniformly and with different effects in terms of individual lives and local as well as various dispersed communities. Such complex cosmopolitan sensoria are at the heart of what might otherwise seem to be very localized conflicts and are profoundly political. What is clear is that a much more nuanced approach to these settings must be taken that is mindful of the complexities of such sensoria—rather than attending to difference as preexisting and self-evident, but as emergent, not just symbolically, discursively, or materially, or reducible to one or the other, but "intra-actively" within specific "material-discursive" settings (following Barad). We need to be attentive to new diverse and cosmopolitan sensoria with their particular capacities to extend, forge, and articulate emergent differences at novel scales and configurations. For this we need new means with which to describe them and through their descriptions to effect their emergence in terms that are more equitable and just, attending to the means by which these phenomena enable as well as disable emergent individuals, groups, and communities. Anthropology and the social sciences are uniquely placed with their ethnographic and eclectic methods focused on the embodied person and intimate communities within such urban settings, to tease out the effects of such cosmopolitan sensoria in the "material-discursive" settings of anthropology's microlevels of analysis that are sustained both at the level of a given localized community and in complex asymmetrical relations beyond.

4

The implacable and excessive materiality of given forms can be seen as the artifactual "effect" of conflicted "commitments," as suggested by Rouse. Or, as Foucault noted in reference to the panopticon: "The carceral network constituted one of the armatures of this power-knowledge that has made the human sciences historically possible. Knowable man (soul, individuality, consciousness, conduct, whatever it is called) is the object-effect of this analytical investment, of this domination-observation" (Foucault 1977: 305).

But these commitments can shift and be refigured to displace the excessive material effects of these commitments. The examples of the *Flaktürme* as well as earlier ones—Stonehenge, the Parthenon, and the like—draw attention to the subtle and effective means by which such implacable materialities can be refigured. The digitization of "bricks and mortar" suggested by Sassen, the immaterial technologies of actuarial practices suggested by Simon, the novel effects of legal instruments such as temporary restraining orders (Merry 2001), and the varying ways in which seemingly implacable empirical forms are reconfigured in novel ways as suggested by the "intra-active" approaches proposed by Barad indicate how novel assemblages emerge, and the shifts of simultaneous multiple registers and their different, and at times conflicted, social effects can refigure and undo what might otherwise seem unambiguously and empirically monumental, unmovable, and fixed.

5 CONSUMPTION STUDIES AND THE HOME

I

In the postwar period, consumption-oriented approaches emerged with particular force. This large body of literature on consumption studies and the home emerged predominantly from an intersection of Marxist analysis, feminist critique, and the rise of consumption studies more widely. Within the Marxian tradition, dwelling and the conditions of everyday life were integral to the analysis of society more broadly. More importantly, the understanding of the Morganian assumption that the conditions of daily life, the home, and family life as outlined in his *Houses and House-Life of the American Aborigines* (1965 [1881]) established an emphasis on the importance of dwelling and daily life as an index of social and technical development within Marxian unilineal schemes. Marx and Engels, as noted before, were close students of Morgan's work, seeing within it the means by which material conditions could be used to understand social life and technical development more broadly, but also, more importantly, how contemporary institutions were the products of specific material and technical circumstances and how changes in the material basis of human life brought about changes in social life. More significantly, Morgan's study indicated that social inequalities were historical, determined by material relations of production, and that those relations have changed over time, as Morgan described in his discussion of "communism in living" with his examples from North America. It is precisely the historical nature of these forms that inspired Marx and Engels (see preface to Engels 1940).

Engels, notably in his work *The Origin of the Family, Private Property and the State* (1940), made clear that gender inequalities were the result of specific modes of production and social organization. In his often-cited assessment of nineteenth-century family life and gender inequality, he observed: "Within the family, he is the bourgeois and the wife represents the proletariat" (Engels 1940: 79). It is within this configuration of interests that early feminism and early Marxism found common cause and a common analytical frame. Under the conditions of the early Soviet state before the rise of Stalinism and in the postwar period in the West, this relationship between feminist and Marxist analysis was very close.

Engels's analysis of living conditions in the industrial towns of England was of singular importance for diagnosing the material effects of capitalist industrialization and suggesting reforms. Earlier nineteenth-century feminists (Hayden 1981) would also study the home and its organization to discover the means by which women could be liberated from the confines of the patriarchal home. With these studies a series of architectural and social reforms were proposed that might help realize a more egalitarian future (see Hayden 1981; Spencer-Wood 2002). It is probably only under the conditions of the first revolutionary Marxist society in the early Soviet state that the issue of proletarian emancipation and women's emancipation went hand in hand. During this period, social and architectural reformers devised and implemented myriad schemes to realize these twinned goals, which were only to be sidelined in the Stalinist period (see Buchli 1999). In the West, these efforts did not reemerge until the years following the Second World War with the rediscovery of Engels's text as a protofeminist tract (see Evelyn Reed's introduction to the 1972 edition [Engels 1972: 21–2]) and, with it, the rise of various Marxist critiques in capitalist Western societies.

Under these conditions in the postwar period, the home takes on a renewed importance as a site where the twinned ills of women's inequality and the inequalities of capitalist consumerism could be diagnosed and where solutions could be proposed. Against such a setting, the almost traditional concern with home and kinship at the heart of ethnographic fieldwork emerged as an important tool for the examination of the wider ills of gender and social inequality in the study of Western homes as well as the homes of more traditional, non-Western ethnographic subjects. In this postwar context, two anthropologists stand out: Pierre Bourdieu and his much-vaunted analysis of the habitus of home life emerging from his study of the Kabyle house (Bourdieu 1977) and Mary Douglas's work on consumerism, and in particular on hygiene, especially in regards to the home, where hygienic norms were seen to be important regulatory practices for the maintenance of social and gender distinctions as well as wider cosmological categories (Douglas 1970b).

Against this backdrop it is vital to consider for the postwar period the importance of consumption studies and the role of Marcel Mauss's concept of the gift and the particular circumstances of its emergence. Mary Douglas, writing in the preface to Mauss's (1990) *The Gift*, offers a critical account of this and the problems facing Western capitalism at the beginning of the twentieth century and the rise of Marxism and the victory of Soviet socialism in the 1920s. Mauss's essay, written in 1923 for *L'Année Sociologique*, represented, according to Douglas, a wider plea at the time to reconsider the alienating effects of modern capitalism and argue for the importance of social ties and relations that were unraveled by the effects of capitalist production so cogently critiqued by Marx and Engels. If Soviet socialism was an attempt to reinstate a moral basis for exchange through the socialization of capital and labor, then *The Gift* functioned as a bourgeois liberal attempt to argue for the maintenance of the social contract under the conditions of capitalism. The English postwar *Gift* was a distinctly Cold War artifact that did not engage with the conflicts between two industrialized economies, the Soviet Union and the United States, over the most equitable terms of social life promised by industrialization (see Marcuse 1958). It represented, instead, a depoliticized and decontextualized discussion of non-Western economies for the moral terms of exchange in nonindustrialized societies.

However, the importance of the text for establishing the moral context of exchange was foundational for the later postwar reassessment of consumerism. Focusing here on the context of domestic consumption, such practices were seen as counter to the alienating effects of wider economic consumerism. Within anthropological accounts of consumerism, rather than reflecting the duping of participants in Western consumer economies, consumption represented the means by which contingent forms of moral authenticity were forged within capitalist societies.

The work of Daniel Miller and his students on consumption stands out (notably Miller 1987). Miller's (1988) article on kitchens on a council estate speaks directly to the force of consumer practices in the home and in the manipulation of the materiality of the home to forge precisely these local and contingent moral orders. Those who opt out of kitchen decoration and the active consumer-driven appropriation of state-sponsored council housing could be seen as asocial beings, unable to participate in provisioning for the moral orders of community and family that the appropriation of kitchens and consumer goods enabled. Similarly, household studies that attempted to understand the nature of women's roles in the home, particular around issues of housework, saw these issues converge on the daily routinized activities of home life and their diagnosis of social ills. Anthropologists were well suited to situate themselves within this nexus of concerns to offer cogent analyses.

The preoccupation with the materiality of consumerist appropriation and the context of use tended to privilege households, and the spheres of action available for individual appropriation—that is, consumer goods and the malleable surfaces of interiors, but not the architectural shells themselves for the most part; this was the domain of the state and the wider economy, not the individual and the household. The situation is quite different in the study of migrants and their remittances and house construction and other self-build traditions. Thus, such consumption-oriented approaches were often done at the expense of the analysis of architectural form. The spatial context, with its arrangement of spaces and its hierarchies, was paramount, but architectural form per se, its materiality, and the processes by which homes were built were relegated to the edges of consumption studies, focusing instead on the activities and processes that took place within the walls and not so much on the walls themselves. Much of this has to do with the simple fact that most Western homes in the industrial and postindustrial period were simply not built by their inhabitants, unlike in vernacular traditions, both Western and non-Western and in certain migrant contexts, with the exception of minority elites who commissioned builders or architects for themselves. A certain tension emerges within these studies as an opposition between built form and lived experience, the shell and its contents, an opposition sustained within domination and resistance paradigms, which saw built form as the purview of wider state and economic forces and the uses of space within as an appropriation of or resistance to these modes of domination. One criticism of such approaches was that they presumed preexisting interests of individuals and the state, anterior to the context of domestic and material life in the twentieth-century West. Later approaches emphasized the close linkage of both these interests not as anterior, but shaped in relation to each other as a result of a mutual commitment to institutions such as the home (albeit an asymmetrical commitment in terms of the distribution of effective power, where increasingly it is the material conditions of home life as a nexus that structures family life, gender, and sexuality as well as the interests of wider powers).

2

Walter Benjamin's evocative description of the bourgeois home enveloped in folds of velvet conveys the power of the fossil metaphor that has long dominated the anthropological study of architectural from. Such a metaphor privileges a visualist form of knowledge whereby the home can be scanned and "read," allowing for identification, assessment, and diagnosis. The rise of photography goes hand in hand with the visual analysis of domestic interiors as portraits or "fossilizations" of their occupants. The wider context and architectural contours are underdetermined at the expense of these surfaces available to the disembodied gaze of the analyst. Csikszentmihalyi and Rochberg-Halton (1981: 138) could still speak of "gastropods" and "shells," while linguistically derived semiotic and structuralist-inspired analysis attest to the "readerly" quality of the analysis of the home.

These surfaces, of course, go hand in hand with the way domestic spaces were to be assessed, analyzed, and acted upon. Early modernist reformers, and in particular Soviet constructivists, saw the material artifacts and surfaces of nonmodern interiors as diagnostic of a particular way of life and sought to eradicate the material effects of these surfaces. In anticipation of Douglas's (1970b) later analysis of hygiene, hygienic norms were produced by which to describe, diagnose, and reform material forms in the home. The heavy drapery, profusion of objects, and elaborate carved designs of nonmodern forms were seen as harboring dust and vermin. In their place, white surfaces, easily cleaned, smooth designs, metal, and expanses of glass ensured that the material effects of bourgeois domestic materiality and their associated filth—vermin and disease—would be dispelled. The health of the body would be ensured without the designs that harbored pathogens. For Soviet reformers, women would no longer be required to constantly and repetitively clean and constitute bourgeois notions of feminine work and cleanliness that enforced a particular form of bourgeois patriarchal feminine moral personhood. Such a habitus of daily repetitive actions, which the materiality of certain forms required, produced an identification and consciousness in relation to the moral orders of the home and family, gender, and social life that were at odds with the socialist project. Instead, easing the repetitive habitus of cleaning meant that women might engage with the wider industrial workforce, freed from the requirements of the bourgeois capitalist home. However, such embodied forms of labor that went toward the maintenance of a specific feminine identification with the materiality of the home would be sacrificed in the realization of more androgynous and masculinist forms of femininity, thus challenging accepted norms of the feminine and, with it, masculine sexuality, ultimately rejected under the conditions of later totalitarian Stalinism.

Numerous studies exist which speak of the constitutive role of material culture and consumerism to make up men and, in particular, women. Design historians have noted how the rise of do-it-yourself (DIY) in the postwar period (see Atkinson 2006) created a new form of heterosexuality in the home, where both men and women, pursuing new complementary gendered activities, would produce the heteronormative values of the postwar nuclear family through their sensuous DIY labors; these activities literally constituted men and women as complementary subjects through their quotidian labors. Gender and heteronormativity was an active, constantly maintained, sensual, and laboring activity.

Addressing a context outside Euro-American societies but in keeping with the rise of gender studies and feminist critiques, Henrietta Moore's (1986) study of the Marakwet in Kenya provides a good insight into how the materiality of domestic practices constitute gender relations and social inequalities, with a particular emphasis on the materiality of domestic dirt and its associated practices. The basic household unit among the rural Marakwet communities in Moore's study was that of a conjugal compound comprised of at least a husband and one wife. Thus, there would be a man's hut and woman's hut and, upon further marriages, additional women's huts. The compound would evolve, however, so that, upon the death of the husband and his parents, his children having moved out, the compound will cease to exist, finalizing the cycle of the compound's use (Moore 1986: 92–8).

Part of Moore's analysis focuses on the importance of waste products in Mara-kwet society for constituting gender and negotiating gender-based inequalities (Moore 1986: 111–20) (echoing the preoccupation with waste products and household maintenance in Western and Soviet discourses). In this case, it is the critical separation of waste products associated with archetypal gendered activities that are at the heart of the negotiation of social and gender inequalities. At issue is the separation of chaff and ash, which is associated with women's activities in the dwelling, from the goat dung, which is associated with men's activities. In Moore's analysis, the architectonic elements of Marakwet dwellings are dominated by the materiality of domestic waste products associated with gendered activities—their flows and regulation—that are key toward the maintenance of gendered relations. The two forms of waste are deposited at opposite ends of the domestic compound. It is vital that the two are held apart from each other. To mix them is profoundly problematic and radically upsets the structure of social and gendered relations. Thus, by the manipulation of these material wastes, women are able to assert a certain modicum of agency in their lives in an otherwise asymmetrical patriarchal order.

As Moore notes ideally, when women are buried, they are buried near the waste products associated with their labor in life—that is, the chaff resulting from the processing of grain—and placed outside the compound; the man will be buried near the goat dung resulting from his pastoral activities, also outside of the compound, to the right (Moore 1986: 102–3). These divisions of space according to waste products are maintained throughout the compound, separating dung/male from ash/female; man's hut from woman's hut, as Moore notes (Moore 1986: 104–5).

The local saying insists on not mixing ash and dung, because this is highly "in-auspicious"; the two must be separated (Moore 1986: 112). This separation, Moore asserts, is associated with the inherent tension between the sexes focused on the com-mon object, the household and house. Although women are subordinate, especially in matters related to the larger social concerns of the patriclan, Moore notes, women acknowledged at the level of the individual household as having a great deal of power. A mature woman's association with the home is profound, enabling her to pursue what Moore refers to as "house-power" (Moore 1986: 112). Her strongest, most fe-male and mature position is where she sits by the hearth cooking (Moore 1986: 113). This is also the source of the tension between male/public/patriclan concerns with female/domestic/family concerns that is embodied in attitudes toward ash. Thus, ash often represents an individualizing tendency that is at odds with the public concerns of men as Moore notes (Moore 1986: 113). Chaff, however, though also female, is related to the group and social activity beyond the domestic unit and is important for the production of beer, which is significant for the maintenance of male/male relations within the patriclan. But since it is "not male," albeit social, it, too, is opposed to the eminently social and public male substance: dung (Moore 1986: 114–16).

Marakwet society being patrilocal, the men are associated with the enduring lineal solidity of villages comprised of domestic compounds and the herding of livestock, which are considered supremely social, communal, permanent, and thereby masculine activities. Women marry in from outside and are considered impermanent and inherently individualizing beings, with their activities focused on the care and maintenance of the individual dwelling. Ash being associated with women's activities can be seen as dangerous to masculine concerns (Moore 1986: 117). Moore notes that if a young girl rejects marriage, she can manipulate the power of these waste products to subvert them—albeit contingently—by smearing her body with ash whereby "this act signifies her desire for the 'death' and/or sterility of the proposed union" (Moore 1986: 117). The deep asymmetries of gendered relations in Marakwet society can be momentarily reworked through this exercise of power over these regulative substances at the micro scale. At the heart of Moore's analysis is the centrality of the regulation of the flows of key substances—seemingly prosaic, though sublime in their constitutive effect on gendered social life, where the architectural context of the dwelling is the nexus in which these regulatory substances are generated and maintained.

The morally constitutive nature of flows of exchanges sustaining daily life as pointed out by Mauss emphasizes the materiality of substances for the regulation of such flows. Their specific material qualities and the embodied responses they elicit are at the heart of the processes by which people are made, kinship is forged, and gender is constituted. Early modernist and Soviet reformers understood instinctively the importance of the materiality of things in homes responsible for the bodily and psychic attachments certain materialities engender (such as the way that glass, metal, and white facilitate a detachment from the constitutive and repetitive materiality of the bourgeois home). This becomes even more clear in other contexts in the wider flows of generative exchanges, where other flows are important besides those associated only with reproduction and commensality, which tend to dominate anthropological accounts. Two more recent contrasting examples by Pauline Garvey and Jean-Sébastien Marcoux suggest how such flows work in urban Euro-American contexts.

Marcoux addresses the peculiarities of the Montreal rental market, which requires most renters to renew their contracts at roughly the same time each year (Marcoux 2001b: 70). The regularity of this cycle becomes the means by which, on a yearly basis, key relationships of locality, affective relations between household members and romantic partners are negotiated (Marcoux 2001b: 83). Decisions to consolidate a household are made in keeping with this cycle, as this becomes the time to either continue to rent or move, initiating a pattern of movement within the city that not only renegotiates relations to place and constitutions of households but, as Marcoux shows (Marcoux 2004), is integral to the negotiation of gendered relations and forms involved in moving. The movement of people across the city and the movement of objects (or their immobility) are all implicated in the production of various forms of gendered personhood. Marcoux's notion of "detachment" (Marcoux 2001b: 82), the ability to disengage, is produced through the syncopation of yearly moves produced through the peculiarities of the Montreal property market. This form of detachability is a desirable quality necessary for the continuous project of the production of selfhood at the heart of consumer societies; the circumstances that enable the renegotiation of relations through these regularized flows (Marcoux 2001b: 83 following Giddens 1991). And, as Marcoux notes, such syncopation is an important component in the way that gender norms are reproduced and sustained.

Similarly, but in almost opposing material fashion, Pauline Garvey (2001) writes not about the movement of bodies and furniture between neighborhoods but of the movement of furniture within homes and their attendant effects on the bodies within, with special emphasis on states of mind. However, the embodied actions of cyclical furniture movement within the home produces a sense of agency and evolving personhood within the home, despite a prevailing normativity that might otherwise stymie this important work of self. Garvey notes that, "Whilst becoming habitual in some cases, rearranging furniture is characterized by its immediacy and therefore acts as a foil to decorative projects which have more 'aspirational' aims" (2001: 65). One can experiment with a guarded individuality without being observed or upsetting conventions.

Garvey describes the subtle work of furniture movement through this exchange between anthropologist and informant:

> Researcher: Do you feel better when you change things around?
> Informant (Lise): When I feel depressed it feels good to move things around. There are some people who have a very clear mind, but have very untidy homes . . . when you have a lot to think about it can help to move things around and clean up or throw things out, and in a way you are always sorting things out in your brain. That's a kind of psychological reason, I don't know why I do it. I just become tired of the way I have it, it's good not to be used to things for so long, right? (Garvey 2001: 53)

Garvey notes selfhood is not understood in terms of distinctive qualities but as part of a sensuous activity of continuing reproducibility in terms of an "ongoing biography"

(Garvey 2001: 56). The artifacts of the home do not function as diagnostic material culture; they are not signifying as earlier linguistic or fossil metaphors would have it. Rather, they are the raw material, the stuff, the means by which sensuous creative flows of activity can take place whereby selfhood is produced within a given moral economy of such flows. The result is that an "identity" might be effected following Strathern: "[o]wnership gathers things momentarily to a point by locating them in the owner, halting endless dissemination, effecting an identity" (Strathern 1999: 177). But Strathern also notes that this identity effect is also the artifact of the anthropological analysis and the wider moral economies which that anthropological analysis serves (Strathern 1990). Or, as Buchli and Lucas (2001) noted in their study of an abandoned council flat, it is the production of a particular morally desirable identity effect that secures housing and state assistance for the troubled family of a single mother in the eyes of council officials.

Similarly, the description of flows in Buchli's (1999) (Figure 22) analysis of post-Stalinist interiors emphasizes how subtle arrangements of furniture between centripetal and centrifugal plans could facilitate Stalinist or post-Stalinist forms and moral orders: centripetal forms focused on the family dining table, producing the individualizing centrality of the nuclear family with its attendant forms of moral personhood. In contrast to this were the centrifugal forms of zoned spaces that accorded with an outward focus beyond the nuclear family and domestic hearth, toward the public realm of socialist life with its attendant materialities. In this postwar and post-Stalinist context, echoing Baudrillard's (1996) observations of Western domestic interiors, this segmentation into rationalized zones referring to the public realm without was facilitated by a materiality of "detachment" (expanding on Marcoux's notion [2001b]) distinct from the "tackiness" described by Gell (1998: 81–2) and the "homeyness" described by McCracken (1998), which, through its smooth, neutral forms produced a certain disembodied "detachment" from the domestic realm and facilitated "attachment" and bodily identification with the wider realm of public socialist construction.

Laurence Douny (2007), in another vein, examined attachment and flow in relation to concepts of hygiene among the Dogon of Mali. Here, dirt in the Euro-American sense facilitates embodied attachment, and cleanliness appears as disembodied death. Douny notes how prosperity is invoked through wishes that one's house will always be dirty (Douny 2007: 314). Dirt indexes the capacity to care, nurture, and grow a family. Sooty walls and ceilings blackened by fires are positive attributes indicating the persistence of the hearth and the corresponding prosperity and longevity of the household. The touching of walls by family members, visitors, and children and the dirt accumulated at these points on the architectural elements of

Figure 22 Postwar Soviet interiors. *Source:* Buchli, 1999.

the home attest to the prosperity and vitality of the household. To be clean would be to be without life and thoroughly undesirable (Douny 2007: 315). Similarly, Douny notes, pots should not be cleaned too quickly while the traces of their life-sustaining contents need to be maintained. Sweat-impregnated clothes attest to the life of their owners and the dung-smeared walls attest to the continuing vitality of domestically cared for animals and their role in the overall economy sustaining life: "They create an ontological security that makes people 'at home'" (Douny 2007: 315). Such waste products that result from the sensuous activities of vital, life-enhancing labor are husbanded and used to then further "feed" and sustain the household (Douny 2007: 314).

Grant McCracken's (1998) seminal work on "homeyness" illustrates in great detail how the relative marginalization of architectural form foregrounding the proliferating and enfolding materiality of the domestic sphere produces a distinctive form of attachment through the materiality of domestic artifacts and materials that are constitutive of that highly emotive and elusive state. What is "homey" in McCracken's analysis are all those objects such as lace curtains, cushions, antimacassars, tablecloths, and collections of objects that cannot be reduced to any one element nor understood in a linguistic fashion as "signs" to be read. Rather, they can only be understood in the terms of the affective qualities of these various material attributes in concert that produce what he refers to as an "encompassment" at the heart of the sensation of "homeyness" (McCracken 1998: 172). This "encompassment," however, is facilitated by these diverse but clearly identifiable attributes of material forms within this setting that produce the affective and emotive attachments of "homeyness" and affirm the moral qualities of family, affective ties, and home life (McCracken 1998: 173). Modernists instinctually understood this in their rejection of the "homey" and the domestic and their use of materials that specifically denied envelopment and attachment—to work instead in the opposite direction and facilitate detachment (Marcoux) through the concert of other material qualities (e.g., light, transparency, whiteness, metal) and with them new forms of sociality, gender, and moral personhood, as exemplified in their ultimate expression in Soviet socialist forms. The "velvet" folds of Benjamin again, do not work as a fossil, except as an external diagnostic and critique; but here, internal to their social context, they function through the concert of their material forms, not in a semiotic "legible" fashion but in an embodied disposition that produces the moral order of the heterosexual nuclear family.

However, recent queer scholarship has reconsidered the effects of such concerts of materiality. Luzia (2011) argues that lesbian families with children similarly require these material attributes in what she refers to as "throwntogetherness" (following Massey), the mess of everyday life, which envelopes young families, heterosexual or homosexual, divorced from earlier preoccupations with gender or sexuality (Figure 23). She argues for the centrality of these messy material attributes as the ground in which children can grow and affective family ties produced. Messiness here is a resource for growth, as Douny (2007) argues cogently in relation to dirt in the Dogon example.

In another vein, Diana Young's discussion of the color white in the London property market (2004) goes a long way toward establishing how forms of attachment and detachment (Marcoux) produced by the color white create value and wider spheres of moral economies where other—bodily—capacities are enhanced through the materialities of architectural form, similar to the contexts just discussed. Here, the materiality of whiteness, used on walls to produce "neutrality," is central to the logic of the late capitalist London property market. Whiteness here performs a certain kind of detachability akin to but distinct from earlier forms of whiteness and their effects in early capitalist modernist contexts (Young 2004: 14) and socialist ones. Here, whiteness creates value through its ability to produce detachment (Marcoux), as it speeds up the circulation of properties within the market. Those properties that are more liquid accrue more value. Any recent home makeover show in Britain will attest to the necessity to depersonalize one's home and make it neutral so as to sell quickly and for more money, as Young notes (2004: 12).

Young (2004: 9, 15) compares the color white to the color red of the *kula* exchange. In the case of *kula* shells, their redness is the effect of the handling producing the red patina that indexes the shells' desirability. In a similar fashion, both materially and in embodied form, whiteness in the London property market enables flats and houses to circulate more quickly, accrue value, and achieve desirability precisely because whiteness facilitates a speedier exchange and enables a more ready assimilation to an individual purchaser's lifestyles and desires (Young 2004: 15). The neutrality of white allows the purchaser to project oneself and one's desires more readily (Young 2004:10). What is detachable (Marcoux) enables a more promiscuous attachability and, with it, desirability. "Homeyness," as evinced by McCracken, works against the production of value within this economy of materials and their qualities. In Young's analysis, an advertisement for a flat showing a quintessentially "homey" home, with its bright and complicated concert of patterned wallpaper, overstuffed and fluffy sofas, and throws, works against this sort of ready promiscuous attachability (Young 2004: 10). It is literally too infused with its previous owner to be readily appropriable. As a result, such a property would need work to be rendered more suitably neutral to circulate within a late capitalist property market and achieve value, as Young notes.

Figure 23 Luzia's "throwntogetherness." *Source*: Karina Luzia.

But Young's analysis suggests that embodied attachments and the sustenance of productive capacities must be sought elsewhere—not in the property per se but, as Gabrielle Ackroyd's work shows (personal communication, 2011), in the mortgage that the circulation of the property produces and enhances. The mortgage here is the direct consequence of a carefully calculated wager a bank makes in relation to the health and steady income-earning potential of the borrower, who, at the right age and life stage, can demonstrate bodily vigor, health, and steady, disciplined employment over a given number of years to pay off the initial mortgage. The mortgaged "white" property of late capitalist property markets, though seemingly disembodied, paradoxically belies its intimate link to the bodily capacities of the mortgagor, as Ackroyd observes. The spate of mortgage collapses and abandoned houses and communities in the wake of the 2008 financial crisis attest to the failure of this wager on both sides, as Ackroyd notes. Because the mortgage, until the financial collapse, was the means by which families could borrow money against a speculative, easily traded, and highly abstracted reification of embodied laboring capacity and use this money to pay for children's education, other forms of mutual support, and collective material and social advancement within the moral economy of the family, such moral projects are left in tatters across various late capitalist economies across the globe (Ackroyd, personal communication; see also Ackroyd 2011). In terms of a moral institution, the fluid materialities of property, enhanced by the detachability of whiteness (Marcoux, Young), sustain the mortgage as resource and sublime substance and incarnation of bodily capacities (Ackroyd). Following Ackroyd, the remarkable fluidity of property and mortgage represents an order of generative power and productive capacity intimately bound up with the sensuous laboring body participating in various nexus of value.

These observations regarding the materiality of interior spaces that marginalize architectural form speak, of course, to the material efficacy of these engagements—that is, the efficacy of these forms of detachability (Marcoux) and disembodiment. In the first instance, they privilege the sphere of individual activity or agency at the expense of the larger architectonic forms of engagement that privilege state interests, as in domination and resistance paradigms, which emphasise "appropriation" (see Buchli 1999; Miller 1988) through the varied uses of space over the "domination" of built forms. Within such discussions that emphasize the efficacy of decorative forms for moral forms of personhood and social relations, there is a tendency to privilege this profoundly embodied understanding of materiality at the expense of disembodied forms of materiality. That is, those forms of materiality that deny the attachment of the body to the object (as Gell [1998: 82] describes in terms of asceticism and other modernist ideals) are dismissed as a dubious exercises of power. The effects of forms

facilitating disembodiment as a specific form of material engagement are rarely actually engaged with (Gell [1998: 81–2] rather cursorily glosses over this in preference
to his wider discussion of ornament). The social effects of disembodied materiality
are profound, not simply at the level of visual forms of regulatory power well rehearsed in postcolonial and feminist critiques but in broader terms where (and to
what purpose) social attachments are to be made. Early Soviet modernists were very
clear about this in terms of engendering attachments to the wider public enterprise
of socialist construction and new forms of embodied socialized labor—hence an
emphasis on a disembodied relation to certain material forms that new industrialized
materials such as glass, metal, whiteness, and so on could facilitate. Late neoliberal
capitalist property markets understand this in terms of the ability to augment value
and sustain the generative capacities of embodied sensuous labor as in the capacities
afforded by the mortgage, as noted by Ackroyd. Detachment (expanding from Marcoux) and disembodied forms of engagements are not a denial of the effects of the
materiality of form; rather, they are the assertion of a different mode in which this
distinctive and powerful sensory mode works, a different material register and sensorial frame, with which to reconfigure human/object relations and effect new forms of
sociality and bodily capacities. As Marcoux's discussion of detachability (2001b: 82)
as necessary for the ongoing production of self echoes Giddens's (as noted by Garvey) emphasis on the flexibility of identity and constant biographical regeneration
inherent in late capitalist contexts, it is in this context that detachability is generative.
It is this detachability and the refusal to attach that Parrott (2005) cogently argues
for in her analysis of psychiatric hospitals and their inmates; and it is the ability to
move on, re-create, and reconfigure relations and not be constantly mired in place
that is at the heart of "happiness" for Parrott's informants in her ethnography of a
South London street (Parrott 2010: 292–3).

The issue of detachability (Marcoux) and attachability in visualist terms
(Young) is key to understanding the significance of the "generic" outside of aesthetic debates, which tend to problematize the issue of the generic or lowbrow
in terms of a lack of social distinction in the manner of Bourdieu (1984) or in
terms of a general malaise of inauthenticity in the minds of many cultural critics. Duyvendak (2011: 13) argues persuasively for the importance of the generic
for "dwelling." The near-interchangeability of architectural forms from Arizona
to China, from South Africa to Russia all point to the emergence of a genericism that is at the heart of one's ability to "dwell" under the mobile conditions
of late capitalism in the world. It is these forms that emerge so cogently within
the global phenomenon of gated communities described by Setha Low and the
communities described by Froud.

As Duyvendak notes, such generic forms serve fluid global elites well (see also Bauman 2000), as also suggested, in somewhat different terms, by Daisy Froud. Describing the seemingly inauthentic and pastiche forms of new vernacular English villages, she notes:

> Moreover, if the shared story is one that we know is false (not *all* may believe it false vis-à-vis England's history, but most know it to be so in the context of this village and their own experience), I suggest that it is thus emptied of much of its historical baggage, making it "owned" in reality by nobody, and thus open to be claimed and played with by all. (Froud 2004: 226)

Thus, these seemingly generic and inauthentic forms provide a "fundamental orientation in space and time in a world of flux where orientation is increasingly tricky" (Froud 2004: 227). In this sense, Froud is optimistic about the capacities of these generic "inauthentic" forms for the generation of meaningful narratives of self and family: "it is possible that an inner sense of narrativity will become more important. And in the absence of great collective stories, maybe personal, domestic ones will matter more" (2004: 229).

Such generic forms, following Duyvendak, can be said, seemingly paradoxically, to enable "habitation" to take place anywhere, easily, legibly, and familiarly, regardless of local circumstances. Their visual banality is part of their ability to emplace, however temporarily, anywhere in the world and thereby make it possible to inhabit such transnational globalized spaces more readily, much as an earlier generic form, the bungalow, discussed by King (1995). Generic forms can also accommodate the requirements of a universal interchangeability as well as very specific local needs. Jane Jacobs (2004) described how diasporic Chinese families in the film *Floating Life* might inhabit many homes of a heterogenous nature in multiple locations; it is their heterogenous forms that enable these homes to serve as iterations of the traditional Chinese ancestral home. The specific form is irrelevant, except in its ability to sustain the ancestral lineage over time and space. It is precisely their appropriable qualities that enable this to work. The house here serves the family as a Lévi-Straussian "illusory objectification" (Carsten and Hugh-Jones 1995) to negotiate seemingly irreconcilable interests through its heterogenous forms and their materiality that facilitate easy detachability and attachability.

Gottfried Semper (1989: 139–42), writing in the middle of the nineteenth century and commenting on the emergence of new generic forms, which were the product of the standardization of planning and construction norms, argued how the American and English home had a powerful universality of appeal and flexibility precisely because of the standardization of these elements that would appeal to the broadest segments of the market. Individual decorative elements could be substituted and replaced with each other at will, the flexibility of such forms ensured universality and, with it, its generic power to accommodate the widest range of tastes, desires, and aspirations. In another vein, Chakrabarty (2000 cited in Maurer 2006: 24) notes how the interchangeability of abstracted labor value emerging in the nineteenth century was made possible by the notion of human equality, interchangeable and equal at all times and in all places. Similarly, as Fox (2005) observes, the twentieth-century universal right to be housed emerges as instrumental in creating the modern universal subject, consider here the United Nations resolution concerning human rights (Article 25 of the United Nations Universal Declaration of Human Rights). What might be seen as the alienating effects of abstracted notions of dwelling are, in fact, the very terms by which a universalizing form of human life can be achieved. But this abstraction has its costs, as the legal scholar Fox (2005) points out in relation to land law. This abstraction according to which legal matters are resolved is problematically emptied of all the nuance and associations of lived homes, especially as they relate to women (Fox 2005; see also Buchli and Lucas 2001). Fox writes: "land law is often regarded as the sine qua non of this legal model of rationality, with leading commentators characterizing it as a 'rational science' in which: 'the perfection of pure reason appears most nearly attainable. English Land Law—more obviously than any other area of the law . . . displays many of the features of a closed system of logic'" (Gray and Gray 2003 cited in Fox 2005: 39). Such generic forms and their abstractions have very complex and problematic effects.

Such interchangeability is evident in Inge Daniels's (2010) recent discussion of the modern Japanese house. The house has significance within a temporal dimension related to several generations of a Japanese family. Houses are built, destroyed, and rebuilt (2010: 154–5) because they serve, in effect, merely as temporary containers for the artifacts and memories associated with different generations of a family. As such, they are relatively disposable as opposed to the contents of such houses that maintain a lineal continuity over time (Daniels 2010: 150). However, the problematic area of concern is the accumulation of mobile objects—collections, kimonos, furniture, and ornaments—which must be delicately negotiated, redistributed along family lines and friends to rearticulate and redirect the flow of objects found in Japanese houses. Houses are repositories for these objects, regulating their flows and the affective ties they produce and sustain. Moving and rebuilding become critical moments. The work of kinship, familial continuity, and wider affective social ties is located in the accumulation, flow, and collection of souvenirs, gifts, dowry items, and so on (Figure 24). These are inherently mobile, small, easily transportable, gifted, and sent, and their mobility and easy accumulation produce what can be argued as "stoppages" (following Gell), which in effect are the embodiment of the affective ties that such mobile and durable objects produce. In many respects, it is the disposability of architectural forms that make lineal connections of several generations possible to maintain. The postwar proliferation of consumer goods and travel and the need to produce kinship ties and wider social networks require the increasing gifting and flow of such artifacts. The result is an accumulation of things

Figure 24 Daniels's Japanese house. *Source:* Susan Andrews.

that are often disliked but difficult to dispose of, clogging Japanese homes with what Daniels calls "troublesome things," gifts that are glossed as "things that one would like to throw away but are difficult to throw away" (Daniels 2010: 174). They are the troublesome excess produced by the work involved in the creation and maintenance of social ties.

Gudeman and Rivera's (1990) work on the household economies of Colombia notes that houses function to differentially regulate flows of animals, foods, bodies, labor, and other generative substances between households and the wider market economy. They describe how Colombian peasants accommodate two economic spheres in their household economies: economic activities that stay within the household and are not traded out that sustain and grow it over the long term and activities that are traded out, with the flow between those two realms enabling the sustenance of household life and its role within the wider market economy of Colombia. These resources are augmented, conserved, and circulated and, in short, fed metaphorically and sometimes literally fed as the pigs of the household, which Gudeman and Rivera note are "piggy banks" that are fed and cared for and, as they grow and reproduce, embody the augmentation of the household's resources and are sold out when needed (Gudeman and Rivera 1990: 86). The embodied labor of the peasant is actively entwined with the sustenance of this nexus of resources, which can at times and with risk be traded out to sustain the household.

The stability of material assemblages in homes as evidenced in collections, heirlooms, photographs, and the like, would typically be curated with great care and would form the basis upon which relationships between family members would be produced and sustained. These processes have been more recently challenged and reconfigured by the emergence of new digital technologies, such as those noted in Fiona Parrott's (2010: 298) work. She demonstrates the importance placed on more fluid, partible, and transportable items such as photos (and particularly digitized photos and music) for the maintenance of memories and social relations rather than less fluid and mobile objects such as furniture—in contrast to what Marcoux and Chevalier have noted—which emerge as less reliable vehicles for memory.

3

As a number of these case studies demonstrate, consumption, home decoration, and the elaboration of the domestic sphere is part of an ongoing concern, as Bloch (1995a, 1995b) so cogently noted in relation to the developing materiality of the Malagasy house. DIY activity, working together through complementary gender roles and their continuous reproduction and rearticulation, literally "grow" relations and gender identifications in relation to one another. Housework and the work of houses maintain these relations.

Moreover, the close examination of consumption practices in the home throughout these studies also indicates that a given sense of moral personhood may not in fact be isomorphic with the dwelling or produced at the site of the dwelling. The examples of the Soviet avant-garde and the importance of the mortgage in Ackroyd's work suggest a different configuration and a different position of the house—one that is "outside" the empirical category of the home as more conventional analyses might consider. This is certainly the insight of Bourdieu (1990: 276) in relation to the production of masculinity in Berber society, where the Berber male is produced "outside the house" but in a distinctive productive relation to it. Similarly, Julie Botticello's (2007) discussion of Nigerians in South London suggests that moral personhood is produced in the back areas of market stalls, which are homelike.

An earlier emphasis on the readable semiotic and durable objectivity of the home gives way in more recent scholarship to flows and their maintenance, and how the regulation of those flows regulates the moral terms of personhood. This emphasis suggests how, in some contexts, such objectivity is problematic and dangerous (having too many things, stoppages that inhibit a "coherent biography" (Garvey 2001 following Giddens 1991), or "the troublesome things" Daniels (2010) speaks of, or the wider importance of flows in Marcoux, Garvey, and Parrott). As Rudi Colloredo-Mansfeld (2003) argues in a related context concerning the materiality of things, liquidity is moral, being able to ensure the correct distribution of moral goods toward the production of persons and social relations.

It is precisely this body of consumption studies, as relate to the materiality of the home, that speaks to these capacities for "continuous revision" (Garvey 2001: 56 following Giddens) and rearticulation—architectural form is not subject to linguistic interpretation as something signifying, or to be read like a fossil, but as a nexus of capacities. But, as Nikolas Rose (1990) notes in his discussion of the "psy disciplines" and the articulation of lifestyle in neoliberal societies, enabling this project of "continuous revision" (Garvey 2001) is part of the contract between neoliberal forms of governance and the production of selfhood through these lifestyle practices. Seemingly incorrigible and immaterial notions of selfhood, such as the Foucauldian notion of the soul, are produced within this wider political economy and the materialities they effect.

6 EMBODIMENT AND ARCHITECTURAL FORM

I

As Carsten and Hugh-Jones (1995) noted, the relationship between the body and built form is difficult to disentangle; it is impossible to clearly say where the body ends and built form begins. What this observation entails, of course, is that this relation is constantly negotiated in many original and innovative ways in terms of local contingencies. This chapter will examine this issue of embodiment and architectural form and consider its corollary of disembodiment for the production of personhood and the kinds of material effects entailed as regards architectural form.

The preoccupation with embodiment emerges with particular force during the 1980s with the rise of feminism and the impact of phenomenological approaches (Bachelard 1964; Norberg-Schulz 1971) that focus on the body and gender as privileged sites of meaning and experience. However, this understanding of the entanglement of bodily and architectural form has a deep lineage in Western thought on architectural form, going back to Vitruvius and the very familiar interpretation of the anthropomorphic basis for classical proportions in the Renaissance interpretation of this relationship (the Vitruvian Man), famously rendered by da Vinci (Figure 25). This image, attributed with asserting the centrality of the body for architectural proportions, was also indicted in the androcentrism of architectonic thought and form (though Laqueur [1990] would assert that in the Renaissance the essentially androgynous or unitary nature of gender, male and female, were degrees of relative expression of one gendered bodily form, which would not bifurcate until the eighteenth century in a binary understanding of distinctly male and female forms).

As Mary Douglas (1970b: 116) would argue in another context: "What is being carved in human flesh is an image of society." It is the negotiation of these distinctions and the images of society that are sustained in bodily and architectonic form, which together are profoundly generative of the terms by which moral personhood and social life are understood in relation to each other. It is analytically quite difficult to segregate one from the other in a meaningful way. This negotiation, however, is at the heart of cultural work, the never-ending terms by which life is made and sustained, requiring

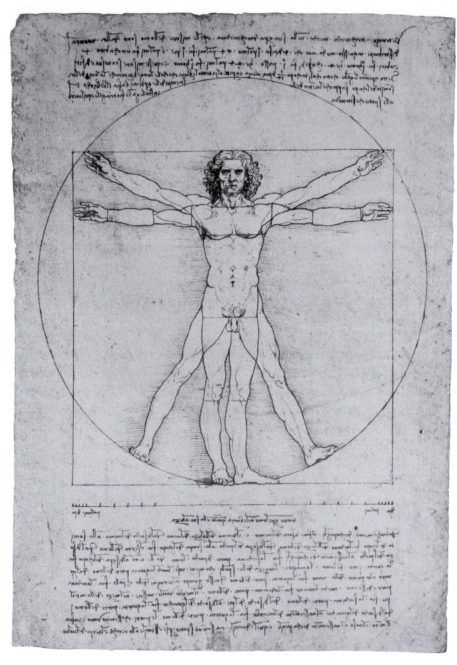

Figure 25 Da Vinci's Vitruvian Man. *Source*: Jakub Krechowicz, Dreamstime.com.

new understandings of embodied form in relation to built form and similarly novel means of disembodiment within the same process—with one comes the other.

Most famously, the question of disembodiment is associated with the rise of Cartesianism in European thought and the oft-cited and oft-critiqued segregation of mind and body at the heart of the European Enlightenment notion of the universal rational subject. But, as a number of observers have noted, this peculiar yet powerful form of European disembodiment has a particular history in terms of the rise of the camera obscura (see discussions in Crary 1992) and an innovative form of social constructivism in terms of a radical new universal subject, as posited by figures such as Brodsky Lacour (1996) in reference to the writing of Descartes.

Crary (1992: 39) argues that the camera obscura provided a means of apperceiving the world that produced the notion of the disembodied subject. The camera obscura produced a compelling metaphor by which objective knowledge and the notion of a universal reasoning subject could be produced in relation to one another as Crary notes (1992: 26–66). Because it worked as a darkened chamber that, through a small aperture, permitted an image of the outside world to be projected onto the inner wall of its chamber in inverse form, it functioned as an analogy by which human thought and apperception functioned (Figure 26). The mind was understood within an architectonic metaphor, where it was like an empty room into which images from the outside world would be delivered through the eyes. Crary notes how Descartes could demonstrate this architectonic metaphor literally, showing the workings of the mind in terms of the working of architectural space and perception:

> Suppose a chamber is shut up apart from a single hole, and a glass lens is placed in front of this hole with a white sheet stretched at a certain distance behind it so the light coming from objects outside forms images on the sheet. Now it is said the room represents the eye; the hole the pupil; the lens the crystaline humour . . . taking the dead eye of a newly dead person (or, failing that, the eye of an ox or some other large animal) . . . cut away the three surrounding membranes at the back so as to expose a large part of the humour without spilling any. . . . No light must enter this room except what comes through this eye, all of whose parts you know to be entirely transparent. Having done this, if you look at the white sheet you will see here, not perhaps without pleasure and wonder, a picture representing in natural perspective all the objects outside. (Descartes 1637 quoted in Crary 1992: 47)

Both mind and architectural form were analogues for one another, but more importantly within this new analog of human thought, the body was radically segregated out (Crary 1992: 40–1), much like the observer/draughtsman in a perspective drawing

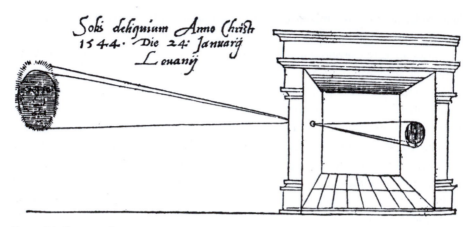

Figure 26 Camera obscura as architectural chamber. First published illustration of a camera obscura observing a solar eclipse in January 1544. Woodcut. Dutch School, sixteenth century. *Source*: Private Collection / The Bridgeman Art Library.

whose "eye," though the central element constitutive of the images, is always physically missing in the final image, as noted by Boulnois (2008: 395). This segregation of mind and body residing at the heart of Cartesian tradition produced the notion of the universal rational subject within this architectonic metaphor (Crary 1992).

This metaphor of disembodiment was also central to other related universalizing projects within the European tradition, namely the creation of the universal Christian subject and the Christian Ecumene. Again, this notion of the mind as a room (Crary 1992: 39), or place as Boulnois (2008: 405) would note, could be exploited in relation to the novel technologies of the printing press in the training of the Jesuit order and its students. The "Exercises" of the order's founder, Ignatius of Loyola, could exploit this analogy and the newfound universality and stability of the printed word, which could be seen to reproduce the "Exercises" in any cultural or geographic context within the colonialist expansion of Catholicism in the wake of the Reformation. The generic Christian monk's cell, now the "study" (see also Crary 1992: 39) of the Jesuit student, could be understood to exploit this nested set of architectonic analogies, the inner chamber of the mind, through to the outer chamber of the study, where the constitution of a universal and stable Jesuit subjectivity could be supervised so long as the innovative and supremely mobile technology of an authorized printed version of the exercises could be used.

2

Phenomenological accounts attempted to come to terms with the prevailing mind/body split that was the product of European modernity. It sought to address the alienating effects of twentieth-century capitalism and the disruptive effects of modernity by reassessing the position of the body within the world, to examine, in fact, how bodily form and architectural form could be more meaningfully integrated to overcome this previously productive dualism. One of its key theoreticians was Martin Heidegger, whose foundational text "Building, Dwelling, Thinking" (1993) was central to this endeavor. It is the rupture produced by modernity that lies at the heart of modernist preoccupations with dwelling both literally and figuratively, but mostly in terms of its profound lack, its essential "homelessness" as Heynen observes (Heynen 1999: 16–18). Heidegger identifies this problem in the following terms: "The proper dwelling plight lies in this, that mortals ever search anew for the essence of dwelling, that they must ever learn to dwell" (Heidegger 1993: 363). It reprises in many respects an earlier observation by Morgan in *Houses and House-Life of the American Aborigines*: "Every institution of mankind which attained permanence will be found linked with a perpetual want" (Morgan 1965: xvi). For Heidegger this means that "[mortals] must ever learn to dwell" (1993: 363), that this is a constant, recurring, and generative process by which the elusive unity of the embodied self with the environment and wider cosmos is constantly in the process of becoming.

Heidegger proposes this unity in terms of his discussion of the fourfold, the essential terms of dwelling comprising the unity of "earth and sky, divinities and mortals" (1993: 360). Heidegger considers this in terms of his discussion of a bridge and how it produces this unity of the fourfold through the intervention of the bridge (1993: 354). The bridge creates the banks, brings the landscapes on both sides of the stream into a novel relationship with each other. "The bridge *gathers* the earth as landscape around the stream" (Heidegger 1993: 354). The bridge, furthermore, leads from the castle to the square and, with that, the road to long-distance trade networks.

What is important, however, in this apparently static account is the element of innovation, as with a new bridge and the perpetual problem of dwelling, as Heidegger describes it as process of integration that never ceases. He notes:

> However hard and bitter, however hampering and threatening the lack of houses remains, the *proper plight of dwelling* does not lie merely in the lack of houses. The proper plight of dwelling is indeed older than the world wars with their destruction, older also than the increase of the earth's population and the condition of the industrial workers. The proper dwelling plight lies in this, that mortals ever search anew for the nature of dwelling, that they *must ever learn to dwell*. What if man's homelessness consisted in this, that man still does not even think of the *proper* plight of dwelling as *the* plight? Yet as soon as man *gives thought* to his homelessness, it is a misery no longer. Rightly considered and kept well in mind, it is the sole summons that *calls* mortals into their dwelling.

> But how else can mortals answer this summons than by trying on *their* part, on their own, to bring dwelling to the fullness of its essence? This they accomplish when they build out of dwelling, and think for the sake of dwelling. (Heidegger 1993: 363; emphasis in original)

The process of dwelling is exemplified in Heidegger's account of the Black Forest hut, an invocation of the "primitive hut" as described by Rykwert (1981), but one which exemplifies how the fourfold of mortals, divinities, earth, and sky are integrated by the material effects of architectural form:

> The essence of building is letting dwell. Building accomplishes its essential process in the raising of locales by the joining of their spaces. *Only if we are capable of dwelling, only then can we build.* Let us think for a while of a farmhouse in the Black Forest, which was built some two hundred years ago by the dwelling of peasants. Here the self-sufficiency of the power to let earth and sky, divinities and mortals enter *in simple oneness* into things ordered the house. It placed the farm on the wind-sheltered mountain slope, looking south, among the meadows close to the spring. It gave it the wide overhanging shingle roof whose proper slope bears up under the burden of snow, and that, reaching deep down, shields the chambers against the storms of the long winter nights. It did not forget the altar corner behind the community table; it made room in its chamber for the hallowed places of childbed and the "tree of the dead"—for that is what they call a coffin there: the *Totenbaum*—and in this way it designed for the different generations under one roof the character of their journey through time. A craft that, itself sprung from dwelling, still uses its tools and its gears as things, built the farmhouse. (Heidegger 1993: 361–2; emphasis in original)

Like the "illusory objectification" of Lévi-Strauss (Carsten and Hugh-Jones 1995), the fourfold attempts to negotiate within a whole otherwise seemingly irreconcilable entities through the process of dwelling. As Heidegger is at pains to note, this is a constant integrative endeavor and one that is never complete—hence its generative power and purpose to provide a contingent, momentary stability by which the terms of dwelling can be enacted.

Heidegger's phenomenological approach does not restrict itself to just dwellings; dwelling occurs in a wider sense in which novel architectural forms such as the bridge assemble humans within new fourfolds, implicating an entirely new embodied engagement: "Bridges and hangars, stadiums and . . . highways, dams and market halls are built, but they are not dwelling places. Even so, these buildings are in the domain of our dwelling" (1993: 347). The body here becomes not just an "encapsulated body" (1993: 359)—but a body of a specific articulation within a particular locale created within space, through the unfolding and constantly emerging process of dwelling. But as the body is rearticulated anew within the unfolding terms of dwelling, so, too, of course, are inner states such as depression, which would seem to be outside the fourfold but nonetheless are contained within it as well, albeit in a pathological way; one is still "staying with things" (1993: 359). Thus, the fourfold reasserts the long-standing interrelatedness of mind, language, and society that the architectural nexus affords ever since Vitruvius's observations of the "gathering," close to two millennia before.

Heidegger's text is a distinctly postwar text. It is in this context that he considers the housing shortage, quite acute especially in postwar Germany. It is also in the postwar period that the rise of feminist scholarship refocused attention on issues surrounding built form, primarily in relation to the home and the problematic and conflicted intimate association of women's roles and identities with the home and its material forms. Because of this intimate association and the general neglect of the question of domesticity, everyday life, and consumption, the issues of women's roles and emancipation in society could be diagnosed and alleviated through the in-depth analysis of this previously underanalyzed realm of scholarly activity.

These feminist concerns were complemented by a broader Marxist critique, such as the one provided by Baudrillard, who addresses postwar forms in his *The System of Objects* (1996). Attending to the material effects and changes of postwar interiors, he draws attention to the way in which a subtle reworking of interior elements suggests profound changes in the way personhood and its social effects might be understood. Baudrillard speaks directly to a prevailing anthropomorphism facilitated by the materiality of interior arrangements: "In their anthropomorphism the objects that furnish it become household gods, spatial incarnations of the emotional bonds and the permanence of the family group" (1996: 16). By contrast, he describes the postwar setting in distinctive terms: new postwar furniture designs "have been stripped down to their most primitive essence as mere apparatus and, as it were, definitively secularized" and "have the freedom to function, and . . . that is practically the only freedom they have" (1996: 18).

He describes a disembodiment that is distinctive from prewar forms where

> [t]he substance and form of the old furniture have been abandoned for good, in favour of an extremely free interplay of functions. These objects are no longer endowed with a "soul," nor do they invade us with their symbolic presence: the relationship has become an objective one, founded on disposition and play. (Baudrillard 1996: 21)

Alluding to Marcel Mauss's (1990: 20) observation that "Souls are mixed with things; things with souls," Baudrillard asserts:

> First of all man must stop mixing himself up with things and investing them
> with his own image; he will then be able, beyond the utility they have for him,
> to project onto them his game plan, his calculations, his discourse, and in-
> vest these manoeuvres themselves with the sense of a message to others, and a
> message to oneself. By the time this point is reached the mode of existence of
> "ambient" objects will have changed completely, and *a sociology of furnishing*
> *will perforce have given way to a sociology of interior design*. (1996: 25; emphasis
> in original)

However, the embodied nature of the connection, radically changed, is changed
only in kind:

> Man is thus bound to the objects around him by the same visceral intimacy, *mu-*
> *tatis mutandis*, that binds him to the organs of his own body, and "ownership"
> of the object always tends virtually towards the appropriation of its substance by
> oral annexation and "assimilation." . . . What we glimpse today in modern inte-
> riors is the coming end of this order of Nature; what is appearing on the horizon,
> beyond the break-up of form, beyond the dissolution of the formal boundary
> between inside and outside and of the whole dialectic of being and appearance
> relating to that boundary, is a qualitatively new kind of relationship, a new kind
> of objective responsibility. (Baudrillard 1996: 28)

Baudrillard argues that the animism of interior objects found in traditional societies is giving way to abstract flows dictated by the logic of postwar industrial capitalism. This is a process anticipated within the socialist modernizing project before the
Second World War, in the 1920s with Benjamin's earlier and similar discussion of
the breakdown of traditional forms and their flows in favor of new ones facilitated by
different material orders, their registers, and their attendant social effects. Benjamin
observes:

> For it is the hallmark of this epoch that dwelling in the old sense of the word,
> where security had priority, has had its day. Giedion, Mendelsohn, Corbusier
> turned the abiding places of man into a transit area for every conceivable kind of
> energy and for waves of light and air. The time that is coming will be dominated
> by transparency. Not just the rooms, but even the weeks, if we are to believe the
> Russians, who want to abolish Sunday and to replace it with moveable days of
> leisure. (quoted in Heynen 1999: 114)

Such a reconfiguration of flows undoing the "animism" or embodied forms of
domestic material life served the creation of a new man and woman within a new
set of attachments and a new set of configurations of bodies within the modernist
materialities of architectonic space.

3

The issue of embodiment was probably most cogently problematized anthropologically in the work of Bourdieu and, in particular, in his discussions of practice—notably in *Outline of a Theory of Practice* (1977), where he developed the notion of habitus in reference to his field research in Kabylia in Algeria. The totality of bodily and architectural form that phenomenological accounts expressed was given further articulation and expansion in his notion of the habitus as a structuring structure.

Like Heidegger, the house is the supreme algorithm for producing the habitus:

> But it is the dialectical relationship between the body and a space structured according to the mythico-ritual oppositions that one finds the form par excellence of the structural apprenticeship which lead to the em-bodying of the structures of the world, that is, the appropriating by the world of a body thus enabled to appropriate the world . . .—and above all the house—is the principal locus for the objectification of the generative schemes; and, through the intermediary of the divisions and hierarchies it sets up between things, persons, and practices, this tangible classifying system continuously inculcates and reinforces the taxonomic principles underlying all the arbitrary provisions of this culture. (Bourdieu 1977: 89)

The house according to Bourdieu is the *opus operatum*, the negotiation of which every child must learn in order to embody a particular cultural habitus (Bourdieu 1977: 90; see also Toren 1999)—an embodied disposition, in which injunctions such as "don't hold your knife in your left hand" (Bourdieu 1977: 94) produce what Bourdieu refers to as a bodily hexis. It is at the locus of this bodily hexis that "totalitarian institutions" (1977: 94) emphasize the minutiae of bodily behaviors for the constitution of social life:

> If all societies and, significantly, all the "totalitarian institutions," in Goffman's phrase, that seek to produce a new man through a process of "deculturation" and "reculturation," set such store on the seemingly most insignificant details of dress, bearing, physical and verbal manners, the reason is that, treating the body as a memory, they entrust it in abbreviated and practical, i.e. mnemonic, form the fundamental principles of the arbitrary nature of culture. The principles em-bodied in this way are placed beyond the grasp of consciousness, and hence cannot be touched by voluntary deliberate transformation, cannot even be made explicit; nothing seems more ineffable, more incommunicable, more inimitable, and, therefore, more precious, than the values given body, made body by the transubstantiation achieved by the hidden persuasion of an implicit pedagogy, capable of instilling a whole cosmology, an ethic, a metaphysic, a political

> philosophy, through injunctions as insignificant as "stand up straight" or "don't hold your knife in your left hand." (Bourdieu 1977: 94)

Refusing such interdictions seems churlish or impolite, considering the modesty of these ostensibly empty actions, but it is precisely because of their banal modesty "a matter of trifles . . . which 'cost nothing' to perform and seem such 'natural' things to demand . . . that abstention amounts to a refusal or a challenge" (1977: 95), which, of course, they in fact are on the most profound level. But in the reproduction of a habitus and its attendant bodily hexis, a certain excess is inherent in the learning process and in the embodied experience of a bodily hexis. As Bourdieu notes, a bodily hexis is produced with a certain degree of a variation, as suggested by the awkward learning efforts of a child or the faux pas a foreigner—yet to be adequately socialized—invariably makes. If the example of the Kabyle house shows how the relation between the body and the cosmos occurs, this process is inherently dynamic addressing several orders of experience. But this dynamism implies an excess beyond that which it attempts to convey; thereby, the reproduction of a habitus can create new things through the subtle manipulation of the bodily hexis—hence, the importance of "style" and the reproductive and dynamic power of the habitus:

> "Personal style," the particular stamp marking all the products of the same habitus, whether practices or works, is never more than a *deviation* in relation to the *style* of a period or class so that it relates back to the common style not only by its conformity—like Phidias, who, according to Hegel, had no "manner"—but also by the difference which makes the whole "manner." (Bourdieu 1977: 86; emphasis in original)

But as Bourdieu's discussion of "totalitarian institutions" suggests otherwise, certain subtle "deviations" can have wide ranging effects.

As this emphasis on style might suggest, embodiment is not felt or practiced in the same sense as one might encounter in a setting such as urban France in the second half of the twentieth century. Here, degrees of embodiment and material entanglement are clearly linked to degrees of power and social status. As Bourdieu discusses in *Distinction* (1984), the bourgeois, because of the mastery of the material necessities of life that status and power affords, can indulge in more immaterial, cerebral practices that engage a restricted range of senses in depth, which exhibit taste and cultural and economic capital. Proletarian tastes are heavier, more embodied and sensory—eschewing the cerebral for the more authentic and down to earth along with the more immediate physical and emotional pleasures that a greater dependence on material resources and their instability engender. This is what Bauman (2000) would refer to as the difference between fluid elites in contrast to the more materially bound, localized and stagnant, nonfluid terms of existence that the poor and marginalized are bound up in. The degree of materiality, its heaviness, contra Rowlands's (2005) discussion, produces disenfranchised subjects.

4

James Fernandez's (1977, 1982) work on the Fang—and, in particular, the architectonics of Bwiti ritual space (1990)—provides an exemplary account of the way in which the anthropomorphic associations of built form with bodily form are intimately related through a process of embodiment and disembodiment at the heart of the production of the Bwiti collective and religious consciousness (1990: 99). Through the denial of direct embodied identification sublimated within the metaphors of Bwiti ritual spatial practices, individual bodily capacities are at once suppressed and healed and reassembled within the collective body that Bwiti ritual performs through the metaphoric use of architectural space. Fernandez (1990) argues that the Bwiti ritual structure in plan represents an androgynous body—at once male and female in its differential use—that produces the collective body of the religious community through ritual engagements within Bwiti architectonic space. Fernandez's schema shows how this is done with the metaphoric identification of various parts of the chapel's architecture with the head, heart, and genitals of what is a collective entity, variously male and female. The central post, at once male and female, is the structural underpinning as well as the site of procreation that both supports and enables the structural form of the chapel as well as produces and supports the collectivity that is the community of Bwiti adherents. Entry to and exit from the chapel space is at once associated with male penetration and nurturance as well as birth and excretion, mirroring understandings of the workings of the human body in androgynous form, understood by Bwiti adherents through their embodied and ritual engagement with the spaces and forms of the chapel. Fernandez is at pains to note that this collective body must be produced by the relative disembodiment of its ritual adherents—that is, the notable prudishness of adherents in terms of their actual bodily engagement in relation to the distinctly sensuous and embodied metaphors of Bwiti ritual practice (1990: 99). Individual bodies and their embodied actions as such do not engage these metaphors directly; rather, it is the metaphors of movement as a gendered collective that produces these distinctly embodied and sensuous interactions at the abstracted level of the collective. The production of this embodied collective requires the individual suppression and disembodied engagement of individual adherents in order to produce this collective, abstracted, and highly sensuous embodiment of the larger-order bodily entity that is the Bwiti collective.

5

Labelle Prussin's work among nomadic African groups offers numerous examples of how nomadic dwellings, their construction, and dismantling are literally productive of gender and sexuality: the dwelling as such is coincident with the embodied reproductive capacities of these nomadic women: "The creation of a marriage house, women's work, is culturally perceived as part of the woman's reproductive process, not as a technological process" (Prussin 1995: 58). In brief, the dwelling is literally the marriage, and, because the construction of the dwelling in the examples provided by Prussin is primarily the work of women and not men, the embodied labor that goes into the construction of these structures is inseparable from their reproductive capacities as wives and mothers. Men, in the case of the Tuareg, Prussin notes, are not constituted within these spaces; they are "guests" in these settings, suggesting an underlying and profound divergence in perspective as regards the dwelling as a common and centrally vital object of masculine and feminine life (1995: 104). In preparation for marriage, a woman constructs and assembles as well as reincorporates existing structural elements given to her by her own mother in the construction of these nomadic structures. Anders Grum notes that, among the Rendille, "to marry" is "to build" (Grum in Prussin 1995: 163). And Prussin observes that, among the Tuareg, "the tent comes into being during the marriage ceremony" (Prussin 1995: 91)—"tent" and "marriage" being synonymous. To make a tent is literally to get married. A man is understood to be married in terms of entering a tent (Prussin 1995: 92). Uta Holter (in Prussin 1995: 147) describes how Mahria tents and their structural qualities are intimately tied with the life cycle of Mahria women, such as when an old woman's tent diminishes in size, indicating a relative disembodiment in relation to her status. Prussin emphasizes how these nomadic forms are profoundly processual, not end points in themselves, and deeply imbricated in the process of assembly, disassembly, and movement. This flow not only produces the extensive horizontal pattens of life across the landscape, but, in vertical genealogical terms, this flow moves women with their buildings in marriage to produce lineal continuity. Movement along both axes is what constitutes and perpetuates the material and social conditions of nomad life. They are transported, but it is the act of transportation, in the case of the Rendille by camel, where the palanquin that contains the woman literally and the elements for dwelling construction come into being as the "tent within a tent" (Prussin 1995: 47). The dyad of tent/woman, at its most powerful reproductively, is part of a wider technology of movement, construction, dismantling, and reconstruction that, through their embodied laboring actions, produce the woman/dwelling in their full mature form as married woman within dwelling. Prussin notes that Rendille tents could be assembled and reassembled almost 1,200 times over the course of seventy-one years (1995: 40). She emphasizes the triad of transportation/dwelling/woman as intimately bound up with and effectively inseparable from one another, especially at the height of a woman's reproductive powers. In the other direction, widows gradually disassemble their structures, occupying increasingly smaller structures, as Grum notes (Prussin 1995: 167). Passing on architectural elements to their daughters (Prussin 1995: 101), mothers enable them to constitute themselves as women/dwellings within another iteration of a matrilineal lineage and reproductive capacity, across generations rather than the iteration of these capacities across space and the lifetime of a single woman. Thus, a process of disembodiment in relation to life cycle is central here.

Prussin notes further that the materiality of the body and the materiality of built form and material culture are deeply implicated in relation to one another. She offers the Somali example where the untying of the wedding basket is related to the infibulation of a woman by her husband (1995: 197). As Talle (1993) notes in a related context of Somali infibulation, patrilineality is understood in the permanence and durable hardness of bones and inseparability. Women, in contrast, through infibulation are understood in terms of their profound separability, and the literal tying up and untying of women's reproductive capacities through rituals of infibulation. Technologies of building, material culture, and the making of gendered bodies are inseparable from one another in what Prussin describes as the linked poetics of gender and architecture (1995: 196).

She notes how sedentization begins to radically affect these poetics with a profound shift in the way gender is understood and the intimacy of body/building forms. The process of continuous iteration required by the frequent movements and transportation of people and dwellings in nomadic societies slows down considerably. With the radical decrease of building frequency, the skills necessary to constantly iterate and rebuild begin to atrophy (Prussin 1995: 201). Similarly, traditional natural materials that emerge from the nomadic landscape and its environment are less accessible. In their stead, modern industrial materials emerge, and prefabricated, specialist-produced materials are incorporated. The gendered activities of women shift into a wider realm of a market, where women serve as "clients" rather than actual providers of the various architectonic elements necessary for making a dwelling and facilitating reproductive life. Similarly with sedentism, the role of movement and transport diminishes for the production of traditional nomadic gender and material life: "the physical attributes of the built environment, which enable nomads to manipulate and carve out the categories they use to deal with the world, are no longer valid for them" (Prussin 1995: 202). To quote Jameson (1984: 80) in relation to the postmodern, "a mutation in the object, unaccompanied as yet by any equivalent mutation in the subject" results. Sedentization may usher in a use of specialist builders outside the traditional triad of transport/woman/dwelling, but the arrangement of space within the now square walls reflects traditional circular arrangements with their specialized arrangements and quadrants, as Prussin notes for recently settled Gabra nomads (1995: 204–5). Control of space shifts from the architectural construction of the dwelling to the arrangement of space within, and with this comes the loss of certain legal rights for women: "[c]onsequently, the architectural value system her gender gave rise to is superseded by that of her male counterpart" (Prussin 1995: 205). A subtle shift and slippage in the materialities by which gender identification is sustained through the materialities of architectural form—seemingly the result of an otherwise 'positive' improvement due to the forces of modernization—result in unexpected forms of disempowerment and disenfranchisement.

6

Suzanne Preston Blier (1987), in her discussion of Batammaliba architectural forms, addresses anthropomorphism and how the architectural forms of the house constitute a larger-order collective of lineal ancestry that individual men and women are literally constitutive of and then later subsumed into through the material form of the house into this larger ancestral entity.

The anthropomorphism of the Batammaliba dwellings is not self-evident. Appearing more castlelike in the imagination of some of the first European observers (Blier 1987: 13), these dwellings in Blier's discussion represented a complex bodily and cosmological entity that literally produces and sustains life through its material forms. The sort of body here is not the unitary, skin-enclosed self, familiar in the guise of the Vitruvian Man, but a multiply gendered genealogical entity whose morphology might appear almost monstrous from a Western perspective, with its appendages of multiple genders. The apparent strangeness of these forms is compounded by the additional observation by Blier that the villages comprising these houses can also be seen to be cemeteries and the houses themselves as graves (Blier 1987: 156). In fact, the association of house and tomb speaks of an important conceptual inversion and the relative insignificance of the living occupants who build and maintain it. The Batammaliba house presences the ancestors and the dead and deities, since "the house is defined primarily as a residence of the gods and deceased elders. Only secondarily, and through inversion, is the house identified with humans" (Blier 1987: 149). As such, the house represents a complete cosmology in a manner befitting Heidegger's fourfold. The construction of the house emplaces and embodies individual men and women within this schema. As Blier notes, the Batammaliba see humans as having "a visible body and an invisible soul, deities have an invisible body and visible soul" (1987: 149). It is the acts of marriage and construction, maintenance and disassembling that literally make such visible souls materially evident. The dwelling acts to presence these absences materially through the embodied actions of men, women, and their wider collective networks to make physically manifest the invisible body, the body of the genealogical collective of ancestors past and future. Those inhabiting, building, and maintaining the structure in the here and now, whose bodies are visible and souls invisible only become visible when they become ancestors and are presenced within the larger lineal collective that is the house. The man within this patrilocal society erects the house at the time of marriage. The construction unites both families, and the work of its maintenance is extended in time by the couple (Blier 1987: 143).

This entity, which one might refer to as "multiply personed," encompassing both ancestors and future descendants of the family of the husband and the wife, is also multiply gendered. Male and female sides of the house, and the storage of substances associated with gendered activities, divide the house along this axis, but the house is also composed of heterogeneous anthropomorphic elements where water spouts are associated with penises; stomachs with granaries; wombs and vaginas with the women's enclosures; nose, testicles, solar plexus, bile, mouth, joints and tongue among others with various other architectonic elements that play distinctive roles in the maintenance of gendered relations and ancestral connections through the habitation of the house. As a body, the house has a skin, and that skin must be decorated and dressed. Patterns incised in the outer plaster of the structure recall the cicatrization patterns used to beautify women's bodies (Blier 1987: 127). The exterior of the house is bathed with oils just as a women's skin would be to ensure its beauty. Granary caps recall the hats of young men. Similarly, the house, like young men and women, experiences initiation (1987: 127–9). When an elder dies, the house is dressed like a youth about to undergo initiation. It is dressed to suggest the same clothes that young men and women would wear in initiation rituals (1987: 130).

> The Batammaliba house thus memorializes each house member at the moment of his or her greatest glory, as a deceased elder ready to leave the Earth to join those who lived and died previously. As portrayed in the house, the physical image of the deceased elder is not that of a person aged fifty-six or over, but someone in the bloom of youth at the time of his or her initiation. (Blier 1987: 130).

Later, their visible souls would be enfleshed in the collective body of the house as in the arrangement of "resting places" within the walls of the house. The "resting places" follow the pattern of the ancestral wandering through the sky, which comes to rest in their gendered patterns within the house walls. "Every afternoon at dusk the resting places are lighted by the rays of the setting sun. At this time the deceased elders are said to leave their sky village to return to their earthly homes on the rays of the setting sun" (Blier 1987: 151–2). Thus, the absent is made physically present and embodied with the modulation of sunlight in relation to these "resting places." The presence of the living relatives is materially less relevant within this greater scale of time and space, where the souls of the dead are manifestly evident and more materially enduring than the briefly existing bodies of the living.

7

Jean-Pierre Warnier (2007) develops an approach to the anthropology of space and embodiment that emphasizes the role of kingship and the circulation of generative flows, but in terms of a notion of containment (not unlike elements of Prussin's analysis), where bodies, buildings, and containers serve as quali-signs for the circulation of generative substances. Here, the body, building, and container are conceptually and pragmatically indistinguishable from one another, except in terms of the specific ways in which they effect the flows of ancestral substance and power. Warnier offers the example of the "pot-king" in Cameroon. He emphasizes how bodies, buildings, cities, and containers are connected in a complex technology of containment and governmentality in the Foucauldian sense, whereby the moral flows of various generative substances are regulated by these "containers" that integrate and embody the king and his subjects. Within this "economy" of substances, some are more endowed with a relative materiality than others in terms of power and efficacy. In a comparable fashion, Rowlands (2005) explores a more intense relation within the materiality of things, as in the figure of the corpulent pot-king described by Warnier, that enables greater power through the monopoly of generative substances. Young, unmarried, low-status men are less materially embodied and implicated within the flows of power; hence, Rowlands's observation of the lure of Christianity for such men who are excluded from these material flows to find their fortunes, lives, and wives (Rowlands 2005).

Marcoux (2001a), in reference to contemporary Western practices, discusses another way in which embodiment is realized and ancestralization occurs. Unlike the Maori, Batammaliba, Tanimbarese, and Malagasy contexts discussed earlier, ancestralization is not the absorption of one's lived experience as an element of architectural space, forming the structure of the dwelling that sustains the lineage over time in one space. Rather, Marcoux describes the process in another direction through other media that exploit the generic interchangeability of modern dwelling forms (as seen in Daniels's [2010] work on Japan) and the fluidity of modern communities in terms of the *casser maison* ("breaking the house") ritual (Marcoux 2001a). The dwelling itself is rather inconsequential in this process. More significantly, it is the generic, interchangeable, and fluid nature of dwelling under the conditions of modernity that places emphasis on mobile property: the furnishings and goods of the home that can be easily transferred but also simultaneously imbued with a certain inalienability because of this capacity to be easily transferred between relatively generic and practically interchangeable architectural contexts. Marcoux, in his ethnographic account, describes how elderly inhabitants, realizing that they must move to smaller, assisted-living facilities or in anticipation of the impending end of life, invest great energy and significance in the distribution among family members of their various household goods, furniture, paintings, crockery, and other such artifacts. He describes this as a process of ancestralization, where the older person desires to produce the ancestral connections with his or her kin in the wake of eventual death. By placing certain objects with certain people, an older person is able to direct how he or she will be remembered and with what objects and under which affective conditions (Marcoux 2001a: 218–20). The specific artifact, with its uses and affordances, produces the terms by which the future ancestor will be incorporated within the lives of the succeeding generation. Marcoux notes that the transfer of certain artifacts also produces rather than reflects gender intergenerationally; traditionally gendered items get passed down from one generation to the next to produce an enduring sense of gendered identity (Marcoux 2001a: 219). Sometimes this produces conflicts—for example, raising questions over why one relative was preferred over another. The claim for ancestralization might also be at odds with a family's living conditions, circumstances, or lifestyles, such as furniture that is too big for a small flat. Key to the movement of such goods is the way they work through a manifest need to divest. Decisions must be made, narratives must be produced because of the imperative of the move, thereby producing and fixing a particular narrative of a life and, with it, the affective means by which ancestors are presenced and accommodated in the lives of subsequent generations and the material terms by which those narratives of subsequent generations are formed. Though there might be remarkable similarities in household arrangements structured by the demands of taste so trenchantly described by Bourdieu (1984), a subtle and deeply complex individuality is produced as well, as Strathern's (1999: 41) observation in another context might suggest: "for individuality lies not so much in the appearance as in the act of assembling. Men dance with assemblages almost identical in appearance, but each will have drawn on their own constellations of relations to do so." It is precisely the relations marshaled to produce what might seem to be a uniform or generic assemblage that are at the heart of the terms by which authenticity and the moral terms of personhood are produced.

In another context, Parrott (2010: 223–6; 2011) describes how controlled divestment functions to create ancestral links in the future. In her case study, a family invests considerable effort in accumulating Christmas decorations; these decorations are collected and displayed on the family Christmas tree during the archetypal ritual holiday in the West, where inalienable family ties are reproduced (Miller 1993). But the process of ancestralization is evident here in how the family then begins to divest itself of these ornaments to other members of the household as they grow older, move out, and establish their own households (2010: 225). At this time, long-curated Christmas ornaments with long and deeply held collective memories of the annual family gathering flow outward to these new households, literally propagating themselves within new fluid and emergent households, thereby establishing those primary links on a cyclical ritual basis. The inherent "partibility" of the ornaments, which must always be small, whose size in concert with other ornaments dissimulate their distinctiveness within the overall composition of the Christmas tree, also allows them to be melded "seamlessly" with other ornaments, producing what one might call an illusory unity (Parrott 2010; see also Parrott 2011). Their annual display invokes the narratives and memories of those ancestral connections across generations, across space, and between previously unrelated extended kin in each iteration of a joint cohabiting household, materially producing a deeply subtle understanding of kinship through the circulation of these easily transported and fluid baubles.

Although the work emerging in this consumption-oriented tradition seems to relegate the materiality of built forms to the margins, it is precisely because of the nature of housing markets and the increasingly minimal labor householders actually put into constructing, expanding, and altering these forms (see also Powell [2009] on the decline of DIY) that the work of kinship is produced in other, more fluid and malleable realms such as those associated with portable artifacts, furniture, Christmas baubles, and so on. But at the same time, it also needs to be argued that it is precisely the increasingly generic, commoditized, and universally substitutable forms of buildings—substitutable shells for the flows of mobile artifacts across time, generation, and space—that enable the sensuous and embodied work of making families and kinship within other more extensive and fluid material registers. The tension between fixity and fluidity evinced in the distinctions between vernacular studies and consumption studies suggests, however, that one cannot be contained in relation to the other. The fixity of forms described in architectural vernacular studies gives way to a preoccupation with flows and processes in anthropological studies of consumption in the home. Although such studies tend to sideline the materiality of architectural form, they suggest how other forms of material engagements are important through those that produce disembodiment and other realms of ontological attachment and the affordances of the banal, "inauthentic," and generic to produce new forms of authenticity and meaning through ever newer flows and engagements.

7 ICONOCLASM, DECAY, AND DESTRUCTION OF ARCHITECTURAL FORMS

1

What is clear from the previous chapter is that bodies and buildings are difficult to disentangle. In some cases, buildings are more animate than living bodies, serving as the repository of ancestral substances and presences preexisting and outliving individual men and women. Ap Stifin (personal communication; see also ap Stifin 2012) notes how the bodies of the victims of 9/11 are literally and inextricably fused with the remains of the building, creating a very complex and unresolved setting in attempts to deal with the aftermath of the World Trade Center's destruction. Without question, the embodiment of built form serves as more than an anthropomorphic representation of a human life or body but is literally that life itself in extended and collective form. As Gell noted in reference to the Maori meeting house (Figure 1): "[t]he living members of the community, gathered in the house, were so to speak, only 'furnishings.' They were mobile appurtenances of its solid enduring structure, into which they would eventually be absorbed as 'fixtures'" (Gell 1998: 253).

It is clear that architectural forms are profoundly animate. Previous chapters have provided numerous examples of how that animacy emerges. This chapter will follow on from those observations regarding the living nature of built forms and human life and consider what happens when those forms are destroyed, either through willful acts of iconoclasm or violent destruction or through orderly normative cultural practices that destroy buildings.

2

But first this chapter will discuss the issues surrounding the decay of architectural forms and the roles that entropy, ruin, and decay play in the constitution of social life. Most of the discussions to this point have emphasized how social relations are constituted and sustained in relation to the construction, maintenance, and use of built forms. The decay of built forms, however, has more recently received more attention. Within archaeology, the issue of preservation and heritage has called into question restoration practices in terms of what these practices do to maintain certain narratives, primarily those surrounding nation-building practices, economic development, and universalizing notions of Euro-American values, as can be understood from within such concepts and institutions as UNESCO World Heritage sites. Such critical works have addressed the problems involved in these preservation attempts that try to stem or preserve built forms at the expense of local understandings and needs concerning the materiality of built forms. Such examples speak to the conflicts that arise between local needs and their attendant material forms and those of heritage and preservation bodies and wider political and economic concerns. Within this body of work, a number of scholars have addressed the problem of decaying built forms in particular and the critical social properties that arise within the deliberation of these decaying forms.

3

Ruins, from the Romantic period to the present day, have had an enduring political significance in social life (see Edensor 2005a, 2005b; Gamboni 2007). One of the persistent characteristics of decaying forms is that they represent a challenge to existing stabilities of built form. Invariably, such approaches emphasize the political dimension in which decay functions in a variety of registers. Such an undoing seems characteristic of the work of entropy and decay (see Bataille et al. [1995: 51–2] on the formless and the academic's obsession with imposing form at all cost). However, this undoing is by no means universal in its effects, as a number of examples attest, but it is without question integral to the material and social effects of the decay and ruination of built forms. Like the actions of disembodiment discussed in the previous chapter, such undoing, either through divestment or gradual disembodiment, is integrally productive toward the forging of new social relations and forms of continuity. Here, too, decay, ruination, and destruction are similarly productive.

In a related vein, Küchler (1999, 2002) describes how the decay, destruction and dissipation of *malanggan* monuments in New Ireland are vitally important for the maintenance of social life, negotiating through the materiality of decayed form the relations between the living and the dead, the production of kinship relations, and access to resources. These ephemeral monuments are a particular type of ritual funerary practice dating back to the colonial period. They are exhibited at the grave for a short period of time. After they have served their purpose, the monuments are abandoned, allowed to decay, or sold off to Western collectors. In fact, they need to decay in order to ensure that the dead remain separate from the realm of the living; their sale to foreigners ensures their separation as well.

As Küchler suggests, the viewing and carving of the *malanggan* in a sense represents a form of intellectual property. The right to reproduce and retain this image is what is transmitted. Along with this information are rights to resources that are associated with the *malanggan*. People are given names at the time of the unveiling of a *malanggan* and thereby are placed within a lineage and come to have ownership over the image of the *malanggan* and its associated rights. The process of decay described by Küchler provides insight into the materiality of the process of decay itself and the means by which social relations can be effected, reproduced, and maintained. Such decay is generative, enabling the naming of persons and access to resources while assuring the necessary separation of the living from the dead. To preserve the carvings would stem such generative processes and do harm—hence their expulsion from the communities of the living. Such destructive practices are not unique to this part of the world. Küchler notes in relation to the Berlin Wall:

> As with the Berlin wall, those who acquire shares in a *malangaan* in the moments after it is revealed, a right to own its memory and to use it as resource for future recollections of what was rendered absent through decomposition—with the notable difference that the fragment of the wall survives physically in the owner's possession, the malanggan only in the mental image. (Küchler 1999: 67–8)

In another context, DeSilvey (2006) observes from the point of view of a heritage professional the decay of a Montana farmstead, abandoned after the death of the youngest son in 1995 (Figure 27). Ruminating on these ruins, DeSilvey invokes Bataille and his descriptions of "unstable, fetid and lukewarm substances where life ferments ignobly" (Bataille 1993: 81 cited in DeSilvey 2006: 319). She describes how "Maggots seethed in tin washtubs full of papery cornhusks. Nests of bald baby mice writhed in bushel baskets" (DeSilvey 2006: 319). Following Bataille, DeSilvey notes the "procreative power of decay" (2006: 320), which engenders contemplation through the decidedly material and bodily responses of "repugnance and attraction." Here, DeSilvey suggests a certain authenticity of experience and meaning associated with these entropic processes recalling, it is contended here, the notion of the abject (*l'abjection*) from Julia Kristeva's (1997) work. This is suggestive of a produced authenticity of experience based on nausea stimulated by the abject. This embodied response is direct, unmediated, and feels supremely authentic, connecting the body to what is observed. This blurring of boundaries illuminates both the threat and power of *l'abjection*. Kristeva elaborates on these qualities further:

Figure 27 DeSilvey's abandoned Montana farmhouse. *Source:* Caitlin DeSilvey.

L'abjection is something that disgusts you. For example, you see something rotting and you want to vomit. It's "abject" on the level of matter. It can also be a notion that concerns moral matters—an *abjection* in the face of crime, for example. But it is an extremely strong feeling which is at once somatic and symbolic, and which is above all a revolt of the person against an external menace from which one wants to keep oneself at a distance, but of which one has the impression that it is not only an external menace but that it may menace us from the inside. So it is a desire for separation, for becoming autonomous and also the feeling of an impossibility of doing so—whence the element of crisis which the notion of abjection carries within it. Taken to its logical consequences, it is

an impossible assemblage of elements, with a connotation of a "fragile limit."
(Kristeva 1997: 372)

DeSilvey notes that conventional conservation and heritage practices work against this notion of abjection. She explains that all the material she was engaging with would have been thrown out by conservationists, yet these materials—in their decaying, abject form—are the basis of their powerful effects, especially in terms of the radical means by which they can establish new forms of knowledge, especially embodied forms of knowledge. Referring to Sloterdijk, DeSilvey notes: "The threshold of discomfort and aversion . . . can also be a threshold to other ways of knowing" (DeSilvey 2006: 321). DeSilvey (2006: 322) notes how these processes of what appears as natural entropy reworked conventional material stabilities that make up one's understanding: "Objects generate social effects not just in their preservation and persistence, but in their destruction and disposal" (DeSilvey 2006: 324).

DeSilvey argues against saving these material forms in the conventional sense to enable this radical interpretive process to take place: "Interpretation requires letting the process run, and watching what happens in the going. Though this might seem wilfully destructive to those who locate the memorial potency of the object in its unchanging physical form" (2006: 324–5). This goes against the Aristotelian concept of memory inhering in the object. Forty (1999) describes this view of memory where objects—either natural of artificial—are analogues of human memory. DeSilvey instead argues against the work of institutional and "socially produced durability" (Buchli 2002) and proposes that "decay itself may clear a path for certain kinds of remembrance despite its (because of its?) destructive energies" (DeSilvey 2006: 326). As such, "Degraded artefacts can contribute to alternative interpretive possibilities even as they remain caught up in dynamic processes of decay and disarticulation. The autonomous exercise of human intention gives way to a more dispersed sharing of the practices of material editing and curation" (2006: 330). With reference to *malanggan*, she writes: "Cultural remembering proceeds not through reflection on a static memorial remnant, but on the process that slowly pulls the remnant into other ecologies of expressions of value—accommodating simultaneous resonances of death and rebirth, loss and renewal" (DeSilvey 2006: 328). In fact, the materiality of decay in and of itself produces a specific and powerful interpretive disposition—as DeSilvey suggests, providing a mute critique of the passing of former economic activities while "weedy trees signal the inexorable 'rewilding' of spaces that are left to their own ecological devices" (2006: 328).

Tim Edensor's work similarly speaks to the political implications of decay and its effects for the production of a political consciousness (Edensor 2005a, 2005b). He examines the ruination of British industrial buildings closed down because of economic downturns and then "dropped from such stabilizing networks" (Edensor 2005b: 313) that normally maintain the integrity of their material forms (Figure 28). As such, the materiality of industrial ruins means they are ideally placed to rebuke the normative assignations of objects, and I highlight the ways in which this disordering of a previously regulated space can interrogate normative processes of spatial and material ordering, and can generate a number of critical speculations about the character, aesthetics, affordances and histories of objects. (Edensor 2005b: 314)

Here, waste and ruin serve to offer a critique of capitalist ideologies of progress and of consumerist expenditure. Regardless, despite attempts to eliminate it, waste always returns to upset categories. Edensor observes how objects decay, merge with each other, become unidentifiable, and fuse with life forms such as fungus and rodents to create monstrous hybrids: "These traces of non-human life-forms on the material textures of ruination reveal other unheralded, non-human ways of existing and interacting with matter . . . This physical deconstruction of objects reveals the artifice through which they are structured to withstand ambiguity" (2005b: 320).

These entropic qualities possess a certain compelling force, a naturalness that belies human processes:

For the ad hoc montages of objects and other scraps found in ruins are not deliberately organized assemblies devised to strike chords and meanings through associations, but are fortuitous combinations which interrupt normative meanings.

Figure 28 Edensor's ruined industrial building. *Source:* Timothy Edensor.

By virtue of their arbitrariness and the evident lack of design, these assortments are difficult to recoup into explanatory or aesthetic frameworks . . . (Edensor 2005b: 323)

These happenstance arrangements, which emerge through their framing by the analyst, perform the critical and politicized task of calling to question the previous human orders that constituted them. A political and material aesthetic emerges, which Edensor describes as an "accidental surrealism" (2005b: 323). Unlike the ruins deliberately constructed by Romantics of another era, Edensor observes that these industrial ruins differ because of the lack of overt control. The Romantic ruin is a highly controlled and contrived edifice, whereas the industrial ruin is not, despite the evident and controlled framing Edensor's method employs: "Neither the elicitation of preferred sentiments and moral lessons nor the contemplative, romantic impulse can be stimulated by contemporary industrial ruins. Instead there is an unpredictable immanence of impression and sensation" (2005b: 324).

Both Edensor and DeSilvey argue for a powerful and authentic immanence afforded by the materiality of ruined forms. Modern spaces, which are smooth, clean, well-maintained, and so on transform bodily experience, according to Edensor, creating a specific kind of "modern body" in keeping with norms of safety and rationality (Edensor 2005b: 324). Such ruins engage the body differently, calling into question high-modern rationalities (such as those surrounding risk, health, and safety standards). Edensor notes (as does DeSilvey similarly), "The ruin *feels* very different to urban space, rebukes the unsensual erasure of multiple tactilities, smells, sounds and sights" (Edensor 2005b: 325). Likewise, it demands a different embodied response that challenges modern urban forms of bodily deportment: "The demise of a stable materiality must be engaged with and learnt, so we become competent in the preservation of life and limb" (2005b: 326).

This is a ludic space of excess, not unlike the Bonaventure Hotel described by Jameson (1984). But here the challenge to the human sensorium is not dystopic but potentially liberating and even utopian:

Stripped of their use and exchange values and the magic of the commodity, they can be reinterpreted anew, perhaps bearing the utopian, collectively oriented visions unconsciously embodied within them by their creators that Benjamin discerned. . . . This disruptiveness of the materiality of the ruin similarly dislocates the normative aesthetic and sensory apprehension of urban space, and undermines the integrity of the fashioned artefact as discrete entity. The political assumptions and desires which lie behind the ordering of matter in space are thus revealed by the effects of objects in ruins, and they provoke the speculation about how space and materiality might be interpreted, experienced and imagined otherwise. (Edensor 2005b: 330)

González-Ruibal (2005) discusses the role of ruins within a modern context, experiencing economic change in another sense. He examines the materiality of ruined farmhouses in the Galician countryside of Spain (Figure 29). Up to the middle of the twentieth century, poor rural farmers from this area migrated abroad. Later returning migrants built new homes. The homes were markedly different from the traditional farmhouses and their former economic roles. New industrially produced materials were used for new houses that gleamed in striking contrast with the older homes that remained. But some older homes remained nonetheless. Despite the benefits of selling a collapsing, ruined, and disused property, rural families clung to the houses jealously; they were simply not for sale. González-Ruibal argues that the evident material contrast of architectural forms, from the decaying old farms and the gleaming new houses, produced an important understanding of time and collective lineal history that was central to the way these families experienced the changing economic and social circumstances of their lives. The contrast of ruin and gleaming form literally reckoned the passage from one condition to the next, providing an ambivalent record of a family's growth, prosperity, and history in these contrasting materialities. The ruins as such produced these new familial, economic, and social forms, and were not available as an alienable commodity for sale. The ruins in material form emplaced these families within a specific history and expanding "spacetime" (following Munn); they were an expression of the expanding laboring and embodied capacities of these extended households over time and space. And as Munn's gleaming, "lightning-like" bodies of young Gawa men attested to their expanding capacities and "spacetime," so, too, did the gleaming finishes of these new architectural forms on the Galician landscape. To restore these decaying buildings would literally deny this expression of familial time and capacity.

The presence of decaying, unfinished and empty buildings on the territory of the former Soviet Union provides another view into the social effects of the materiality of ruination. Mathijs Pelkmans (2003) describes the presence of empty structures in post-Soviet Ajaria. The construction of these buildings stopped; financing was gone, political will was not available to complete them, and some of these buildings started to decay in place before even beginning their lives as inhabited structures. However, Pelkmans notes the significance these buildings have in this postsocialist environment. Because of their emptiness, they offer the chance to envision an open-ended futurity that is available to everyone to participate in—in effect, they become generative of new possibilities. The building process was a fraught one under the conditions of postsocialism, plagued by widespread corruption and profiteering. These empty structures provide a collective hope and index of the possibility of an open future that has not been claimed by any one interest yet; they remain anticipatory for all to participate in.

Figure 29 González-Ruibal's abandoned farmhouse, Galicia, Spain. *Source:* Alfredo González-Ruibal.

Nikolai Ssorin-Chaikov (2003: 110–39), in another manner, describes the distinctive architectural qualities of rural Siberian settlements. In their constant state of unfinished construction, they are incomplete, incessant building sites that evoke what he refers to as the "poetics of unfinished construction," a political and poetic material disposition inscribing a distinctive understanding of time and materiality. This is a time of constant unfolding into the future of a materially indexed, constantly deferred futurity that is close but not at hand, always moving forward but never realized—in short, a material embodiment of an incessant Marxian progress, always in construction, and, as such, constructing itself ceaselessly toward the unrealizable goal of communism.

Both Pelkmans and Ssorin-Chaikov's analyses of the materiality of built form demonstrate the significance of Susan Buck-Morss's (2002) observations concerning socialist time and its implication for a specific socialist form of materiality. She quotes Lenin at the time of the Treaty of Brest Litovsk in March 1918: "I want to concede space . . . in order to win time" (Lenin quoted in Buck-Morss 2002: 24). Space, time, and materiality have specific material registers under the evolving conditions of Soviet socialism that are distinct from corresponding bourgeois nationalist notions. The capitalist nation-state is predicated on the idea of territorial integrity, consolidated through its markets, the containment of people, and the consolidation of national territory in geographic, spatial, ethnic, and material cultural terms. This is the invention of the national vernacular, as Marcel Mauss mused at the Treaty of Versailles of June 1919. It was a time that could see ethnic nation-states suggested by the prevalence of a given vernacular roof type over another, characterizing this understanding of fixed, stabilized, and vernacular forms, consolidating bourgeois nationalist space and time. Socialist time, however, according to Buck-Morss's schema, eschews the stabilization of space in the conquest of time, which in material terms is seen as continuous and unfolding within a constantly developing futurity. Socialist time is prospective and expansive rather than retrospective and intensive bourgeois nationalist time. The unstable decaying or empty material forms described by Pelkmans and Ssorin-Chaikov index this form of time and produce it.

4

The destruction of built forms stands in contrast to the various sustaining practices involved in the use of built forms—everything from housework to building maintenance and moving. All these actions refigure social relations and reconfigure or reaffirm gender relations and other aspects of status. Moving and divestment disembody in relation to a certain architectural context. Similarly, the evacuation of meaning in built form rendering it alienable as a commodity in the property market and/or as an abstract universal principle in English property law enables its wider, more attenuated flow and, with it, the reconfiguration of the material terms in which human relationships are forged and sustained. Problematically, this may amount to a critical disembodiment, as Fox (2005) argues and as Young (2004) has shown. At one level, moving involves the dismantling and destruction of a previously inhabited context, such as the moving of houses in Malaysia discussed earlier or the various nomadic peregrinations in which personhood and life-cycle stage are actively produced through the dismantling of architectural forms. These dismantlings and reassemblings are done in different fashions and via different material means (everything from simply moving the furniture around, to tearing down and rebuilding). Status, continuity, and time are reconfigured within the material terms of these actions. And sometimes buildings simply die, such as the Ye'cuana chieftain's house (Rivière 1995), or they are killed, like the holy houses of Malagasy villages (Bloch 1995a, 1995b) and the Neolithic houses described by Tringham (2000).

It should be clear from the earlier discussion that the animacy attributed to built forms and their intimate relationship to the body in a variety of configurations is by no means a non-modern phenomenon but rather is one that characterizes the complex human relationship to built forms. Non-modern forms outside of the Euro-American sphere may appear to exhibit a certain coherence in terms of this association, which, I might hazard, is more of an artifact of the nature of ethnographic writing than the lived reality of these contexts. Modern urban contexts within the Euro-American sphere, however, might be contrasted with their own distinct complexities surrounding the animacy of built forms. Harris (1999), in his discussion of twentieth-century urban forms, discusses how buildings undergo "building surgery" through the reworking of infrastructure such as plumbing, electricity, and air conditioning to extend the life of a building. He also considers the calculation of depreciation over the life span of a building in terms of materials "allotting wooden structures, for example, ten years, concrete, brick, and steel frame twenty-five years, and corrugated iron siding structures a six year life" (Harris 1999: 125) and how they constitute very specific lives for buildings in terms of the investment of resources into their upkeep in relation to the durability of their material forms.

In many ways buildings are about thinking and working through things that cannot be adequately cognized and presenced in the here and now: the past, the future, ancestors, resolutions of social conflict, and contradiction. Buildings in many ways are about what is not there or what cannot possibly be physically or conceptually realized as being there: the cosmos, communist utopia, the ideal nuclear family, the "primitive hut," the hero/ancestor's home, the totality of ancestors and descendants. As Gell has noted in reference to the Maori meeting house, it is the "cognitive process writ large," thus helping us understand "mind" collectively: "transcending the individual *cogito* and the coordinates of any particular here and now" (1998: 258; emphasis in the original).

However, the actual death of buildings, their physical collapse, and destruction are vitally important occasions for collective thought and action. Collapses, as Harris (1999) says, are opportunities for a postmortem, as death refigures social relations, creating new ones and new temporalities. The deaths of buildings, when they are in fact animated by human understandings with an attribution of embodiment and thereby die, help us understand the terms of physical as well as social life. By salvaging bits and pieces as relics, the Berlin Wall (or fragments of the Bastille in another era [Gamboni 2007: 32]) does not really die. It is merely redistributed in different form: attenuated, more immaterial, and probably with a greater degree of immortality—just as the World Trade Center took on an unexpected monumentality not in durable form but when it shifted in material register into the ephemeral and highly attenuated visual images of its eternally collapsing structures.

The study of buildings in terms of lives or kinds of bodies is hard to grasp ethnographically. Often we do not know what these bodies really are because of the limitations of the ethnographic moment. We can only begin to understand this historically or archaeologically, as these lives are beyond immediate grasp, being much larger than individual perceptions or even temporally limited collective ones (which is really all we are able to understand ethnographically). The moment of their death, of their destruction, however, does give us a sense. The study of iconoclasm allows this, providing just such a window, even though it does not really give us a sense of what the long-term implications are of destruction in terms of renewal or the renegotiation of relations and bodies and selves—ideally, archaeology, is situated towards this task (as well as various forms of ethnohistory).

The destruction of a building produces, it would seem, a paradoxical effect, rendering something previously seen as inanimate suddenly animate. In effect, such moments reveal the essentially hybrid nature of our ontologies where people and things are deeply intertwined despite our "hard-won" modernity, as Strathern (1996: 518) observes, that would insist otherwise. How can purporting to kill something endow an object with animacy at the time of its death? This might be understood in terms of the evident excess that the iconoclastic act or the intention to kill confers. To kill something inanimate is to attribute it with an animacy beyond its normative objective status. Gell's analysis of the vandalism of Velázquez's painting *The Rokeby Venus* at the National Gallery in London is instructive as to how this process works: slashed by the suffragette Mary Richardson in 1914, the painting existed in this vandalized form temporarily, until it was restored. During this period, Gell refers to the picture as the " 'Slashed' Rokeby Venus by Richardson" (Gell 1998: 62–5) and in so doing discusses it as an immensely potent work with an excess of meaning that the process of restoration and preservation served to stem and stabilize.

Gell describes how Richardson attacked the painting with a kitchen knife, instigating a form of "art making in reverse," an iconoclasm with "artistic-agency" (Gell 1998: 64), something Latour, in a similar vein, refers to as "iconoclash" (Latour and Weibel 2002). Gell notes how Mary Richardson stabbed Venus in the heart, destroying in her words, "the most beautiful woman in mythological history," to protest the imprisonment of "the most beautiful character in modern history" (Gell 1998: 64), the suffragette leader Emmeline Pankhurst. In the course of this "art-making in reverse,"

> Richardson endowed the Rokeby Venus with a life it never possessed before by "killing" it and turning it into a beautiful corpse. The restoration of the picture to its original condition, though of course necessary and desirable, was also a means of re-erecting the barrier which prevents such images troubling us unduly, politically, sexually, or in any other way. (Gell 1998: 64)

The act, by the very virtue of its perpetration, Gell notes, invoked a form of volt sorcery that through its intention to kill imbued an animacy and excess above and beyond that which was normally attributed to it. To maintain the slashed painting would have been to sustain this violent excess indefinitely; as Gell states, it was certainly desirable from the point of view of a wide range of interests to stem this excess and stabilize it. However, it is arguable, as Gell notes, that the "Slashed Rokeby Venus," as short-lived as it was, was clearly the more powerful and affecting of the two, imbued with this violent animate excess produced by Mary Richardson's actions.

In Gell's example, the animacy of *The Rokeby Venus* is stabilized institutionally in order to stem the excess effected by destruction. Pietz (2002) argues in his discussion of the sin of Saul, that destruction always produces an excess that is the result of the particular affordances of the fragment and ruin. Unless complete destruction is achieved, which arguably is never possible, the fragment always returns with destabilizing effects. It is the fragment's radically promiscuous assimilability that in itself can never be adequate to its context, in either origin or assimilation. Thus, this excess is available, and available in particular ways, to create new material registers with often unexpected social effects.

Forty (1999: 10–12) and Yampolsky (1995) describe such interpretive excess created by the destruction of statues in the context of post-Soviet iconoclasm. Both discuss how the destruction of statues created voids in the urban environment that suddenly gained significance because of their absence, indexed by the empty plinths and niches that once supported them. The empty space drew attention to the absence, which suggested a presence no longer there. In short, the destruction of these statues produced an excess, a presence beyond that which was immediately perceptible; and because of this materially produced excess through absence, a more powerful evocation resulted.

When people are killed within buildings, the sites become imbued with a spiritual dimension through death and suffering that was not there before. The site is the only way to presence the absented individual (for instance, the extermination camps of the Holocaust, the site of a murder, and roadside memorials). There is a transference; the site becomes animated because of the way it draws people in relation to it and then begins to have its own independent, somewhat spectral life. It serves as the empty plinths as an index of that absence. And an index, according to Peircean semiotics, is a natural sign that invariably participates in a physically connected way with that which it represents—such that smoke as an index is physically connected to and a direct consequence of fire. In this way, seemingly empirically banal forms can subtly serve to conjure and sustain and produce absent life.

The destruction of something ascribed with permanence becomes traumatic or imbued with iconicity (see Coward 2009 on "urbicide" and Drakulic 1993). As in the case of the World Trade Center, a building that within the normal scheme of things would have had an actuarial life of a certain number of years is paradoxically animated by its sudden death (Figure 30). The separation of persons and things, buildings and people—those hard-won battles of our modernity, as Strathern (1996: 518) would have it—are suddenly lost, and violently and irredeemably conflated as elements of unidentifiable but clearly human genetic material are tragically fused with the building debris at the World Trade Center (ap Stifin personal communication).

The Twin Towers might have been, in fact, the embodiment of global capitalism, built according to its terms of rationality and profit maximization, a profoundly "rational" building, even redundantly so (as Baudrillard [2002] is at pains to note, a simulacrum of itself, hence two). But their destruction revealed a profound social truth about the structures as productive of a new collective body; in fact, the souls of the dead and the building as well as the physical qualities (quite gruesomely) are now irrevocably intertwined. If, say, *malanggan* carvings produce social truth through their revelation and subsequent destruction, so do the Twin Towers reveal a truth about our thoroughly unmodern understandings of how bodies and things are intertwined. They produced a greater truth about the world order than had been understood or acknowledged before. And as with any death, be it the death of a loved one or a collective one as in the death of a building, it becomes a means of reorganizing people and things, rethinking social order, rethinking continuity—it is for this reason that we live in a post-9/11 world.

The fact that what was destroyed on 9/11 were buildings was important for the way we cognize our relations. As Gell states, buildings represent a public/collective cogito, distributed beyond the individual one, and temporally they extend into the past and into the future beyond a particular body, as they are extensions of a body and bodies, distributed beyond the individual and any discrete time (such as the lifetime of a person). Because buildings as such are extensions of individual and collective minds, when they are destroyed, much more than the individual or the building is killed.

It may be that the Holocaust in its monstrousness is graspable because of the camp. This is what Agamben (1998) suggests in his discussion of the camp as constitutive of the exceptional process that could create a life to be killed. These exceptions reveal the basic structure of social life, and viable and nonviable lives ("bare life"). This could only be known spatially and architecturally through the materialities of the terrible enclosure that was the camp and the terrifying truth of the relations it created through its destructive forces. But as the monument is believed to be the enemy of remembering, it is the artist Christian Boltanksi's contention that a true memorial to the Holocaust must be made every day to be remembered, which really means that the previous memorial must be destroyed to

Figure 30 World Trade Center. *Source:* Americanspirit, Dreamstime.com

thereby reassert the memory within a new set of relations every day (see the discussion in Forty 1999: 6).

Without such materialites as afforded by enclosures or buildings, it is difficult to assess meaning, to think through and collectively grasp the significance of these events. Buildings are the most effective and immediate means with which to presence such absences—be they absences of origins, absences of idealized futures, or absences of people—as the intimacy between people and buildings insists upon and which destruction affirms.

5

However, iconoclasm and destruction work to produce new forms of material excess and, with them, novel social effects. Adrian Forty (1999: 9–10) observed in relation to the destruction and reconstruction of the Frauenkirche in Dresden the process of iconoclasms and counter-iconoclasms and their attendant effects on memory and history. The church was destroyed by Allied bombs during the Second World War, in February 1945. Later, under the socialist government of the postwar East German state (GDR), the site was left empty and became a site to observe the anniversary of the destruction of the city by Allied forces and quietly protest socialism. After the end of communism, many Soviet- and GDR-era monuments were razed, but the Frauenkirche was rebuilt. As Forty notes, the church was rebuilt to forget socialism and the memory of wartime trauma. Forty observes how the rebuilding, then, paradoxically silenced two distinct memories in the experience of twentieth-century history.

Similarly, Forty notes that, in Moscow, the Cathedral of Christ the Savior underwent a comparable form of "counter-iconoclasm" (Figure 31). Sidorov (2000) describes how the structure, commissioned by Emperor Nicholas I was razed under Stalin in 1931. It was meant to make way for the famous Palace of the Soviets; however, due to the subsequent war effort the proposed palace was never built. A hole was left in the ground, which, in 1960, became a great outdoor swimming pool, very popular during the Soviet period. Later, with the collapse of communism, the new post-Soviet Russian state and the Russian Orthodox Church rebuilt the original Cathedral of Christ the Savior in a manner to suggest that it had been there all along, effectively silencing the iconoclasm that was foundational for the establishment and consolidation of the Soviet state. The materiality of the new structure, however, belies this counter-iconoclasm. According to critics, original materials were not reproduced but rendered in inappropriate media. However, the wider image of the resurrected Cathedral sustained this wider counter-iconoclasm and was only undone upon close inspection by a few observers and critics for whom this expression of what would seem to be inappropriate construction methods indexes the inauthenticity of the rebuilt structure and wider issues concerning the legitimacy of the post-Soviet state and the Russian Orthodox Church. Here, too, a complex and multiply registered materiality of architectural fabric is actively productive in the wider issues of historical and social memory and legitimacy.

Dolff-Bonekämper's (2002) discussion of the Berlin Wall and its remains attests to the extraordinary complexity of the materialities associated with the wall, especially from the point of view of a conservator and heritage professional (Figure 32). Such a contested structure was probably at its least problematic materially while it was the active dividing wall between West and East Berlin. As Dolff-Bonekämper notes, from the western side, the wall was rather unproblematically approached by West Berliners, who could approach and touch this physical manifestation of the deep political divide between East and West Berlin and between the capitalist West and the socialist East. From the East German side, the experience was decidedly different: East Berliners could only peer over the wall from a distance separated by a death strip of raked earth, poisoned to kill plants, and of course the real threat of death if one should step on to it and approach the actual wall. After the opening of the wall on November 9, 1989, it was famously and gradually dismantled. People spontaneously chipped away at it, carrying off pieces; whole sections were removed, with the result that smaller and larger pieces of it began to circulate all over the world as souvenirs of the wall. In the meantime, the wall itself and the divides it produced were only visible in a few sections. Various calls to preserve the remains resulted in what are now only four remaining protected sections that are the focus of Dolff-Bonekämper's discussion. These four sections, for her, constitute *lieux de discorde*, or "sites of dispute," following Pierre Nora's terminology of "sites of memory" (2002: 247). The nature of the fragment and ruin takes on a decidedly complex role socially and politically in this context.

Dolff-Bonekämper notes that in the aftermath of the dismantling of the wall and Berliners' desire to remove it from their lives, preservationists were only able to negotiate four remaining sections and two watch towers, whose complex material conditions produce these "sites of dispute" in various registers. The first section, in Bernauer Strasse, was divided among competing preservation and community interests, with the result that a resolution was not satisfactorily achieved and the remains decayed in different ways in relation to the different types of conflict surrounding their preservation. As such, the remnants of the wall here, Dolff-Bonekämper notes, are not a testimony to the wall that separated East from West but a monument to the complex and highly conflicted responses to it and to its legacy among various constituencies. In the end, remains seem to be engulfed by the surrounding landscape or are decaying in situ, a testimony to the irresolvable nature of the legacy of the Berlin Wall.

The second section, the East Side Gallery, was once covered by graffiti art, but to consolidate the graffiti as a memorial proved difficult and the original artists were

Figure 31 Cathedral of Christ the Savior, Moscow. *Source*: Sailorr, Dreamstime.com

asked to restore their original interventions. A decade later, the impetus to do this on the part of the artists was considerably lost and some refused, leaving space for other artists to intervene.

The third section was along a canal behind the eighteenth-century Cemetery of the Invalids, but due to its position in relation to an existing boundary, the canal, this section of the wall, Dolff-Bonekämper notes, serves more as a picturesque backdrop to the restored eighteenth-century cemetery rather than as a curated monument to the wall that separated East from West. It has become incorporated as an element of a picturesque view within a curated eighteenth-century landscape instead.

The fourth section, Dolff-Bonekämper describes, is in Niederkirchnerstrasse. This is the best-preserved section and was the site where "wallpeckers" would hammer away to mine small fragments. At one point, hammers were rented out so people could chip off small fragments for souvenirs. Since then, a number of unsuccessful barriers have been put up to prevent people from approaching the site and pecking away at it. Because this section is now protected behind a tall fence like the ones used at construction sites, the wall is in a rather good state of preservation despite the earlier activities.

These fragmented sections and their varied contexts of engagement produce a diverse set of "sites of dispute," as Dolff-Bonekämper notes:

> It allows one to make a difference between consensual and dissensual situations and to accept a monument's capacity to create dissensus—or to make it visible— as a positive quality, a social value. A monument that is argued about becomes

Figure 32 Berlin Wall fragment. A section of the original East–West Berlin border and walls, viewed from the tower of the Berlin Wall Documentation Center in Bernauer strasse. *Source*: iStockphoto LP.

precious *because* it does not embody cultural and social consensus on historic or present events. (Dolff-Bonekämper 2002: 247; emphasis in the original)

Dolff-Bonekämper is keen to hope that the preservationists will persevere in their attempts to maintain what is left of the wall. She insists on the importance of its ambivalence and irresolvability as a value in and of itself as a "site of dispute" in an ongoing working of historical memory and the material forms that sustain it—in a sense insisting on the sections' presence as a preserved fragment to displace any pre-vailing consensus in an open-ended process of enabling continuous dissensus. This is not dissimilar to the inherently displacing effect of Moshenska's (2008) shrapnel of the Second World War and Tringham's (2000) ceramic fragments. This work on the Berlin Wall can be contrasted with the work of Palestinian artist Khalil Rabah on the wall the Israeli state is building at the West Bank. His 2004 work, *The 3rd Annual Wall Zone Sale* (see discussion in De Cesari 2012: 89), auctioned off material associated with the wall to raise consciousness about its presence and—through what might be seen as an attempt at sympathetic magic by auctioning off and dispersing the materials—aid in the eventual dismantling of the wall itself through the frag-menting effects of this intervention.

Such iconoclasms and counter-iconoclasms produce a material register of many conflicting commitments and, with it, a particular intensity that one might consider the implacability of the material but which, it is argued, is the contingent material effect of these conflicted commitments. Yiftachel (2009), in his discussion of "gray space" in relation to the repeatedly destroyed Bedouin settlements in Israel, describes an unexpected agency as a result of the concatenation of these repeated acts of de-struction, construction, destruction, and construction, again and again. Yiftachel notes how the materiality of the destroyed settlements are productive of a distinctly new political engagement that is outside of established political conventions and thereby produces an unexpected enduring political agency and radicalization of po-litical interests when before there was none. He quotes a Bedouin activist in relation to the repeated destruction inflicted by Israeli authorities:

We know this is a long haul, and that this new mosque will probably be fol-lowed by further demolitions and legal penalties . . . but we also know that the attempts to remove us will never fully succeed, like the failure in burning and resisting Gaza. This is because we are sons of this soil, and we know how to survive on it, and we will. . . . The state calls us "criminals" just for living in our localities . . . this does not matter, as we'll always remain the people of this place, not for the state, but for our own communal future. (quoted in Yiftachel 2009: 253–4)

Such repeated destruction and construction produces an anticipated political commitment and engagement. Yiftachel notes this process of constant destruction and construction and its unwitting productive effects enables "the rise of informal and autonomous leadership 'from below' against an ethnocratic hard-line policy of denial and forced removal . . . It has thereby gradually institutionalized their long-term future in gray space, while setting the foundations for incipient forms of indigenous sovereignty" (Yiftachel 2009: 253).

Similarly, the World Trade Center, in its vast and still-to-be-played-out complexity, assumes unexpected registers in the case of the Tulsa, Oklahoma, structure that was designed by the same architect and has the same appearance (see Sulzberger 2011). Despite being so many miles away from New York, the building's visual similarity and common architect renders it suddenly and unexpectedly vulnerable. The images of the original towers collapsing or of the planes crashing into them circulate ceaselessly in the press and the Internet and especially on the anniversary of 9/11. Office workers in Tulsa live in fear that the same fate will befall them, as these images circulate and the visual and physical connection, which was never prominent, is constantly invoked, with real on-the-ground consequences in terms of security, and reluctant occupants. The promiscuous, fragmented images circulating in digitized space promote a visual contagion with another distant building, linking the two and mimetically animating one as a result of these digitized images of ruination and destruction. The circulating digitized fragments of this destruction animate in an unexpected manner, just as the ruins of Bedouin houses animate a political discourse and new collectivity that is increasingly intractable in terms of present politics but increasingly present in stubborn ways as a result of the specific materialities and excesses of destruction that forge these new collectivities in unexpected form—as Pietz (2002) had invoked with his discussion of the sin of Saul in relation to the fragments resulting from the sacked city of Benin. All these examples point to the remarkably productive and unexpected consequences of destructive acts, which, by their inherently conflicted nature, produce new material intensities and investments that might suggest a certain implacable "thingness" but which attest to the inherently conflictual nature of material forms and the relations they negotiate and effect—their novel thingness being just an effect of these conflicted investments.

POSTSCRIPT

I

Having considered the home and architectural form in fragments and ruins and the complex effects of the wider circulation of these disintegrated forms and their flows and shifting registers, how might we then consider the wider sense of their materiality and the terms under which dwelling takes place? A certain strain of the literature on vernacular form bemoans the loss of "authentic" traditions in the face of modernization or the violence of political and social life that has been intensely felt in the modern period. New forms and practices are often marginalized, hidden in footnotes, or briefly discussed against the increasingly threatened and diminishing forms of authentic traditions. However, if one considers the work of the house as an "illusory objectification" (Carsten and Hugh-Jones 1995), these objectifications can take on new forms and participate in new flows to facilitate the social work of the making and unmaking of people and social relations. Numerous migration studies have shown how this process can work, placing particular emphasis on the nature of flows in relation to the generative substances both prosaic and sublime that sustain social life and the role material culture and architectural forms play to sustain and constitute these flows.

The fixity of the dwelling in terms of its formal characteristics and its normative institutions have tended to dominate understandings of architectural forms within the social sciences. We have been held in the thrall of these analytical categories—these "illusory objectifications" (Carsten and Hugh-Jones 1995)—ever since Lévi-Strauss's first observations. The reasons, of course, are numerous, as we have seen in the many examples presented here. The analytical category has at times obscured attention to the process of flows that architectural forms regulate and produce as a result of the materiality of their forms. The discussions presented here have attempted to chart how the materiality of architectural forms regulates and produces these flows that sustain social life. The next section summarizes some of these insights.

2

As regards the architectonic regulation of flows, by way of conclusion, one might take the opportunity to engage again with the representation of such architectonic forms and the issue of abstraction, particularly as it concerns new technologies and new ways of circulating and iterating architectural forms and their flows. It is under the conditions of these emerging technologies that the status of the artifact itself and its relative stability within such flows is called into question, resonating with the numerous examples presented here. It might be worthwhile to consider here briefly the question of printing—in particular, three-dimensional printing—of architectural forms, as its ability to stabilize form and facilitate its wider flow takes on a new dimension. It is useful to return to Hyde Park and the site of the Crystal Palace and Semper's encounter with the Carib hut to consider another structure proposed by the Rabih Hage Gallery in London (Figure 33). A crumpled piece of paper is digitally scanned, scaled up in a computer-aided design (CAD) program, and printed three-dimensionally to produce a pavilion for Hyde Park. As the gallery's March 2008 press release straightforwardly suggests: "the CAD data (drawings) can be sent

Figure 33 Hage's pavilion. Exhibition pavilion designed by Rabih Hage, architect, 2008. Built using layer manufacturing technology (3D printing) components built by EOS Electro Optical Systems Ltd. *Source*: Rabih Hage Ltd.

via email. This data can be used to manufacture the pavilion on an E-Manufacturing machine anywhere in the world, therefore, incurring no shipping cost, taxes or duties." Whole realms of space, geography, time, the nation-state, tax regimes, and labor markets, and, with them, union agreements are overcome with the click of a mouse. The "vicious bifurcation" of nature observed by Whitehead (2000: 185) that has constituted our understandings of the empirical world and girded the productive dualisms constituting social life, and the "objects" and "subjects" forged therein are almost conflated and entirely obliterated in the creative and manufacturing processes underlying rapid manufacturing, when the immaterial digital code and material physical artifact are difficult to differentiate meaningfully in time and space.

In this light, the act of drawing forms on paper, circulating, and then assembling them is reconfigured again in a new fashion that calls into question established notions of distance, time, and material form (see Latour 1990). The material artifact itself in this respect is the least stable, as many of the more traditional ethnographic examples of architectural form discussed so far have demonstrated. It is the "immaterial" digital code that is most stable, circulates most widely, and stabilizes the various "material" and unstable iterations of form. But as Blanchette (2011) demonstrates, the relatively immaterial quality of the code is an artifact of the wider network of hardware, circuits, electrical infrastructure, and so on; its immateriality is an effect of this wider sphere of material "intra-actions" (Barad 2007). I would argue that its apparent transcendent, immaterial qualities are an effect of the sorts of productive dualisms that would render those two realms of experience separate and distinctive and the ontological and social work such a transcendent immaterial sphere of action serves to maintain. Thus, transcendental qualities are valorized at the expense of the material circumstances that would produce such transcendental effects and the political economies sustained therein.

It is precisely such networks whose constitutive effects are belied by the preoccupation with form per se that are very much in evidence in the ethnographic literature of migrant homes. With reference to examples presented here earlier, Hodder (1994) notes, how the socially constitutive registers of architectural forms change from experiential to referential; Prussin (1995) notes how in relation to migratory nomadic groups, it is the cumulative network of numerous iterations over a time-space that produces dwelling; and Gell (1998) remarked, how it is the totality of the iterations of the Maori meeting house that is the socially relevant scale, not its ethnographic snapshot outside of the "spacetimes" (Munn) of a given Maori lineage.

Horst (2008), in her ethnography of returning Jamaican migrants and their homes in Jamaica, as well as Dalakoglou (2010), in his account of Albanian migrants between Greece and Albania, show how dwelling is constituted within complex networks of transportation, roads, and travel—wider "spacetimes," to use Munn's term, in which dwelling takes place and the multiple and extended iterations in which homes emerge to facilitate dwelling. Along these networks, substances both sublime and prosaic, human reproductive capacities, building materials chosen to fit into cars that travel on roads (as in Dalakoglou's ethnography [2010]), remittances, and so on facilitate the wider "spacetime" (Munn) of architectural form. It is often the generic and interchangeable nature of architectural forms in their apparently banal and unremarkable material qualities that actually enable novel kinds of habitation. Wider social networks and horizontal ones exploit specific material registers that are often unremarkable from a perspective that privileges the dwelling as opposed to those nonarchitectural contents within that Empson describes (2007). Prussin (1995) describes how the contraction of wider female relations associated with certain nomadic forms are undone when urban building materials replace traditional ones, and women's networks and productive capacities are superseded by masculine ones within a more sedentary and monetized economy. Waterson (1997 [1990]) also describes how the replacement of concrete for wood can upset traditional hierarchies of power and prestige in Indonesia.

In another vein, Buchli (forthcoming) discusses how archaeologists at the Neolithic site of Çatalhöyük have shown that a shift from an elaboration of architectural form to elaborate ceramics indicates how different registers facilitate different forms of social life, from intensive (architectural) to extensive (ceramic). Architectural models (tectomorphs) can at once locate and house ancestors so that they become portable or, as in the case of the Carib hut, serve as ciphers to create wider forms of sociality, such as those evinced by the nineteenth-century Euro-American notion of the psychic unity of man. Different registers thus facilitate different forms of intensive or extensive forms of sociality. As "resting places" in the houses of the Batammaliba accommodate invisible ancestors presencing them with light, Dalakoglou describes empty houses in Albania activated by ringing phones dialed from Greece, indicating the future presence of family and descendants and the extended and reproduced households of Albanian migrants (2010: 761). Similarly, Krit (2013; see also forthcoming) describes the empty rooms of British migrants in Spain waiting for children and grandchildren who never come to visit as enabling at once the separation of generations and life projects that lifestyle migration entails, while maintaining the ideal of intergenerational continuity through empty rooms. Thus, various material registers facilitate technologies of presence in relation to architectural form in both extensive and intensive manners that a strict preoccupation with architectural form per se would obscure. Similarly, we have seen how homes can be regarded as merely disposable and interchangeable shells to facilitate the continuity of families over differing spatial and temporal scales, where mobile artifacts within these interchangeable architectonic shells facilitate the generative capacities of families and lineages. This process is described with heirlooms and jewelry by McKinnon (1995, 2000), Christmas ornaments by Parrott (2011), and the regulation of furniture by Chevalier (1999) in French contexts. Generic forms, rather than being inauthentic, actually help sustain the work of the house in other material registers as an interchangeable shell that enables the work of dwelling in other registers such as through partible and mobile artifacts. It is precisely the interchangeability of generic architectural forms, that sustain a particular flow and the maintenance of more mobile artifacts, that work "houselike" to produce kinship and moral personhood. This must be seen, as the examples here have demonstrated, as a hybrid context sustaining the necessary flows that constitute social life.

But as the home and the lifestyle projects associated with it are conceived as the terms by which alliances are forged within neoliberal forms of governance, when considering the contemporary issue of ecological sustainability and the ambiguous and contradictory penumbra of practices the notion of sustainability encompasses (Dickson 2011), then the scales of occupation, tenure, and migration associated with the home render it problematic at the wider scales required for sustainable development—the home at this scale of affairs appears to be not such an easy tool of governance (Dickson 2011).

3

As Lévi-Strauss notes in relation to the structure of the Bororo village, the illusory unity of the material forms that sustain social life are belied by the opposition of male and female and clan perspectives in relation to that unity (Lévi-Strauss 1963: 141–2). Similarly, this unity of opposites is elaborated upon in Bourdieu's discussion of the inversions of architectural space in relation to male and female habitus and the productive nature of that differential "misrecognition." Bourdieu (1977) describes how the relational oppositions that structure space within the house are, in fact, the same oppositions that are

> established between the house as a whole and the rest of the universe, that is, the male world, the place of assembly, the fields and the market. It follows that each of these two parts of the house (and, by the same token, each of the objects placed in it and each of the activities carried out in it) is in a sense qualified at two degrees, first as female (nocturnal, dark, etc.) insofar as it partakes of the universe of the house, and secondarily as male or female insofar as it belongs to one or the other divisions of that universe. (Bourdieu 1977: 90–1)

Thus, Bourdieu argues for the flexibility of these arrangements in relation to perspective and position, which inverts one in relation to the other, producing a different material register depending on the perspective of a man or a woman:

> But one or the other of the two systems of oppositions which define the house, either in its internal organization or in its relationship to the external world, is brought to the foreground, depending on whether the house is considered from the male point of view or the female point of view: whereas for the man, the house is not so much a place he enters as a place he comes out of, movement inwards properly befits the woman. (Bourdieu 1977: 91)

An almost magical transformation of registers occurs:

> Through the magic of a world of objects which is the product of the application of the same schemes to the most diverse domains, a world in which each thing speaks metaphorically of all the others, each practise comes to be invested with an objective meaning, a meaning with which practices—and particularly rites—have to reckon at all times, whether to evoke or revoke it [. . .] The mind is a metaphor of a world of objects which is itself but an endless circle of mutually reflecting metaphors. (Bourdieu 1977: 91)

Within the tightly rule-bound system of the dispositions of the habitus, there is a structured flexibility or movement between one principle or another, between a female register and a masculine one, that reconfigures registers in relation to one another and obviates tensions between them through these structured inversions, maintaining two principles of register in structured movement between them. Thus, one can consider how two registers can coexist without contradicting the other (albeit, in Bourdieu's schema, they are held in fluid, structured complementarity) and how one register can be converted from one to another, having "to reckon at all times, whether to evoke or revoke it" (Bourdieu 1977: 91).

These shifts in registers also involve shifts in materiality along anaphoric chains of association and with wider commitment to the mutual object of their entailments—a notion discussed in the introduction (Rouse 2002). Recalling this discussion in relation to Munn and Bataille, Bourdieu describes how agricultural cycles and seasonality and the "union" of sexual opposites that convert the qualities of one into the other are part of the wider productive resolution of opposites and opposite material qualities in relation to otherwise seemingly stable entities: "Marriage rites and ploughing rites owe their numerous similarities to the fact that their *objective intention* is to sanction the union of contraries which is the condition of the resurrection of the grain and the reproduction of the group" (Bourdieu 1977: 137–8). Thus, "Ploughing and sowing mark the culmination of the movement of the outside into the inside, the empty into the full, the dry into the wet, sunlight into earthly shadows, the fecundating male into the fertile female" (Bourdieu 1977: 137). These material qualities and their transformed material registers are summed up with Bourdieu's citation of Kabyle sayings such as "'Something dead out of something living'—an egg. 'Something living out of something dead'—a chick" (1977: 138). These sayings expose the slippages between anaphoric associations securing the overall commitment to the terms of material and social life.

4

At another level, the practices of iteration in relation to dwelling—the constant reiteration of previous occupations seen in the earlier examples discussed here in Tringham (2000), Borić (2002), and Hodder (1994) within intensive modes of habitation or the extensive modes that are facilitated by anaphoric slippages—suggest the importance of the palimpsest or trace in terms of the continuous iteration in direct form or anaphoric form toward the maintenance and transformation of social life. Povinelli's (2011) discussion of "endurance"—just as the repeated process of destruction, construction, destruction, and construction in Yiftachel's (2009) "gray spaces"—produces novel forms of subjectivity through their enduring reiterations. These reiterations exemplify the critical faculty of "endurance" identified by Povinelli, an endurance despite the powers that be, which, in effect, produces an excess at whose margins new and unexpected forms of social life can emerge. Yiftachel (2009) shows how the cumulative palimpsest over time of each destroyed Bedouin settlement requires a rebuilding, and the cumulative destruction and rebuilding produces a new identification and politics that is posterior and unanticipated in relation to these multiple buildings and rebuildings—an architecture and identification that is literally forged out of multiple and repeated destruction within this palimpsest of tracings. Similarly, the fragment, the souvenir, the ruin—in their promiscuous and open-ended manner—produce a reengagement with unexpected turns. Thus, in reference to earlier examples discussed here, the "remains" in the sin of Saul (Pietz 2002), the shrapnel found in Moshenska (2008), we can see how the pottery fragments encountered by Tringham's (2000) farmers require a retracing of the prehistoric past in the contemporary and recent past of villagers. Reiterations are therefore produced precisely because of the inherently destructive practices that produce them and the excessive margins they forge and, with them, the very terms by which habitable life is tentatively possible and enabled.

The object of destruction and its rearticulation is the common object of a conflicted commitment—an object that is produced and sustained within this conflicted commitment and its generative force (objectified, establishing a new set of relations toward its conflicted constituents and, with it, a new tentative identification that the objectified house produces, albeit illusory; a unity out of conflicted duality). And because of its conflicted nature, it is always subject to articulation, a "not this"/"not that" (following Povinelli 2011: 191), something that is anterior to ideology or identity but inherently productive of it, as Yiftachel (2009) has shown and as Povinelli aspires to inculcate, which always produces and enables and ensures different forms of habitation, however tentative or precarious. These conflicted commitments produce an excess that is at times considered to describe a recalcitrant materiality (e.g., Keane 2005; Pinney 2005; Sansi-Roca 2005); but this materiality is merely the effect of this conflicted investment and excess that is at the heart of its productive sociality and that exceeds any given material register. This harkens back to the notion at the heart of this book that built form is a fetish as conceived by Lévi-Strauss, an "illusory objectification" (Carsten and Hugh-Jones 1995) attempting to contain and extend the conflicted commitments that enable social life and that can then emerge from this productive misrecognition.

At the beginning we discussed the nineteenth-century project of the psychic unity of man, which attempted to account for the universality of human being and expand it. This project of expansion is continued in more recent critical theory in its efforts to expand the myriad forms of life that are emergent within an agonistic and ever-expanding universalism in the present, as suggested by Butler (2000) and the writings of Ernesto Laclau and Chantal Mouffe (see Smith 1998) in their radical democratic politics. Within this expansion of the terms by which human life is understood, anthropology has always played a central and constitutive role, and because architectural forms have always been integral to this life-constituting process, anthropology has always been attentive to the material processes by which the architectural process of life making has taken place. The numerous examples in this book in their respective registers and transformations hopefully attest (and the book itself) to the novel material forms and registers by which architecture makes people.

NOTES

Introduction

This book could not have been written without the help of a number of people. Chief among them have been my students, both undergraduate and graduate, here at University College London, whose conversations and work over the years have deeply inspired me. I am particularly indebted to Jan Geisbusch and his patient and good-humored help in assembling this manuscript, and especially grateful to Ian Buck at Bloomsbury for his exceptional care and patience, as well as the well-considered suggestions of anonymous reviewers; however, all inadequacies in the book are entirely my own.

1. I am indebted to Anna Hoare for demonstrating the usefulness of the "parallax" to describe the conflicted vested interests that converge on the "house."
2. See Hume's *Treatise on Human Nature* (1739–40) though note Rouse's critique of Hume and Humeans who assume the a priori nature of objects to be related rather than as phenomena produced within specific sustained intra-actions (Rouse 2002: 312–13).
3. I am very grateful to Anna Hoare for drawing my attention to the work of Locke and the metaphysical nature of substance.

BIBLIOGRAPHY

Ackroyd, G. (2011), "The 'Financialization' of the Home and the Institution of the Mortgage: Characterising Contemporary Home Ownership in the Irish Republic," paper delivered at the Centre for Studies of Home Post-Graduate Workshop, Geffrye Museum, London, November.

Adamson, G., and Pavitt, J. (eds) (2011), *Postmodernism: Style and Subversion, 1970–1990*, London: V&A Publishing.

Agamben, G. (1998), *Homo Sacer: Sovereign Power and Bare Life*, Palo Alto, CA: Stanford University Press.

Alder, K. (1998), "Making Things the Same: Representation, Tolerance and the End of the Ancien Regime in France," *Social Studies of Science*, 28/4: 499–545.

Althusser, L. (2006a), *Lenin and Philosophy and Other Essays*, Delhi: Aakar Books.

Althusser, L. (2006b), *Philosophy of the Encounter, Later Writings, 1978–87*, London: Verso.

Amerlinck, M.-J. (ed.) (2001), *Architectural Anthropology*, Westport, CT: Bergin and Garvey.

ap Stifin, P. (2012), "The Resonating Voice: Materialities of Testimony at Ground Zero," panel presentation on The Materiality of Sound, Cultural Studies Association General Meeting, University of California, San Diego, March.

Atkinson, P. (2006), "Do It Yourself: Democracy and Design," *Journal of Design History*, 19/1: 1–10.

Augé, M. (1995), *Non-Places: Introduction to an Anthropology of Supermodernity*, London: Verso Books.

Bachelard, G. (1964), *The Poetics of Space*, New York: Orion Press.

Bailey, D. (2005), "Beyond the Meaning of Neolithic Houses," in D. Bailey, A. Whittle, and V. Cummings (eds), (*Un*)*settling the Neolithic*, Oxford: Oxbow Press.

Barad, K. (2003), "Posthumanist Performativity: How Matter Comes to Matter," *Signs: Journal of Women in Culture and Society*, 28/3: 801–31.

Barad, K. (2007), *Meeting the Universe Halfway: Quantum Physics and the Entanglement of Matter and Meaning*, Durham, NC: Duke University Press.

Bataille, G. (1987 [1928]), *Story of the Eye*, San Francisco: City Lights.

Bataille, G. (1993), *The Accursed Share: An Essay on General Economy*, New York: Zone Books.

Bataille, G. et al. (1995), *Encyclopaedia Acephalica*, London: Atlas Press.

Baudrillard, J. (1996), *The System of Objects*, London: Verso.

Baudrillard, J. (2002), *The Spirit of Terrorism*, London: Verso.

Bauman, Z. (2000), *Liquid Modernity*, Cambridge: Polity.

Belk, R. (2001) *Collecting in a Consumer Society*, London: Routledge.

Bender, B. (1998), *Stonehenge: Making Space*, Oxford: Berg.

Benjamin, W. (1999), *The Arcades Project*, Cambridge, MA: Belknap Press.

Bennett, T. (1995), *The Birth of the Museum: History, Theory, Politics*, London: Routledge.

Binford, L. R. (1972), *An Archaeological Perspective*, New York: Seminar Press.

Binford, L. R. (1978a), "Dimensional Analysis of Behavior and Site Structure: Learning from an Eskimo Hunting Stand," *American Antiquity*, 43/3: 330–61.

Binford, L. R. (1978b), *Nunamiut Ethnoarchaeology*, New York: Academic Press.

Birdwell-Pheasant, D., and Lawrence-Zúñiga, D. (1999), *House Life: Space, Place and Family in Europe*, Oxford: Berg.

Blanchette, J.-F. (2011), "A Material History of Bits," *Journal of the American Society for Information Science and Technology*, 62/6: 1042–57.

Blier, S. (1987), *The Anatomy of Architecture: Ontology and Metaphor in Batammaliba Architectural Expression*, Cambridge: Cambridge University Press.

Blier, S. (2006), "Vernacular Architecture," in C. Tilley et al. (eds), *Handbook of Material Culture*, London: Sage.

Bloch, M. (1995a), "Questions Not to Ask of Malagasy Carvings," in I. Hodder et al. (eds), *Interpreting Archaeology: Finding Meaning in the Past*, London: Routledge.

Bloch, M. (1995b), "The Resurrection of the House amongst the Zafimaniry of Madagascar," in J. Carsten and S. Hugh-Jones (eds), *About the House: Lévi-Strauss and Beyond*, Cambridge: Cambridge University Press.

Borić, D. (2002), "'Deep Time' Metaphor: Mnemonic and Apotropaic Practices at Lepenski Vir," *Journal of Social Archaeology*, 3/1: 46–74.

Botticello, J. (2007), "Lagos in London: Finding the Space of Home," *Home Cultures*, 4/1: 7–24.

Boulnois, O. (2008), *Au-delà de l'image: une archéologie du visuel au Moyen-Âge V e–Xvi e siècle*, Paris: Editions de Seuil.

Bourdieu, P. (1977), *Outline of a Theory of Practice*, Cambridge: Cambridge University Press.

Bourdieu, P. (1984), *Distinction: A Social Critique of the Judgement of Taste*, London: Routledge and Kegan Paul.

Bourdieu, P. (1990), *The Logic of Practice*, Cambridge: Cambridge University Press.

Brandom, R. (1994), *Making It Explicit: Reasoning, Representing, and Discursive Commitment*, Cambridge, MA: Harvard University Press.

Brodsky Lacour, C. (1996), *Lines of Thought: Discourse, Architectonics and the Origins of Modern Philosophy*, Durham, NC: Duke University Press.

Brown, B. (2001), "Thing Theory," *Critical Inquiry*, 28/1: 1–22.

Buchli, V. (1999), *An Archaeology of Socialism*, Oxford: Berg.

Buchli, V. (2000), "Constructing Utopian Sexualities: The Archaeology and Architecture of the Early Soviet State," in R. Schmidt and B. Voss (eds), *Archaeologies of Sexuality*, London: Routledge.

Buchli, V. (2002), "Introduction," in V. Buchli (ed.), *The Material Culture Reader*, Oxford: Berg.

Buchli, V. (2004), "General Introduction," in V. Buchli (ed.), *Material Culture: Critical Concepts in the Social Science*, vol. 1, London: Routledge.

Buchli, V. (2006), "Astana: Materiality and the City," in C. Alexander, V. Buchli, and C. Humphrey (eds), *Urban Life in Post-Soviet Asia*, London: UCL Press.

Buchli, V. (2010a), "La Culture Matérielle, La Numérisation et Le Problème de L'Artefact," *Techniques et Culture*, 52: 212–31.

Buchli, V. (2010b), "Presencing the Im-Material," in M. Bille, F. Hastrup, and T. Flohr Sørensen (eds), *An Anthropology of Absence: Materializations of Transcendence and Loss*, New York: Springer.

Buchli, V. (2013), "Surface Engagements at Astana," in G. Adamson and V. Kelley (eds), *Surface Tensions: Surface, Finish and the Meaning of Objects*, Manchester: Manchester University Press.

Buchli, V. (forthcoming),"Material Register, Surface and Form at Çatalhöyük," in I. Hodder (ed.), *Religion and the Transformation of Neolithic Society: Vital Matters*, Cambridge: Cambridge University Press.

Buchli, V., and Lucas, G. (2000), "Children, Gender and the Material Culture of Domestic Abandonment in the Late 20th Century," in J. Sofaer-Derevenski (ed.), *Children and Material Culture*, London: Routledge.

Buchli, V., and Lucas, G. (2001), "The Archaeology of Alienation," in *Archaeologies of the Contemporary Past*, London: Routledge.

Buck-Morss, S. (2002), *Dream Worlds and Catastrophe: The Passing of Mass Utopia in East and West*, Cambridge, MA: MIT Press.

Butler, J. (1993), *Bodies That Matter: On the Discursive Limits of "Sex,"* New York: Routledge.

Butler, J. (2000), "Restaging the Universal: Hegemony and the Limits of Formalism," in J. Butler et al. (eds), *Contingency, Hegemony, Universality*, London: Verso.

Carpo, M. (2001), *Architecture in the Age of Printing: Orality, Writing, Typography in the History of Architectural Theory*, Cambridge, MA: MIT Press.

Carsten, J. (1995), "Houses in Langkawi: Stable Structures or Mobile Homes," in J. Carsten and S. Hugh-Jones (eds), *About the House: Lévi-Strauss and Beyond*, Cambridge: Cambridge University Press.

Carsten, J. (2004), *After Kinship*, Cambridge: Cambridge University Press.

Carsten, J., and Hugh-Jones, S. (eds) (1995), *About the House: Lévi-Strauss and Beyond*, Cambridge: Cambridge University Press.

Chapman, W. R. (1985), "Arranging Ethnology: A.H.L.F. Pitt Rivers and the Typological Tradition," in G. W. Stocking Jr. (ed.), *Objects and Others: Essay on Museums and Material Culture*, Madison: University of Wisconsin Press.

Chevalier, S. (1999), "The French Two-Home Project," in I. Cieraad (ed.), *At Home: An Anthropology of Domestic Space*, Syracuse, NY: Syracuse University Press.

Childe, V. G. (1950), "Cave Men's Buildings," *Antiquity*, 24: 4–11.

Cieraad, I. (ed.) (1999), *At Home: An Anthropology of Domestic Space*, Syracuse, NY: Syracuse University Press.

Classen, C., and Howes, D. (2006), "The Museum as Sensescape: Western Sensibilities and Indigenous Artifacts," in E. Edwards et al. (eds), *Sensible Objects: Colonialism, Museums and Material Culture*, Oxford: Berg.

Colloredo-Mansfeld, R. (2003), "Introduction: Matter Unbound," *Journal of Material Culture*, 8: 245–54.

Coole, D., and Frost, S. (eds) (2010), *New Materialisms: Ontology, Agency, and Politics*, Durham, NC: Duke University Press.

Coward, M. (2009), *Urbicide: The Politics of Urban Destruction*, London: Routledge.

Crary, J. (1992), *Techniques of the Observer: On Vision and Modernity in the Nineteenth Century*, Cambridge, MA: MIT Press.

Csikszentmihalyi, M., and Rochberg-Halton, E. (1981), *The Meaning of Things: Domestic Symbols and the Self*, Cambridge: Cambridge University Press.

Dalakoglou, D. (2010), "Migrating-Remitting-'Building'-Dwelling: House-Making as 'Proxy' Presence in Postsocialist Albania," *Journal of the Royal Anthropological Institute*, 16/4: 761–77.

Daniels, I. (2010), *The Japanese House: Material Culture and the Modern Home*, Oxford: Berg.

Daryll Forde, C. (1934), *Habitat, Economy and Society*, London: Methuen.

De Certeau, M. (1998), *The Practice of Everyday Life*, Minneapolis: University of Minnesota Press.

De Cesari, C. (2012), "Anticipatory Representation: Building the Palestinian Nation (-State) through Artistic Performance," *Studies in Ethnicity and Nationalism*, 12/1: 82–100.

Deetz, J. (1977), *In Small Things Forgotten: The Archaeology of Early American Life*, New York: Doubleday.

DeSilvey, C. (2006), "Observed Decay: Telling Stories with Mutable Things," *Journal of Material Culture*, 11/3: 318–38.

Dickson J., with Buchli, V. (2011), "Green Houses: Problem-Solving, Ontology and the House," in S. Lehman and R. Crocker (eds), *Designing for Zero Waste: Consumption Technologies and the Built Environment*, London: Routledge.

Dillon, S. (2007), *The Palimpsest*, London: Continuum.

Dolff-Bonekämper, G. (2002), "The Berlin Wall: An Archaeological Site in Progress," in J. Schofield, W. Gray Johnson, and C. M. Beck (eds), *Materiél Culture: The Archaeology of Twentieth Century Conflict*, London: Routledge.

Douglas, M. (1970a), *Natural Symbols: Explorations in Cosmology*, London: Barrie & Rockliff.

Douglas, M. (1970b), *Purity and Danger: An Analysis of the Concepts of Pollution and Taboo*, Harmondsworth: Penguin.

Douglas, M. (1991), "The Idea of a Home: A Kind of Space," *Social Research*, 58/1: 287–307.

Douny, L. (2007), "The Materiality of Domestic Waste: The Recycled Cosmology of the Dogon of Mali," *Journal of Material Culture*, 12/3: 309–31.

Drakulic, S. (1993), "Falling Down: A Mostar Bridge Elegy," *The New Republic*, December 13: 14–15.

Duyvendak, J.W. (2011), *The Politics of Home: Belonging and Nostalgia in Europe and the United States*, Basingstoke: Palgrave Macmillan.

Edensor, T. (2005a), *Industrial Ruins: Space, Aesthetics and Materiality*, Oxford: Berg.

Edensor, T. (2005b), "Waste Matter—The Debris of Industrial Ruins and the Disordering of the Material World," *Journal of Material Culture*, 10/3: 311–32.

Edwards, E., Gosden, C., and Phillips, R. (eds) (2006), *Sensible Objects: Colonialism, Museums and Material Culture*, Oxford: Berg.

Empson, R. (2007), "Separating and Containing People and Things in Mongolia," in A. Henare, M. Holbraad, and S. Wastell (eds), *Thinking Through Things: Theorising Artefacts Ethnographically*, London: Routledge.

Engels, F. (1940), *The Origin of the Family, Private Property and the State*, London: Camelot Press.

Engels, F. (1972), *The Origin of the Family, Private Property and the State*, New York: Pathfinder Press.

Epstein, D. (1973), *Brasília, Plan and Reality: A Study of Planned and Spontaneous Urban Development*, Berkeley: University of California Press.

Fernandez, J. (1977), *Fang Architectonics*, Working Papers in the Traditional Arts, no. 1, Ann Arbor: Institute for the Study of Human Issues, University of Michigan.

Fernandez, J. (1982), *Bwiti: An Ethnography of the Religious Imagination in Africa*, Princeton, NJ: Princeton University Press.

Fernandez, J. (1990), "The Body in Bwiti," *Journal of Religion in Africa*, XX/1: 92–111.

Forty, A. (1999), "Introduction," in A. Forty and S. Küchler (eds), *The Art of Forgetting*, Oxford: Berg.

Foucault, M. (1977), *Discipline and Punish: The Birth of the Prison*, London: Penguin.

Foucault, M. (1986), "Space, Knowledge, and Power," in P. Rabinow (ed.), *The Foucault Reader: An Introduction to Foucault's Thought*, London: Harmondsworth Press.

Foucault, M. (1991), "Governmentality," in G. Burchell, C. Gordon, and P. Miller (eds), *The Foucault Effect: Studies in Governmental Rationality*, Hemel Hempstead: Harvester Wheatsheaf.

Fox, L. (2005), "The Idea of Home in Law," *Home Cultures*, 2/1: 25–50.

Froud, D. (2004), "Thinking Beyond the Homely: *Countryside Properties* and the Shape of Time," *Home Cultures*, 3/1: 211–34.

Gamboni, D. (2007), *The Destruction of Art: Iconoclasm and Vandalism since the French Revolution*, London: Reaktion Books.

Garvey, P. (2001), "Organized Disorder," in D. Miller (ed.), *Home Possessions: Material Culture behind Closed Doors*, Oxford: Berg.

Gell, A. (1998), *Art and Agency: An Anthropological Theory*, Oxford: Clarendon Press.

Gibson, T. (1995), "Having Your House and Eating It: Houses and Siblings in Ara, South Sulawesi," in J. Carsten and S. Hugh-Jones (eds), *About the House: Lévi-Strauss and Beyond*, Cambridge: Cambridge University Press.

Giddens, A. (1991), *Modernity and Self-identity: Self and Society in the Late Modern Age*, Cambridge: Polity.

Gillespie, S.D. (2000), "Maya 'Nested Houses': The Ritual Construction of Place," in R.A. Joyce and S.D. Gillespie (eds), *Beyond Kinship: Social and Material Reproduction in House Societies*, Philadelphia: University of Pennsylvania Press.

Glassie, H.H. (1975), *Folk Housing in Middle Virginia: A Structural Analysis of Historical Artifacts*, Knoxville: University of Tennessee Press.

González-Ruibal, A. (2005), 'The Need for a Decaying Past: An Archaeology of Oblivion in Contemporary Galicia (NW Spain)," *Home Cultures*, 2/2: 129–52.

Goodfellow, A. (2008), "Pharmaceutical Intimacy: Sex, Death and Methamphetamine," *Home Cultures*, 5/3: 271–300.

Groys, B. (2008), *Art Power*, Cambridge, MA: MIT Press.

Gudeman, S., and Rivera, A. (1990), *Conversations in Colombia: The Domestic Economy in Life and Text*, Cambridge: Cambridge University Press.

Gullestad, M. (1984), *Kitchen-Table Society: A Case Study of Family and Friendships of Young Working-Class Mothers in Urban Norway*, Oslo: Universitetsforlaget.

Hacking, I. (1983), *Representing and Intervening: Introductory Topics in the Philosophy of Natural Science*, Cambridge: Cambridge University Press.

Harris, N. (1999), *Building Lives: Constructing Rites and Passages*, New Haven, CT: Yale University Press.

Harrison, R., and Schofield, J. (2010), *After Modernity: Archaeology Approaches to the Contemporary Past*, Oxford: Oxford University Press.

Hayden, D. (1981), *The Grand Domestic Revolution: A History of Feminist Designs for American Homes, Neighborhoods, and Cities*, Cambridge, MA: MIT Press.

Heidegger, M. (1993), "Building, Dwelling, Thinking," in D. F. Krell (ed.), *Basic Writings from "Being and Time" (1927) to "The Task of Thinking" (1964)*, London: Routledge.

Helliwell, C. (1992), *Good Walls Make Bad Neighbours: The Dayak Longhouse as a Community of Voices*, Oceania, 62/3: 179–93.

Helliwell, C. (1996), "Space and Sociality in a Dayak Longhouse," in M. Jackson (ed.), *Things as They Are: New Directions in Phenomenological Anthropology*, Bloomington: Indiana University Press.

Hermann, W. (1984), *Gottfried Semper: In Search of Architecture*, Cambridge, MA: MIT Press.

Heynen, H. (1999), *Architecture and Modernity: A Critique*, Cambridge, MA: MIT Press.

Hicks, D., and Horning, J. (2006) "Historical Archaeology and Buildings," in D. Hicks and M. Beudry (eds), *The Cambridge Companion to Historical Archaeology*, Cambridge: Cambridge University Press.

Hillier, B., and Hanson, J. (1984), *The Social Logic of Space*, Cambridge: Cambridge University Press.

Hillier, B., and Vaughan, L. (2007), "The City as One Thing," *Progress in Planning*, 67/3: 205–30.

Hodder, I. (1986), *Reading the Past: Current Approaches to Interpretation in Archaeology*, Cambridge: Cambridge University Press.

Hodder, I. (1994), "Architecture and Meaning: The Example of Neolithic Houses and Tombs," in M. Parker Pearson and C. Richards (eds), *Architecture and Order: Approaches to Social Space*, London: Routledge.

Holston, J. (1989), *The Modernist City: An Anthropological Critique of Brasília*, Chicago: University of Chicago Press.

Horst, H.A. (2008), "Landscaping Englishness: Respectability and Returnees in Mandeville, Jamaica," *Caribbean Review of Gender Studies*, 2/2: 1–18.

Howes, D. (ed.) (2004), *Empire of the Senses: The Sensual Culture Reader*, Oxford: Berg.

Humphrey, C. (1974), "Inside a Mongolian Tent," *New Society*, 31: 13–14.

Hvattum, M. (2004), *Gottfried Semper and the Problem of Historicism*, Cambridge: Cambridge University Press.

Ingold, T. (2007), "Materials against Materiality," *Archaeological Dialogues*, 14/1: 1–16.

Jacobs, J. M. (2004), "Too Many Houses for a Home: Narrating the House in the Chinese Diaspora," in S. Cairns (ed.), *Drifting: Architecture and Migrancy*, London: Routledge.

Jameson, F. (1984), "Postmodernism, or the Cultural Logic of Late Capitalism," *New Left Review*, 146: 53–92.

Janowski, M. (1995), "The Hearth-group, the Conjugal Couple and the Symbolism of the Rice Meal Among the Kelabit of Sarawak," in J. Carsten and S. Hugh-Jones (eds), *About the House: Lévi-Strauss and Beyond*, Cambridge: Cambridge University Press.

Johnson, M. (1993), *Housing Culture: Traditional Architecture in an English Landscape*, London: UCL Press.

Johnson, M. (1996), *An Archaeology of Capitalism*, Oxford: Blackwell.

Joyce, R. A., and Gillespie, S. D. (eds) (2000), *Beyond Kinship: Social and Material Reproduction in House Societies*, Philadelphia: University of Pennsylvania Press.

Keane, W. (2005), "Signs Are Not the Garb of Meaning: On the Social Analysis of Material Things," in D. Miller (ed.), *Materiality*, Durham NC: Duke University Press.

Kent, S. (1984), *Analyzing Activity Areas: An Ethnoarchaeological Study of the Use of Space*, Albuquerque: University of New Mexico Press.

Kent, S. (1990a), "A Cross-Cultural Study of Segmentation, Architecture and the Use of Space," in S. Kent (ed.), *Domestic Architecture and the Use of Space: An Interdisciplinary Cross-Cultural Study*, Cambridge: Cambridge University Press.

Kent, S. (ed.) (1990b), *Domestic Architecture and the Use of Space: An Interdisciplinary Cross-Cultural Study*, Cambridge: Cambridge University Press.

King, A. (1995), *The Bungalow: The Production of a Global Culture*, Oxford: Oxford University Press.

Kristeva, J. (1997), *The Portable Kristeva*, ed. K. Oliver, New York: Columbia University Press.

Krit, A. (2013), "Lifestyle Migration Architecture and Kinship in the Case of the British in Spain," unpublished PhD thesis, Department of Anthropology, University College London.

Krit, A. (forthcoming), "New Interpretation of Old Notions: Architecture, Property and Belonging in Lifestyle Migration," *Mobilities*.

Küchler, S. (1999), "The Place of Memory," in A. Forty and S. Küchler (eds), *The Art of Forgetting*, Oxford: Berg.

Küchler, S. (2002), *Malanggan: Art, Memory, and Sacrifice*, Oxford: Berg.

Laqueur, T. (1990), *Making Sex: Body and Gender from the Greeks to Freud*, Cambridge, MA: Harvard University Press.

Laszczkowski, M. (2011), "Building the Future: Construction, Temporality and Politics in Astana," *Focaal: Journal of Global and Historical Anthropology*, 60: 77–92.

Latour, B. (1990), "Visualisation and Cognition: Drawing Things Together," in S. Woolgar and M. Lynch (eds), *Representation in Scientific Practice*, Cambridge, MA: MIT Press.

Latour, B. (1999), *Pandora's Hope: Essays on the Reality of Science Studies*, Cambridge, MA: Harvard University Press.

Latour, B. (2005), "From Realpolitik to Dingpolitik," in B. Latour and P. Weibel (eds), *Making Things Public: Atmospheres of Democracy*, Cambridge, MA: MIT Press.

Latour, B., and Weibel, P. (eds) (2002), *Iconoclash: Beyond the Image Wars in Science, Religion and Art*, Karlsruhe: ZKM; Cambridge, MA: MIT Press.

Laugier, M. A. (1977), *An Essay on Architecture*, Los Angeles: Hennessy and Ingalls.

Lefebvre, H. (1991), *The Production of Space*, Oxford: Blackwell.

Leone, M. (1984), "Interpreting Ideology in Historical Archaeology: Using Rules of Perspective in the William Paca Garden in Annapolis, Maryland," in C. Tilley and D. Miller (eds), *Ideology, Power and Prehistory*, Cambridge: Cambridge University Press.

Lévi-Strauss, C. (1963), *Structural Anthropology*, New York: Basic Books.

Lévi-Strauss, C. (1982), *The Way of the Masks*, trans. S. Modelski, Seattle: University of Washington Press.

Lévi-Strauss, C. (1987), *Anthropology and Myth: Lectures, 1951–1982*, Hoboken, NJ: Wiley-Blackwell.

Locke, J. (1975), *Essay Concerning Human Understanding*, ed. P. H. Nidditch, Oxford: Clarendon Press.

Low, Setha (1997), "Urban Fear: Building the Fortress City," *City and Society*, 9/1: 53–71.

Low, Setha (2003), *Behind the Gates: Life, Security and the Pursuit of Happiness in Fortress America*, London: Routledge.

Low, S., and Lawrence-Zúñiga, D. (eds) (2003), *The Anthropology of Space and Place: Locating Culture*, Oxford: Blackwell.

Lucas, G. (2000), *Critical Approaches to Fieldwork: Contemporary and Historical Archaeological Practice,* London: Routledge.

Luzia, K. (2011), "Growing Home: Reordering the Domestic Geographies of 'Throwntogetherness'," *Home Cultures*, 8/3: 297–316.

Malinowski, B. (1961 [1922]), *Argonauts of the Western Pacific*, New York: E. P. Dutton.

Mallgrave, H.F. (1989), "Introduction," in G. Semper, *The Four Elements of Architecture*, Cambridge: Cambridge University Press.

Marchand, T. (2009), *The Masons of Djenné*, Bloomington: Indiana University Press.

Marcoux, J.-S. (2001a), "The 'Casser Maison' Ritual: Constructing the Self by Emptying the Home," *Journal of Material Culture*, 6/2: 213–35.

Marcoux, J.-S. (2001b), "The Refurbishment of Memory," in D. Miller (ed.), *Home Possessions: Material Culture behind Closed Doors*, Oxford: Berg.

Marcoux, J.-S. (2004), "Body Exchanges: Material Culture, Gender and Stereotypes in the Making," *Home Cultures*, 1/1: 51–59.

Marcuse, H. (1958), *Soviet Marxism*, New York: Columbia University Press.

Markus, T. (1993), *Buildings and Power: Freedom and Control in the Origin of Modern Building Types*, London: Routledge.

Marx, K. (1954), *The Eighteenth Brumaire of Louis Bonaparte* (3rd rev. ed.), Moscow: Progress; London: Lawrence & Wishart.

Marx, K. (1977), *Karl Marx: Selected Writings*, ed. D. McLellan, Oxford: Oxford University Press.

Marx, K. (1986), *An Introduction to Karl Marx*, ed. J. Elster, Cambridge: Cambridge University Press.

Maurer, B. (2006), "In the Matter of Marxism," in C. Tilley et al. (eds), *Handbook of Material Culture*, London: Sage.

Mauss, M. (1990), *The Gift*, London: Routledge.

Mauss, M. (2006), *Techniques, Technology and Civilisation*, ed. N. Schlanger, New York: Durkheim Press; Oxford: Berghahn Books.

McCracken, G. (1989), "Homeyness—A Cultural Account of One Constellation of Consumer Goods and Meanings," in E. Hirschman (ed.), *Interpretive Consumer Research*, Provo, UT: Association of Consumer Research.

McGuire, R. H. (1991), "Building Power in the Cultural Landscape of Broome County, New York, 1880–1940," in R. H. McGuire and R. Paynter (eds), *The Archaeology of Inequality*, Oxford: Blackwell.

McKinnon, S. (1995), "Houses and Hierarchy: A View from a South Moluccan Society," in J. Carsten and S. Hugh-Jones (eds), *About the House: Lévi-Strauss and Beyond*, Cambridge: Cambridge University Press.

McKinnon, S. (2000), "The Tanimbarese *Tavu*: The Ideology of Growth and the Material Configurations of Houses and Hierarchy in an Indonesian Society," in R. A. Joyce and S. D. Gillespie (eds), *Beyond Kinship: Social and Material Reproduction in House Societies*, Philadelphia: University of Pennsylvania Press.

Melhuish, C. (ed.) (1996), "Architecture and Anthropology," *Architectural Design* [special issue], 66/11–12.

Merry, S. E. (2001), "Spatial Governmentality and the New Urban Social Order: Controlling Gender Violence through Law," *American Anthropologist*, 103/1: 16–29.

Meskell, L. (ed.) (1998), *Archaeology under Fire: Nationalism, Politics and Heritage in the Eastern Mediterranean and Middle East*, London: Routledge.

Meskell, L. (2012), *The Nature of Heritage: The New South Africa*, Oxford: Wiley-Blackwell.

Miller, D. (1987), *Material Culture and Mass Consumption*, Oxford: Blackwell.

Miller, D. (1988), "Appropriating the State on the Council Estate," *Man* (New Series), 23/2: 353–72.

Miller, D. (ed.) (1993), *Unwrapping Christmas*, Oxford: Clarendon Press.

Miller, D. (ed.) (2005), *Materiality*, Durham, NC: Duke University Press.

Miller, D. et al. (eds) (1995), *Domination and Resistance*, London: Routledge.

Miller, M. (1956), *Archaeology in the USSR*, London: Atlantic Press.

Moore, H. (1986), *Space, Text and Gender: An Anthropological Study of the Marakwet of Kenya*, Cambridge: Cambridge University Press.

Morgan, L. H. (1965 [1881]), *Houses and House-Life of the American Aborigines*, Chicago: University of Chicago Press.

Morgan, L. H. (1978 [1877]), *Ancient Society*, New York: Labor Press.

Moshenska, G. (2008), "A Hard Rain: Children's Shrapnel Collections in the Second World War," *Journal of Material Culture*, 13/1: 107–25.

Munn, N. D. (1977), "The Spatiotemporal Transformations of Gawa Canoes," *Journal de la Société des océanistes*, 54–55/33: 39–53.

Munn, N. D. (1986), *The Fame of Gawa: A Symbolic Study of Value Transformation in a Massim Papua New Guinea Society*, Durham, NC: Duke University Press.

Murphy, M. (2006), *Sick Building Syndrome and the Problem of Uncertainty: Environmental Politics, Technoscience, and Women Workers*, Durham, NC: Duke University Press.

Myers, F. (2004), "Social Agency and the Cultural Value(s) of the Art Object," *Journal of Material Culture*, 9/2: 203–11.

Neich, R. (1996), *Painted Histories: Early Maori Figurative Painting*, Auckland: Auckland University Press.

Norberg-Schulz, C. (1971), *Existence, Space and Architecture*, London: Studio Vista.

Oliver, P. (ed.) (1997), *Encyclopedia of Vernacular Architecture of the World*, Cambridge: Cambridge University Press.

Ong, W. (1967), *The Presence of the Word*, New Haven, CT: Yale University Press.

Parker Pearson, M., and Richards, C. (eds) (1994), *Architecture and Order: Approaches to Social Space*, London: Routledge.

Parrott, F. R. (2005), " 'It's Not Forever': The Material Culture of Hope," *Journal of Material Culture*, 10/3: 245–62.

Parrott, F. R. (2010), "The Transformation of Photography, Memory, and the Domestic Interior," unpublished PhD thesis, University College London.

Parrott, F. R. (2011), "Death, Memory and Collecting: Creating the Conditions for Ancestralisation in South London Households," in S. Byrne et al. (eds), *Unpacking the Collection: Networks of Material and Social Agency in the Museum*, New York: Springer.

Pearce, S. (ed.) (1995), *Art in Museums*, London: Athlone Press.

Pelkmans, M. (2003), "The Social Life of Empty Buildings: Imagining the Transition in Post-Soviet Ajaria," *Focaal: Journal of Global and Historical Anthropology*, 41: 121–36.

Pietz, W. (1985), "The Problem of the Fetish, I," *Res*, 9: 5–17.

Pietz, W. (2002), "The Sin of Saul," in B. Latour and P. Weibel (eds), *Iconoclash: Beyond the Image Wars in Science, Religion and Art*, Karlsruhe: ZKM; Cambridge, MA: MIT Press.

Pinney, C. (2005), "Things Happen: Or, From Which Moment Does That Object Come?" in D. Miller (ed.), *Materiality*, Durham, NC: Duke University Press.

Pitt Rivers, A.L.F. (1867), "Primitive Warfare," *Journal of the Royal United Services Institute*, 612–43.

Pitt Rivers, A.L.F. (1875a), "On the Evolution of Culture," *Proceedings of the Royal Institute of Great Britain*, 7: 496–520.

Pitt Rivers, A.L.F. (1875b), "On the Principles of Classification," *Journal of the Anthropological Institute of Great Britain and Ireland*, 4: 293–308.

Povinelli, E.A. (2001), " 'Radical Worlds': The Anthropology of Incommensurability and Inconceivability," *Annual Review of Anthropology*, 30: 319–34.

Povinelli, E.A. (2011), *Economies of Abandonment: Social Belonging and Endurance in Late Liberalism*, Durham, NC: Duke University Press.

Powell, H. (2009), "Time, Television and the Decline of DIY," *Home Cultures*, 6/1: 89–108.

Preziosi, D. (1983), *Minoan Architectural Design: Formation and Signification*, Berlin: De Gruyter Mouton.

Prussin, L. (1995), *African Nomadic Architecture: Space, Place, and Gender*, Washington, DC: Smithsonian Institution Press.

Purbrick, L. (ed.) (2001), *The Great Exhibition of 1851: New Interdisciplinary Essays*, Manchester: Manchester University Press.

Rabinow, P. (1989), *French Modern: Norms and Forms of the Social Environment*, Chicago: University of Chicago Press.

Rapoport, A. (1969), *House, Form and Culture*, Englewood Cliffs, NJ: Prentice Hall.

Rivière, P. (1995), "Houses, Places and People: Community and Continuity in Guiana," in J. Carsten and S. Hugh-Jones (eds), *About the House: Lévi-Strauss and Beyond*, Cambridge: Cambridge University Press.

Rorty, R. (1970), "Incorrigibility as the Mark of the Mental," *Journal of Philosophy*, 67: 399–424.

Rorty, R. (1991), *Essays on Heidegger and Others*, Cambridge: Cambridge University Press.

Rosaldo, R. (1986), "From the Door of His Tent: The Fieldworker and the Inquisitor," in J. Clifford and G. Marcus (eds), *Writing Culture: The Poetics and Politics of Ethnography*, Berkeley: University of California Press.

Rose, N. (1990), *Governing the Soul: The Shaping of the Private Self*, London: Routledge.

Rose, N. (1996), *Inventing Ourselves: Psychology, Power and Personhood*, Cambridge: Cambridge University Press.

Rouse, J. (2002), *How Scientific Practices Matter: Reclaiming Philosophical Naturalism*, Chicago: University of Chicago Press.

Rowlands, M. (2005), "A Materialist Approach to Materiality," in D. Miller (ed.), *Materiality*, Durham, NC: Duke University Press.

Rykwert, J. (1981), *On Adam's House in Paradise: The Idea of the Primitive Hut in Architectural History*, Cambridge, MA: MIT Press.

Sadler, S. (1998), *The Situationist City*, Cambridge, MA: MIT Press.

Samson, R. (ed.) (1990), *The Social Archaeology of Houses*, Edinburgh: Edinburgh University Press.

Sansi-Roca, R. (2005), "The Hidden Life of Stones: Historicity, Materiality and the Value of Candomblé Objects in Bahia," *Journal of Material Culture*, 10/2: 139–56.

Sassen, S. (2006), *Territory, Authority, Rights: From Medieval to Global Assemblages*, Princeton, NJ: Princeton University Press.

Schnapp, A. (1996), *The Discovery of the Past: The Origins of Archaeology*, London: British Museum Press.

Semper, G. (1989), *The Four Elements of Architecture*, Cambridge: Cambridge University Press.

Service, E. R. (1962), *Primitive Social Organisation: An Evolutionary Perspective*, New York: Random House.

Shanks, M. (2004), "Three Rooms: Archaeology and Performance," *Journal of Social Archaeology*, 4/2: 147–80

Sidorov, D. (2000), "National Monumentalization and the Politics of Scale: The Resurrections of the Cathedral of Christ the Savior in Moscow," *Annals of the Association of American Geographers*, 90/3: 548–72.

Simon, J. (1988), "The Ideological Effects of Actuarial Practices," *Law and Society Review*, 22/4: 771–800.

Skeates, R., McDavid, C., and Carman, J. (eds) (2012), *The Oxford Handbook of Public Archaeology*, Oxford: Oxford University Press.

Smith, A.M. (1998), *Laclau and Mouffe: The Radical Democratic Imaginary*, London: Routledge.

Spencer-Wood, S. (2002), "Utopian Visions and Architectural Designs of Turn-of-the-Century Social Settlements," in A. Bingaman et al. (eds), *Embodied Utopias: Gender, Social Change and the Modern Metropolis*, London: Routledge.

Ssorin-Chaikov, N. (2003), *A Social Life of the State in Subarctic Siberia*, Palo Alto, CA: Stanford University Press.

Stafford, B.M. (1999), *Visual Analogy: Consciousness as the Art of Connecting*, Cambridge, MA: MIT Press.

Stocking, G.W. (1995), *After Tylor: British Social Anthropology, 1888–1951*, Madison: University of Wisconsin Press; London: Athlone Press.

Stocking, G.W. (1999), "The Spaces of Cultural Representation, circa 1887 and 1969: Reflections on Museum Arrangement and Anthropological Theory in the Boasian and Evolutionary Traditions," in P. Galison and E. Thompson (eds), *The Architecture of Science*, Cambridge, MA: MIT Press.

Strathern, M. (1990), "Artefacts of History: Events and the Interpretation of Images," in J. Siikala (ed.), *Culture and History in the Pacific, Transactions of the Finnish Anthropological Society*, no. 27, Helsinki: Finish Anthropological Society.

Strathern, M. (1996), "Cutting the Network," *JRAI*, 2/3: 517–35.

Strathern, M. (1999), *Property, Substance and Effect: Anthropological Essays on Persons and Things*, London: Athlone Press.

Sulzberger, A.G. (2011), "A Lone Oklahoma Tower's Clear but Uncomfortable Links to 9/11," *New York Times*, August 27.

Talle, A. (1993), "Transforming Women into 'Pure' Agnates: Aspects of Female Infibulation in Somalia," in V. Broch-Due, I. Rudie, and T. Bleie (eds), *Carved Flesh/Cast Selves: Gendered Symbols and Social Practices*, Oxford: Berg.

Thomas, N. (1991), *Entangled Objects: Exchange, Material Culture and Colonialism in the Pacific*, Cambridge, MA: Harvard University Press.

Thomas, N. (1997), *In Oceania: Visions, Artifacts, Histories*, Durham, NC: Duke University Press.

Thrift, N. (2005), "Beyond Mediation: Three New Material Registers and Their Consequences," in D. Miller (ed.), *Materiality*, Durham, NC: Duke University Press.

Tilley, C. et al. (eds) (2006), *Handbook of Material Culture*, London: Sage.

Toren, C. (1999), *Mind, Materiality and History: Explorations in Fijian Ethnography*, London: Routledge.

Traugott, M. (2010), *The Insurgent Barricade*, Berkeley: University of California Press.

Trigger, B. (1989), *A History of Archaeological Thought*, Cambridge: Cambridge University Press.

Tringham, R. (2000), "The Continuous House: A View from the Deep Past," in R. A. Joyce and S. D. Gillespie (eds), *Beyond Kinship: Social and Material Reproduction in House Societies*, Philadelphia: University of Pennsylvania Press.

Van der Hoorn, M. (2005), *Indispensable Eyesores: An Anthropology of Undesired Buildings*, Utrecht: Universiteit Utrecht.

Van der Hoorn, M. (2009), *Indispensable Eyesores: An Anthropology of Undesired Buildings*, New York: Berghahn Books.

Vellinga, M. (2009), "Going beyond the Mud Hut and Noble Vernacular: The Need for Tradition in Sustainable Development," *Space Magazine*, 493.

Venturi, R., Scott Brown, D., and Izenour, S. (2000), *Learning from Las Vegas: The Forgotten Symbolism of Architectural Form*, Cambridge, MA: MIT Press.

Vitruvius (1914), *The Ten Books on Architecture*, Cambridge, MA: Harvard University Press.

Vidler, A. (2000), "Diagrams of Diagrams: Architectural Abstraction and Modern Representation," *Representations*, 72 (Autumn): 1–20.

Vilaça, A. (2005), "Chronically Unstable Bodies: Reflections on Amazonian Corporalities," *Journal of the Royal Anthropological Institute*, 11: 445–64

Viveiros De Castro, E. (1998), "Cosmological Deixis and Amerindian Perspectivism," *Journal of the Royal Anthropological Institute*, 4: 469–88

Vogt, A. (1998), *Le Corbusier, the Noble Savage: Toward an Archaeology of Modernism*, Cambridge, MA: MIT Press.

Vuyosevich, R. D. (1991), "Semper and Two American Glass Houses," *Reflections*, 8: 4–11.

Warnier, J.-P. (2007), *The Pot-King: The Body and Technologies of Power*, Leiden: Koninklijke Brill NV.

Waterson, R. (1997 [1990]), *The Living House: An Anthropology of Architecture in South-East Asia*, London: Thames and Hudson.

Werrett, S. (1999), "Potemkin and the Panopticon: Samuel Bentham and the Architecture of Absolutism in Eighteenth-Century Russia," *UCL Bentham Project Journal of Bentham Studies*, 2: 1–25.

Whitehead, A. N. (1978), *Process and Reality*, New York: Free Press.

Whitehead, A. N. (2000), *Concept of Nature*, Cambridge: Cambridge University Press.

Yalouri, E. (2001), *The Acropolis: Global Fame, Local Claim*, Oxford: Berg.

Yampolsky, M. (1995), "In the Shadow of Monuments: Notes on Iconoclasm and Time," in N. Condee (ed.), *Soviet Hieroglyphics: Visual Culture in Late Twentieth-Century Russia*, Bloomington: Indiana University Press.

Yaneva, A. (2012), *Mapping Controversies in Architecture*, Farnham: Ashgate.

Yiftachel, O. (2009), "Critical Theory and Gray Space: Mobilization of the Colonized," *City*, 13/2–3: 240–56.

Young, D. (2004), "The Material Value of Colour: The Estate Agent's Tale," *Home Cultures*, 1/1: 5–22.

Žižek, S. (2006), *The Parallax View*, Cambridge, MA: MIT Press.

INDEX

abandoned farmhouses, 160*f,* 165*f*
"accidental surrealism," 163
the Acropolis, 68, 69*f,* 108
actuarial regulation/practices, 4, 107–8, 115
agnatic relations, 84–6
Albanian migrants, 181
Althusser, Louis, 14, 15–16
American Indians, 33
anaphoric chains, 14–17, 84, 88, 184–5
ancestors and house form, 83–4, 151–2
ancestralization process, 152–4
Ancient Society (Morgan), 32, 33, 44
The Andaman Islanders (Radcliffe-Brown), 39
Anglo-American anthropology, 39–42
animacy, 144, 157, 167, 170
anthropological archaeology, 47–8
anthropology
    artifacts in, 29–30
    material culture studies, 11
    sensory capacities and, 112
    of space, 40, 152–5
    see also social anthropology
anthropomorphism
    of architectural form, 4, 150–1
    of built form, 147, 157
    of household objects, 143
    in Renaissance form, 137
    in *tavu* house posts, 83
Arab decorative elements, 95
archaeology
    anthropological archaeology, 47–8
    architectural thinking with, 35
    artifacts in, 29–30
    ethno-archaeology, 2–3, 47, 51
    materiality of built form, 47–8, 66–7

material registers and, 70
New Archaeology, 47, 51–2
see also architecture and archaeology;
    artifacts; ruins
architectonic objects, 101–2, 180–1
architectural forms
    of American Indians, 33
    anthropomorphism of, 4, 150–1
    the body and, 139, 141
    British colonial administration and, 42–4
    consumption studies and, 120
    diachronic time in, 65
    digitized globalization impact on, 111–13
    house form, 37–9, 179
    human forms of habitation, 44–5
    institutional context in, 106–7
    linguistics and, 54–6, 58
    materiality of, 111
    metaphor in, 120
    ornament in, 26, 132, 154, 183
    of paper, 180–1, 180*f*
    phenomenological approaches of, 61
    poststructuralism and, 62–7
    textile partitioning of, 25
    understanding of, 29
    unilineal evolutionism and, 48
    see also built forms; embodiment and
        architectural form; house forms
architectural forms, iconoclasm, decay and
    destruction
    animacy and, 157
    loss of life with, 170
    materiality of built forms, 166–72
    reconstruction and preservation, 172–8
    role in social life, 157–8

architectural forms, iconoclasm, decay and
    destruction (*continued*)
  ruins and, 158–66, 160*f*, 162*f*, 165*f*
  World Trade Center destruction, 157, 168,
    170–1, 171*f*, 177
architecture and archaeology
  anthropological archaeology, 47–8
  binary unity of, 53
  built forms and, 28, 67–70
  linguistics and, 54–6
  material registers, 70
  medieval architectural forms, 56–8
  poststructuralist approaches to, 58–62, 67
  prehistory discipline, 48–50
Argonauts of the Western Pacific (Malinowski), 39
Art and Agency (Gell), 8, 65
artifacts
  degrading of, 161
  effect and materiality, 115–16
  of the eighteenth century, 35
  influence of, 29–30
  material-discursive phenomena and, 113
  as mobile, 182–3
  weaponry, 31*f*
artifactual effect, 115–16
Astana, Kazakhstan, 99–100, 101*f*
Austrian National Library, 108–9
Autonomous Soviet Socialist Republic
    of Ajaria, 164
Avebury monument, 68
Aztecs, 33

Bailey, Douglass, 66
Barad, Karen, 6, 11, 112–14, 116
barbarism periods, 33
Bastian, Adolph, 30–1
Bataille, Georges, 16–17, 88, 184
Batammaliba architectural forms, 150–2, 182
Battle of the Beanfield (1985), 68
Baudrillard, Jean, 125, 143–4
Beaulieu Park estates, 104
Bedouin settlements, destruction, 177,
    178, 185
Bender, Barbara, 67, 69, 108
Benjamin, Walter, 34, 35, 92, 120, 144
Bentham, Jeremy, 3, 92

Berlin Wall, 5, 159, 168, 173–6, 175*f*
Beyond Kinship (Joyce, Gillespie), 79
Binford, Lewis, 51
Birdwell-Pheasant, Donna, 1
Black Forest hut, 142
Blier, Suzanne, 1, 150–2
Bloch, Maurice, 77, 103
Boas, Franz, 39
Boasian tradition, 37
the body
  architectural form and, 139, 141
  built form and, 27, 58, 73, 137, 139, 167
  health and, 121
  in house form, 73, 143
  inherent ambiguity between, 3, 4
  material registers and, 105
  nomadic dwellings, 149
  ruins and, 163
  space and, 58, 80, 145
  technology of power over, 94
Boltanksi, Christian, 172
Bonaventure Hotel, 96–8, 97*f*, 163
Boric, Dušan, 62–3, 185
Botticello, Julie, 135
Bourdieu, Pierre, 4–7, 37–8, 58, 72, 184
Brandom, R., 14–15
Brasília, Brazil, 99, 100*f*
Brazilian architectural forms, 98–9
British colonial administration, 42–4
British industrial ruins, 162–3, 162*f*
British social anthropology, 42, 50, 73
Brown, Scott, 96
Buchli, Victor, 86, 182
Buck-Morss, Susan, 66, 166
building materials, 1, 6, 63–4, 182
built environment
  challenges in, 96
  consumption studies and, 4
  man and nature in, 43
  origin myths and, 76
  past, present and future uses, 53
  physical attributes of, 149
  psychic unity of (man) mankind, 67
  social relations and, 103
built forms
  animacy of, 167

anthropomorphism of, 147, 157
architecture and, 28, 67–70
the body and, 27, 58, 73, 137, 139, 167
embodied nature of, 61, 80
gendered roles and, 7
house form and, 55–6, 72
maintenance/regulation of, 26, 88
Neolithic and, 3
psychic unity of man, 66
social life and, 19
Western examples of, 4
see also materiality of built forms
Burned House Horizon, 64
Butler, Judith, 67
Bwiti ritual space, 147

cabinets of curiosities, 29, 31
camera obscura, 4, 139, 140*f*
Candomblé stones, 10, 13
canoes, material qualities of, 16
Carib hut, 24*f,* 25, 31, 182
Carpo, M., 22
Carsten, Janet, 3, 7, 58, 73–4, 77, 137
Cartesianism, 4, 21–3, 43, 139, 140
casser maison ritual, 153
Çatalhöyük site, 182
Cathedral of Christ the Savior (Moscow), 172, 174*f*
chest furniture, 83–6
Childe, Gordon, 42, 50
China, 130
Chomsky, Noam, 55–6
Christian Ecumene, 140
Christianity, 68, 152
Christian Venetian forces, 69
citationality in poststructuralism, 62–3
clay as material, 63–4
cobblestones as barricades, 90–2, 91*f*
Collège de France, 34
Colloredo-Mansfield, Rudi, 135
Columbian household economies, 134
comfort notion, 19, 79, 104–5
communism, 33–4, 41, 117, 166, 172–3
computer-aided design (CAD) program, 180–1
concrete as building materials, 1, 14, 108, 110, 167

consumption studies
anthropological studies and, 154
built environment and, 4
detachability concept, 124, 130–1
home and, 117–20
interior spaces, materiality, 129–30
Japanese modern house, 132–4, 133*f*
as ongoing concern, 135–6
waste products in Marakwet society, 122–3
Crary, J., 139
Crystal Palace
architectural forms and, 25, 26*f,* 27–30
industrial form of, 89–90
modern consumerism understanding, 3
psychic unity of mankind, 30–1
Csikszentmihalyi, M., 35, 119, 120

Dalakoglou, D., 182
Daniels, Inge, 132, 133*f*
da Vinci, Leonardo, 137, 138*f*
Dayak longhouse, 78
de Castro, Viveiros, 11
De Certeau, M., 94
Deetz, James, 42, 54–5
DeSilvey, C., 159–62
detachability concept, 124, 128–32
diachronic time, 41, 48, 65–6, 79
digitized globalization, 111–13
Dillon, Sarah, 62
Ding as "thing," 17, 31
dirt concept, 121, 126–8
Distinction (Bourdieu), 146
disurbanist forms, 50
Dogon of Mali, 126–7
do-it-yourself (DIY) culture, 121, 135
Dolff-Bonekämper, G., 173–6
domestic space *see* space
Douglas, Mary, 4, 17, 118, 137
Douny, Laurence, 126–7
Druids, 68
Duyvendak, J. W., 131
dwellings
importance of, 43, 74, 150
institutions and, 179
Lake Zurich dwellings, 35, 36*f*
of Neolithic period, 43–4

dwellings (*continued*)
  nomadic dwellings, 148–50, 181–2
  of Paleolithic period, 49
  perpetual problems, 4–5, 45, 141–2
  wattle-and-daub houses, 64
  wood hut, 19, 20*f*
  Ye'cuana dwellings, 76–7, 167
  see also house forms

East German state (GDR), 172, 173
Ecochard, Michel, 96
Edensor, Tim, 162–3
Efimenko, Petr Petrovich, 49
egalitarianism, 50, 118, 121
Egenter, Nold, 28
The Eighteenth Brumaire of Louis Bonaparte (Marx), 90
embodiment and architectural form
  ancestralization, 152–4
  anthropology of space, 152–5
  anthropomorphism, 150–2
  disembodiment and, 147
  habitus notion and, 145–7
  nomadic dwellings, 148–50, 181–2
  phenomenological approaches, 140–4
  relationship between, 137–40
Empson, R., 84, 86
Engels, Friedrich, 32–3, 90, 117–19
English Land Law, 132
Enlightenment era, 23, 139
Eskimos, 21
ethno-archaeology, 2–3, 47, 51
Euro-American society, 7
evolutionism, 30, 41, 48, 50–1
extrasomatic collective form, 51, 71

feminism, 4, 105, 117, 137
Fernandez, James, 147
fertility, 81, 123
fetishization notion
  of generic forms, 59–60
  house form as, 38, 72
  in material culture phenomenon, 14
  misrecognition of, 7–8
  production of, 17
field tent, 40*f*

First World War, 38
Folk Housing in Middle Virginia (Glassie), 55
Forty, Adrian, 172–3
fossilizations of lifeways, 35, 120
fossil metaphor, 2, 50–1, 62, 70
Foucault, Michael, 3–4, 59, 92, 94
Frauenkirche (Dresden), 172
Froud, Daisy, 104, 131
furniture/furnishings
  accumulation of, 133, 135
  chest furniture, 83–6
  from clay, 64
  from cobblestones, 92
  diversity of choice in, 44
  Mongolian connection to, 84–5
  movement of, 124–5, 153–4
  postwar designs, 143
  soft furnishings, 106

Gabra nomads, 150
Garvey, Pauline, 124–5
gated communities, 102–4, 103*f*
Gawa people, 16, 164
Gell, Alfred
  architectural forms and, 5, 65
  destruction of buildings, 170–1
  detachment and, 125, 130
  Maori meeting house, 6, 8, 157, 167
  small-scale material changes, 60
  vandalism of paintings, 168
generic forms, 59–60, 131–2, 183
Giddens, Anthony, 58, 135
Gillespie, Susan, 79–81
Glassie, Henry, 42, 54–6, 73
González-Ruibal, A., 164
Goodfellow, A., 87
Great Exhibition, 29, 32
Great Notley Garden Village, 104
Greek philosophy, 11
Groys, Boris, 41
Grum, Anders, 148
Gudeman, S., 134

habitus notion, 6, 145–7
Hall, Edward T., 42, 51
Hanson, J., 53–4

Harris, N., 168
Heidegger, Martin
    dwelling importance, 42–3, 74, 150
    habitus notion and, 145
    housing shortage, 143
    problem of dwelling, 4–5, 45, 141–2
Helliwell, C., 78–9
Hillier, B., 53–4
Hispaniola (Haiti), 21
Hodder, Ian, 56–7, 70, 181, 185
the Holocaust, 170, 172
Holston, James, 98–9
Horst, H. A., 181
house forms
    ancestors and, 83–4, 151–2
    as an illusory objectification, 72
    anthropomorphism and, 150–2
    architectural forms, 37–9, 179
    the body and, 73, 143
    built forms and, 55–6, 72
    consumption studies and, 117–20
    as fetishization notion, 38, 72
    habitus notion and, 145–7
    house societies and, 38–9
    institutions and, 7, 38, 71–4, 84
    Japanese modern, 132–3
    lateral continuity of, 75
    Maori meeting house, 6, 8, 9f,
        157, 167
    material registers of, 78–88
    Mongolian connection to, 84–5
    primitive and pre-industrial, 43
    primitive hut, 24f
    selfhood in, 125
    universality of, 44–5
    see also dwellings
"house-power," 122–3
Houses and House-Life of the American Aborigines
    (Morgan), 44, 117, 141
house societies see Lévi-Strauss, Claude, house
    societies
Hugh-Jones, Stephen, 3, 7, 58, 73–4, 77, 137
human evolution theory, 32
Human Relations Area Files, 52–3
human reproductive processes, 74
Humphrey, Caroline, 73

Hvattum, M., 23–4, 26–7
hygiene concept, 4, 118, 121, 126–7

iconoclasms, 168, 172, 177
Ignatius of Loyola, 140
illusory objectification, 5, 6, 142,
    179, 183
imbrication
    analysis of, 87
    anthropology and, 12
    architectural forms and, 108
    built forms and, 4, 27
    defined, 114
    of technologies, 112
immobility, 3, 80–1, 88, 124
industrialization, 32, 34, 118–19
Industrial Revolution, 29, 30
Ingold, Tim, 6
institutions
    anthropologies and, 5
    architectural forms and, 107–10
    clothing, as expression of, 106
    community and, 3, 16–17, 89–90, 94
    context in architectural forms, 106–7
    dwellings and, 179
    home decoration and, 105
    house form and, 7, 38, 71–4, 84
    as illusory, 72
    maintenance of, 96
    material conditions of, 114–15, 117
    personal objectives and, 107
    prison structure, 92–4
    "totalitarian institutions," 145–6
    understanding of, 3
interior spaces, materiality, 129–30
International Association for the Study of
    Traditional Environments, 1
intra-action notion, 113–15
Iroquois longhouse, 33, 33f, 50

Jacobs, Jane, 131
Jameson, Fredric, 96, 149–50, 163–4
Japanese modern house, 132–3, 133f
Johnson, Matthew, 56
Joint Tenement house, 32
Joyce, R. A., 79

Kabyle house, 6, 146
Kazakhstani nation state, 86
Kazakh yurt, 86
Kent, Susan, 44, 52–3
Klemm, Gustav, 27
Kristeva, Julia, 160
Krit, A., 182
Küchler, S., 158–9
kula, shell body decorations, 16, 128–9

l'abjection, defined, 160
Laclau, Ernesto, 186
Lake Zurich dwellings, 36–7, 36*f*
land law, 132
Laszczkowski, M., 100
Laugier, Abbé, 2, 21, 23, 25, 32
Lawrence-Zúñiga, Denise, 1
Lefebvre, H., 94, 98
Leone, Mark, 54, 59–60
Lévi-Strauss, Claude, house societies
    cultural logic of, 55
    emergence of theories, 34
    fetishization notion and, 5, 8, 14, 17
    house form and, 38–9
    illusory objectification of, 5, 6, 142,
        179, 183
    regulation and, 99
    social anthropology, 71–4
    structuralism of, 73
lieu de discorde (site of dispute), 174
linguistics
    analogies of, 47, 77
    analyses of, 60, 120
    archaeological theory and, 54
    architectural form and, 54–6, 58
    linguistic turn, 2, 42
    space impact on, 89
Locke, J., 11, 13
Low, Setha, 1, 102–3, 106

Malagasy house, 83, 103, 167
malanggan funeral monuments, 158–9, 161
Malay Langkawi houses, 74
Malinowski, B., 39–40
Malinowskian tradition, 37

Maori meeting house, 6, 8, 9*f,* 157, 167
Marakwet communities, 121–3
Marchand, Trevor, 1
Marcoux, Jean-Sébastien, 124–5, 152–3
Marr, Nicholai, 41
Marx, Karl, 32, 90, 117–19
Marxian legacy (Marxists), 10–11, 32, 37, 117
mass-industrialized housing, 1
material culture studies, 14, 42, 52, 149
material-discursive phenomena, 113
materiality of built forms
    archaeology and, 47–8, 66–7
    architectural forms and, 166–72
    artifactual effect and, 115–16
    attention to specifics of, 95
    British industrial buildings, 162, 162*f*
    concepts of movement, 79–80
    consumerist appropriation and, 119–20
    consumption-oriented traditions, 154
    decay of, 160, 163
    defined, 8–9, 17
    destruction of, 166–72
    healing power of, 104, 105–6
    illusory unity of, 183
    interior spaces, 129–30
    in Malay Langkawi houses, 74
    material registers of, 1–2, 186
    modalities of, 16
    nomadic dwellings, 149
    problematic role of, 96
    security and, 106–7
    sensorial effects of, 79
    social form and, 32–3, 179
    space and, 102
    understanding of, 6, 29, 63
    in urban environment, 101
    whiteness and, 129–30
    see also built forms
material registers
    agnatic relations in, 84–6
    anaphoric chains and, 14–17, 84, 88,
        184–5
    archaeological preoccupation of, 70
    the body and, 105
    as diverse, 15–16

generic forms and, 59–60, 131–2, 183

of house form, 78–88

overview, 1–2

social effects of, 86–7, 182

transformation of, 184

Mauss, Marcel, 4, 37–8, 118, 143, 166

Mayan nested houses, 79–82

McCracken, Grant, 125, 127, 128

McFadyen, Lesley, 10

McGuire, R. H., 101

McKinnon, S., 82–3

medieval architectural forms, 56–8

Melhuish, Claire, 1

Merry, S. E., 106–7

middling modernism, 95

Miller, Daniel, 119

modernist ideals, 2, 164

Mongolian yurt, 84

Mongol interior space, 73, 84–5

monumental forms of tells, 64–5

Moore, Henrietta, 121–2

Moore, Henry, 56

moral personhood, 71

Morgan, Lewis Henry

"anthropology of space," 40

artifacts and, 37

embodiment and architectural form, 141

house form and, 44

material culture studies, 32

practice of communism, 33–4

savagery and matriarchy, 49

unilineal evolutionism, 34, 48

Moroccan building forms, 95–6

Moshenska, Gabriel, 65

Mouffe, Chantal, 186

mud as building materials, 1

Munn, Nancy, 16–17, 88, 184

Murphy, Michelle, 104

Muslim Malays, 78

Mutterrecht ("mother right") principle, 33

National Gallery (London), 168

Nazi bunkers, 108–9

neocolonial decorative motifs, 102

Neolithic period

built forms of, 3

dwellings of, 44

houses in, 57–8, 66, 167

palimpsests and, 62–3

social life, 182

nested houses phenomenon, 79–82

New Archaeology, 2, 47, 52

nineteenth-century European architectural
forms, 19–27, 27–30

noble savage, 23

nomadic dwellings, 148–50, 181–2

non-Catholic ritual practices, 10

Nora, Pierre, 175

Oliver, Paul, 1

On Adam's House in Paradise (Rykwert), 28

*The Origin of the Family, Private Property and the
State* (Engels), 117

ornament in architectural forms, 25, 133,
154, 183

Ottoman forces, 68

Outline of a Theory of Practice (Bourdieu),
145

Paleolithic period, 42, 48–9, 49f

palimpsests, 3, 62–4, 70, 185

Pankhurst, Emmeline, 169

panopticon structure, 92–4, 106, 107, 115

paper and architectural forms, 180–1, 180f

Paris arcade, 93f

Paris barricades, 90–2, 91f

Parrot, Fiona, 105–6, 130, 134, 154

the Parthenon, 70, 115

patrilocal communities, 121–3

Pearson, Mike Parker, 1

Pelkmans, Mathijs, 164–5, 166

phenomenological approaches to architectural
forms, 61, 140–4

"philosophy of progress," 30

phonetic alphabet, invention, 33

Pietz, William, 7, 14

Pitt Rivers, A.L.F.

"anthropology of space," 40

artifacts, 29–31

material culture, 42, 62

Pitt Rivers, A.L.F. (*continued*)
  primitive warfare illustration, 15
  weaponry, 31*f*
Portman, John, 96
postmodern spaces, 98–100
poststructuralism, 10, 58–63, 62, 67
postwar period architectural forms, 42
postwar Soviet interiors, 126*f*
prehistory discipline, 48–50, 57, 66
preservation of architectural forms,
      172–8
prewar forms, 143
Preziosi, D., 54
primitive hut, 22*f*
prison structure, 92–4
processualism, 51
Prussin, Labelle, 148–50, 181–2
psychic unity of (man) mankind, 2, 30–3,
      36, 67

queer scholarship, 127

Rabah, Khalil, 176
Rabih Hage Gallery (London), 180, 180*f*
Rabinow, Paul, 95–6
radicalism, 29, 40
Rapoport, Amos, 42–4, 52
Reclus, Élie, 41
reconstruction of architectural forms, 172–8
Reformation movement, 140
Richards, Colin, 1
Richardson, Mary, 168–9
rituals
  architecture and, 27, 57
  Bwiti ritual space, 147
  casser maison ritual, 153
  communal rituals, 85
  decorations as, 154
  of divestment, 15
  household rituals, 83
  of infibulation, 149
  of initiation, 151
  monuments as, 158
  non-Catholic ritual practices, 10
  objects in, 61

Rivera, A., 134
Rivière, P., 65, 76
Rochberg-Halton, E., 35, 120
Rokeby Venus destruction, 168–9
romanticism, 69, 158, 163
romantic ruins, 163
Rorty, R., 12
Rose, Nikolas, 88, 135
Rouse, Joseph, 12–13
Rowlands, M., 152
ruins
  abandoned farmhouses, 160*f*, 165*f*
  as architectural forms, 158–66, 160*f*,
      162*f*, 165*f*
  British industrial ruins, 162–3, 162*f*
  modern context of, 164
  political aesthetics of, 5
  romantic ruins, 163
  Soviet Union ruins, 16, 164–6
Russian Orthodox Church, 173
Russian Revolution, 50
Rykwert, Joseph, 21, 28, 43

Samson, Ross, 1, 47
Sassen, Saskia, 110–13
savagery, 33, 49
Science Museum (London), 32
Second World War, 65, 108, 118, 144, 176
sedentism, 3
sedentization and body/building forms,
      149
selfhood in house form, 126
Semper, Gottfried
  architectural forms and, 23–7, 24*f*
  the Crystal palace and, 27–30
  generic forms, 131
  psychic unity of man, 32
sensoria
  cosmopolitan sensoria, 112, 114, 115
  diversity of, 62
  of materiality, 79
  sensorial dimension, 87, 94
  space and, 54
Shanks, Michael, 56, 61
shanyrak (bent wood structure), 86

shrapnel collection, 65, 176
siblingship, 75, 85
sick building syndrome, 4, 104, 105, 111
Simon, Jonathan, 107–8
social anthropology
   architectural studies within, 70
   British social anthropology, 42, 50, 73
   Lévi-Strauss "house societies" and, 3, 71–4
   man's relation to nature, 41
   social structure and, 2
social forms/formations
   architectural forms and, 48
   material forms and, 29, 32
   origin of, 21
   of ruins, 164
Social Logic of Space (Hillier, Hanson), 53
social reform, 2–3, 29, 50, 118
soft furnishings, 106
Somalian infibulation, 149
Soviet Marxists, 37
Soviet socialism, 118
Soviet Union, 16, 86, 164–6
space
   the body and, 58, 80, 145
   impact on linguistics, 89
   materiality of built form, 102
   sensoria and, 54
   spatial arrangement, 34
Ssorin-Chaikov, Nikolai, 165–6
Stalinism, 117–18, 173
status of the "real," 8–9
STM atom, 12
Stocking, G. W., 39–40
Stonehenge monument, 67, 68, 68*f*, 108, 115
Story of the Eye (Bataille), 16
Strathern, Marilyn, 7
street culture, 99
structuralism, 2, 42, 47, 51, 54, 73

tavu (house post), 82–3, 82*f*
Ten Books on Architecture (Vitruvius), 19
thingness concept, 13, 17
Thomas, Nicholas, 37, 178
Thompson, E.P., 108

Tilley, Christopher, 56, 58
"totalitarian institutions," 145–6
Traditional Dwellings and Settlements Review (journal), 1
Traugott, M., 91
Tringham, Ruth, 63–4, 185
Tschumi, Bernard, 70
Tzotzil Maya, 79–80

UNESCO World Heritage sites, 158
unilineal evolutionism, 30, 34, 36, 48
United Nations Universal Declaration of Human Rights, 132
universalism, 21, 41–2
University College London (UCL), 52
Upper Paleolithic, 48–9, 49*f*
urbanist forms, 50, 163
urban planning/environment, 95, 99–100, 101
urbicide, 5, 78, 170
U.S. Government Printing Office, 44

Van der Hoorn, Melanie, 108–9
Velázquez's painting vandalism, 168
Versailles Peace Conference, 38
Victoria & Albert Museum, 32
Victorian legacy, 37–9
Vidler, Anthony, 34
Viennese *Flaktürme,* 108–9, 110*f,* 115
visual form, 23, 34, 35, 130
Vitruvius (Roman author/architect), 19–23, 137, 143
Vogt, Evon, 35–7, 80
Volkov, Feodor Kondrat'evich, 49
Volksgeist notion, 26
Vuyosevich, R.D., 25

Warnier, Jean-Pierre, 152
waste products in Marakwet society, 122–3
wattle-and-daub houses, 64
The Way of the Masks (Lévi-Strauss), 71
weaponry, 15, 31*f*
Whitehead, Alfred North, 10–13, 113
whiteness, materiality, 129–30

William Paca Garden, 59, 60*f*
wood as building materials, 1
wood hut, 19, 20*f*
World Trade Center destruction, 157, 168,
    170–1, 171*f,* 177

Yalouri, Eleana, 69, 108
Yampolsky, M., 169, 170

Yaneva, Albena, 112
Ye'cuana dwellings, 76–7, 167
Yiftachel, O., 177, 185–6
Young, Diana, 127–9
Yucatec Maya, 81
yurts, 73, 84, 86

zoning laws, 103, 106